Praise for Jon S. Lewis

"Flying motorcycles, shape-shifting aliens, comic book superscience, and mind-control technology . . . a fun read."

—PUBLISHERS WEEKLY

"Brisk pace, aliens, and jet-packs . . . Lewis is a veteran of the comic book industry, and his plot is a domestic read-alike of Alex Rider."

—KIRKUS

"*Invasion* is a page-one blast off into the top secret realms that want to control our lives. My paranoia was seriously spiking until new hero on the block, Colt McAllister, started chasing the truth like an unstoppable cyborg mix of Jason Bourne and Fox Mulder. Read Invasion with your eyes wide open. No blinking or you might miss a shapeshifting alien as it blows past you en route to a total planetary take-over."

—FRANK BEDDOR, *New York Times* bestselling author of
The Looking Glass Wars

"More twists and turns than a rollercoaster. Comic books sprung to life. Armies of brain-controlled assassins. Heroes worth rooting for and some of the scariest villains you'll ever encounter—and all of it spun into a fantastic adventure by a truly gifted storyteller. Jon S. Lewis deftly balances mystery and action, fun and frights. It all boils down to one thing: *Invasion* is a blast!"

—ROBERT LIPARULO, bestselling author of the
Dreamhouse Kings series

INVASION

A C.H.A.O.S. Novel

JON S. LEWIS

THOMAS NELSON
Since 1798

NASHVILLE   DALLAS   MEXICO CITY   RIO DE JANEIRO

Published in Nashville, Tennessee, by Thomas Nelson. Thomas Nelson is a registered trademark of Thomas Nelson, Inc.

Thomas Nelson, Inc., books may be purchased in bulk for educational, business, fund-raising, or sales promotional use. For information, please e-mail SpecialMarkets@ThomasNelson.com.

Jon S. Lewis is represented by the literary agency of Alive Communications, Inc., 7680 Goddard Street, Suite 200, Colorado Springs, CO 80920, www.alivecommunications.com.

Publisher's Note: This novel is a work of fiction. Names, characters, places, and incidents are either products of the author's imagination or used fictitiously. All characters are fictional, and any similarity to people living or dead is purely coincidental.

ISBN 978-1-40168-542-3 (Trade Paper)

Library of Congress Cataloging-in-Publication Data

Lewis, J. S. (Jon S.)
Invasion / J.S. Lewis.
    p. cm.
Summary: After his parents are killed in an automobile accident, sixteen-year-old Colt McAllister moves to Arizona where he is recruited by a secret organization to join the battle against malevolent, supernatural creatures from another world.
ISBN 978-1-59554-753-8 (hard cover)
[1. Secret societies—Fiction. 2. Adventure and adventurers—Fiction. 3. Supernatural—Fiction. 4. Arizona—Fiction.] I. Title.
PZ7.L58662In 2011
[Fic]—dc22   2010038942

Printed in the United States of America

11 12 13 14 15 QG 5 4 3 2 1

For Nana, who taught me that
giants could be slain.

:: CHAPTER 1 ::

I t's a military academy."

Colt McAlister looked at his dad sideways. They were in Washington, D.C., on what was supposed to be a summer vacation, but this didn't look like the kind of place tourists would visit—especially a sixteen-year-old tourist like Colt. "I thought you said this was a camp."

"It's more like a prep school."

"Are you thinking about sending me away?"

"Don't worry," Dad said, and reached over to tousle Colt's hair. "You're just taking a tour, that's all. Besides, they won't admit you until you're eighteen."

"So why am I here?"

"Because you were invited."

"By who?"

"The same people who invited your brothers. This is an elite school. You can't even apply—it's strictly invitation-only."

"What if I don't want to go into the military?"

"That's up to you." As Colt's dad rolled his window down, a panel opened up on one of the brick columns. A mechanical arm unfolded with a sphere like an eyeball attached to the end. Then a green light flared to life before it scanned Colt and his father. Moments later a buzzer sounded, and the gate opened up.

"Is this place owned by Trident Industries or something?" Colt asked as the green beam shone in his eyes. He was referring to the multinational conglomerate that had its hand in everything from weapons manufacturing and robotics to capital investment and biotechnology.

"I doubt it. Why?"

"You know what they say, Trident is watching," Colt said with a shrug. "I mean, if scanners like this exist, I wonder what kind of spy equipment is out there."

"You've been listening to too many conspiracy theories."

"Maybe, but I want one of those for my room," Colt said as they drove through the opening and down the winding drive.

"It might be a little out of your price range."

"I was thinking you could buy it for me."

"I'll have to talk to your mother." Dad didn't hide the sarcasm in his tone.

It wasn't long before they pulled up to the front steps, but when his dad didn't get out of the car, Colt frowned.

"Sorry, but this tour is for potential cadets only," Dad said. "Trust me, it's more fun that way."

"Is there something you're not telling me?"

"I'll be back to pick you up this afternoon."

Colt hesitated before he opened the car door. He stepped onto the sidewalk, shut the door, and then stood there until his dad rolled down the window. "Why aren't there any signs?"

"It's a top-secret facility."

"What kind of school is top secret?"

"You'll be fine, son, I promise."

Colt looked over his shoulder at the massive building and felt his chest tighten.

"Look, if this is anything like the tour your brothers took, you're going to spend most of the day playing video games," Dad said. "I hear you even get to watch a movie."

"Seriously?"

"Have I ever lied to you?"

"When I was six you told me it wouldn't hurt when you pulled my tooth out."

"That was different."

"How?"

"Pain is relative."

"What does that mean?"

"You're just stalling."

"Dad?"

"Yes?"

"You're coming back, right?" Colt knew that didn't sound very macho, but something felt off.

"Of course. And make sure you say hello to Lieutenant Lohr for me." Dad rolled up the window and pulled away.

After the car disappeared behind a bank of trees, Colt took a deep breath and walked up the front steps. Another buzzer sounded, followed by a click that released the lock. Colt pulled on the handle and walked inside.

The foyer was stark, reminding him of an office building or maybe a bank. There was no art on the walls, the floor was covered in large marble tiles, and a man in a military uniform stood behind the reception area.

"Name?" he asked, his voice monotone as though the answer didn't matter.

"Colt McAlister."

The man pushed a button, activating a metal sphere that rose from the countertop. It flew over Colt's head, where it hovered. There were no strings holding it in the air, and once again, he was distracted by thoughts of Trident Industries spying on the entire world with their top secret network. The Internet was filled with rumors about how they were using it to gather intelligence so they could become the most powerful entity in the world. Sure, Colt thought it was ridiculous. Still, if technology like this hovering scanner existed, then anything was possible.

"What is that?"

"Stand still, please," the man said as he looked at a monitor.

"It's flying."

An aperture opened beneath the belly of the sphere, bathing Colt in a green spotlight as the sphere spun slowly in place. A dimensional replica of Colt flickered to life next to him. It reminded Colt of an X-ray. He could see his skeleton, as well as the change in his front pocket.

"How is it doing that?"

The man ignored Colt's question. "Do you have a phone, camera, or any other type of recording device?" he asked.

Colt shook his head.

The man pushed the button once more, and the holographic image of Colt disappeared. The aperture closed and the sphere returned to the desk as the man picked up a duffel bag from the floor and handed it to Colt. "You can change in the locker room at the end of the hall."

"Thanks." Colt paused, looking at the sphere, then at the man, who didn't return his gaze. He had all the warmth of a robot, and there was clearly no point in asking more questions.

Colt walked down a long corridor before reaching the boys' locker room. He was expecting more science-fiction gadgetry, but there was nothing extraordinary—at least nothing that stood out. There were walls of stacked lockers, hooks filled with towels next to open shower stalls, and long benches. A dozen boys about his age were in various states of undress as they changed into black T-shirts with matching cargo pants and combat boots.

Colt was strong, but most of them looked like professional athletes. They were tall, their shoulders were broad, their chests thick, and their stomachs taut. Without a word, Colt walked over to a quiet corner and unzipped his bag to find the same uniform.

He dressed quickly, embarrassed to find the bag even had new underwear. Since there was no belt, Colt had to use his own to keep his pants from falling down.

"Where are you from?"

Colt turned around to find a tall boy with dark skin and black hair smiling at him.

"San Diego."

"So that explains it."

"Explains what?"

"Your hair."

"What's that supposed to mean?"

"You're a surfer dude, right? You have the tan, the blue eyes, and the shaggy blond hair. All you need is a set of puka shells and you could be the poster boy for southern California."

"I guess," Colt said before stuffing his old clothes into his duffel bag. He wanted the kid to go away but he decided to be polite. "Where are you from?"

"I was born in Virginia, but I've lived in Germany, Japan, Washington, Texas, and a few other places. Right now I live in Arizona."

"My grandpa lives there."

"Yeah, I get that a lot. By the way, I'm Romero," the boy said, offering Colt his enormous hand.

"I'm Colt."

"So you're a gunslinger or something?"

"Not exactly."

As the boys shook hands, another man in uniform walked into the locker room. "Put your personal items in one of the lockers and follow me."

"I didn't bring a padlock," Colt said.

"You don't need one," Romero said. "Just put your thumb on that sensor."

Colt raised his thumb to a small black pad next to one of the lockers, but he paused when he saw a Trident Security logo.

"What's wrong?"

"Nothing," Colt said, thinking his dad was right. Maybe reading all those conspiracy blogs was getting to him. He pressed against the sensor and a green light glowed as the door clicked open. Romero took Colt's duffel bag, stuffed it inside, and shut the door. Then Colt placed his thumb back on the sensor, but this time a red light flashed three times. The door didn't open.

"Now you try it," Romero said.

Colt put his thumb on the sensor, and just like before, the door clicked open. "How does it work?"

"It's a biometric scanner," Romero said. "They reset them every night, but for today that's your locker. The only way someone could break in is if they cut your thumb off."

Colt shut the door before trying to open it again.

"We'd better get going," Romero said. "Lohr is going to make us run laps until we throw up if we're late for orientation."

"How do you know so much about this place?"

"My dad is kind of in charge."

"He's the principal?"

"Not exactly. He's the director of the entire agency."

"What agency?"

"CHAOS."

"Wait," Colt said. "As in the CHAOS Agency that protects the world from alien invasions?"

"Yep."

Colt hesitated. "I don't get it. I mean, isn't that just in comic books and movies?"

"You'll see."

Romero led Colt through a series of corridors before they came to a set of double doors that slid open like an elevator, revealing a room that looked like an amphitheater. Six rows of desks were filled with quiet boys all dressed in the same gear. Nobody was talking, and Colt could see why.

In the front of the room, standing on a small stage, was a monster at least seven feet tall.

CHAPTER 2

Is that a . . . I mean . . ."

"Technically he's a Tharik from the planet Nemus," Romero said, "but yeah. It's Bigfoot."

From head to foot the creature was covered in fur the color of a sunrise, and it looked like a mad scientist had performed strange experiments on it. There was a second head made out of iron bolted over its left shoulder, and a mechanical arm that connected to a series of metal plates covered its rib cage.

Colt was having a difficult time forming coherent thoughts. Advanced technology like biometric scanners was one thing, but living cryptids that were straight out of his comic books? "It's a guy in a costume, right?"

Romero shook his head.

"It has to be," Colt said.

"Why?"

"Because Bigfoot isn't real."

"If you think it's just a mask, I'll give you a thousand bucks if you walk up there and take it off."

Colt looked at Bigfoot. "How?"

Romero shrugged. "He came through one of the gateways, the same as all the other aliens."

"There are more?"

"Look," Romero said. "There's an entire world hidden in the shadows. Most people don't know things like Lohr exist, and they never will. It's our job to keep it that way."

"So you're a CHAOS agent?"

"Not yet."

"But . . ." Colt's voice trailed off as the giant beast with the robotic head turned to look at him.

"Trust me, this is only the beginning," Romero said.

"Nice of you to show up," the Bigfoot said. Its voice was so deep that it sounded like two boulders scraping together. "Why don't you two find a seat? There's space in the front row waiting for you."

"Did you brush your teeth this morning?" Romero asked.

"What does it matter? It's not like I'm going to kiss you."

A smattering of nervous laughter told Colt that he wasn't the only one in the room who was uncomfortable.

"That's a relief," Romero said before leaning over to whisper to Colt. "Thariks don't like to bathe, so you might want to plug your nose."

"I heard that," the Bigfoot said.

Romero bounded down the stairs to take his front row seat. Colt hesitated, caught between fear and excitement, and then followed, each step slow and deliberate.

"My name is Lieutenant Lohr," the monster said, "and yes, I'm a living, breathing Sasquatch—or if you prefer, Bigfoot. So now that we have that out of the way, who can tell me why I'm stuck babysitting a bunch of humans?"

"You got a promotion?" Romero said. There was more nervous laughter.

"I realize you think that you're special, Romero, but from here on out you'll address me as Lieutenant."

"Yes, Lieutenant," Romero said with a salute that didn't look terribly sincere.

"Most of you have grown up believing that the monsters in your closets were part of your imagination, but I'm living proof that they're real," Lohr said. "The CHAOS Agency exists to protect the world from creatures that make me look like a teddy bear—and believe me, there are more of them roaming around than you know."

"Where are they, Lieutenant?" asked a boy with a thick Texas accent. "I mean, if there're so many, shouldn't we be able to see them?"

"What's your name?"

"Lawson, sir. Tyrese Lawson."

"Well, Lawson, if we do our job, you never will," Lohr said. "It's up to CHAOS to hunt those monsters down before they crawl through your windows in the middle of the night."

"Where do they come from, Lieutenant?"

"Name?"

"Dante DiMaggio."

"Care to guess where they come from, DiMaggio?"

DiMaggio shrugged.

"Anyone?" Lohr's robotic head scanned the room looking for someone to respond, but no one did. "Come on, don't any of you read comic books anymore?"

Colt raised his hand, though only high enough for Lohr to see. The mechanical eye on the monster's second head spun left, then right, and left again, like a camera lens trying to focus.

"You're one of the McAlister boys, right?"

"Yes, sir. My name is Colt."

"Did you know that I served with your grandfather in the Second World War?"

Colt frowned as he tried to do the math in his head.

"I'm older than I look. Besides, why do you think I have all this fancy machinery?" Lohr wiggled his mechanical fingers and rotated his robotic head. "The Nazis bombed our position, and I took a direct hit. Your grandpa was part of the team that saved my hide. Without him, I wouldn't be here today."

"I had no idea."

"That's the way it's supposed to be," Lohr said. "All of our missions during the war were classified. Your grandpa was lucky, though. He made it to retirement, but I've been stuck here long enough to train your father and all seven of your brothers too. With hair like that, are you sure you're a McAlister?"

"People say I take after my mom."

A few of the boys snickered.

"Hey, he's from California; cut him some slack," Romero said. "Everyone looks like that out there."

"Is that so?" Lohr smiled. "You're the one they call Runt?"

There was more laughter.

"I guess so," Colt said as he shrank down in his chair.

"You had some fairly impressive test scores," Lohr said. The laughter stopped, and all eyes focused on Colt. "Then again, so did everyone sitting in this room."

"What test scores?" Colt asked.

"You've all taken them, you just didn't know what they were for," Lohr said. "Your score is a culmination of everything from the standardized tests you take at the end of the school year to the fitness tests you take in your gym classes. We even ran samples of your DNA that were taken moments after you were born."

"Is that legal?" a boy with a shaved head asked.

"Excuse me . . . ?"

"The name's Simon Fletcher."

"Would you like to rephrase that, Fletcher?"

"Is that legal, Lieutenant?"

"We have certain privileges that other government agencies don't share," Lohr said. "In fact, today we're going to put you through a few more tests to determine if you have what it takes to save the world. If you pass, you'll be admitted into the CHAOS Military Academy."

Colt raised his hand. "What if we don't want to go, Lieutenant?"

Lohr smiled, revealing a set of incisors that looked like they could puncture steel. "Over the next few weeks more than a thousand young men and women will come through these doors. We'll be lucky if a dozen qualify, so I wouldn't worry about that just yet."

There was a murmur through the room, but it quieted when Lohr raised his hand. "Those who qualify will get to pick a specialty from things like space exploration, counterintelligence, weapons systems, piloting, and espionage. We even have teams of scientists and engineers, so there's room for everyone. Well, everyone except Romero, anyway."

"You should really leave the comedy to the professionals," Romero said.

Lohr smiled again before he turned his attention back to Colt. "You were going to tell us where all the creepy crawlies that go bump in the night come from."

For a moment Colt lost his train of thought, but he recovered. "I have a question first," he finally managed to say.

"Go ahead."

"Is this the same CHAOS agency as the one in the comic book?"

"You mean *Phantom Flyer and the Agents of CHAOS*?" Lohr asked. He held up his hand to show Colt a Phantom Flyer signet ring that would have been big enough to fit around Colt's neck. "Yeah, you could say that."

"In that case," Colt answered, "according to the official *CHAOS Guidebook*, monsters and aliens come to Earth through invisible gateways that connect us to other worlds. They're kind of like bridges, I guess, and they allow us to go places we couldn't reach by spacecraft."

"Like my home world of Nemus?" Lohr asked.

"That's the world with all the trees, right?"

"You know something, you may not be as big as your brothers, but you're a heck of a lot smarter," Lohr said. "Now all we have to do is get you a haircut, and you just might turn into the soldier that everybody's been hoping for."

Colt pushed his long bangs out of his eyes. "Does that mean my brothers are CHAOS agents?"

"That's classified."

"What about my dad?"

"All I can tell you is that he graduated from the academy," Lohr said before turning back to the rest of the group. "Now I hope you were paying attention, because McAlister is right. We've shut most of the major gateways down, but small ones pop up all the time. It's up to us to find them before anything dangerous escapes into our world."

"Some of the gateways are still open, Lieutenant?" Fletcher asked.

"Only a few, but they're heavily regulated," Lohr said. "We've even built settlements on planets that can sustain human life."

"Then everything in the Phantom Flyer comic books is real? Hitler had an army of werewolves, robots, and supersoldiers?"

"More or less," Lohr said. "And don't forget the flying saucers and the shape-shifting aliens."

"You mean the Thule?" Colt asked.

Lohr nodded. "In their natural form, those blighters look like walking lizards with six arms, but they can shift into just about anything. In fact, for all you know, I could be one of the Thule."

"But you're not," DiMaggio said. He was on the edge of his chair, and looked ready to bolt as he waited for Lohr to respond.

"You better hope not," Lohr said. "When we opened the gateway to their home world, it nearly cost us everything. The Thule decided to send a fleet of warships to exterminate everyone on Earth so they could colonize this little rock we call home. Luckily we closed the door before too many broke through."

"Hitler was one of the Thule, right?" another boy asked. "I mean, he was in the Phantom Flyer comic anyway."

"Don't believe everything you read," Lohr said. "Those comics are like movies based on true stories. The creators took liberties to make the story more exciting. That being said, they're still pretty close to the truth."

"Why hasn't any of it been documented? I mean, comic books aren't exactly used in history class."

"It has, but those files are classified," Lohr said. "Think about it. What would happen if you saw someone like me walking down the street in your hometown?"

Everyone laughed, and for the first time they sounded relaxed.

"Exactly," Lohr said. "It would cause mass hysteria. So our job as CHAOS agents is to keep a lid on all of this so people like your parents don't have to worry. They have enough problems putting up with the music that you listen to—that is, if you want to call it music. We don't need to add an alien invasion to the list."

:: CHAPTER 3 ::

Lieutenant Lohr wrapped up his orientation by breaking the boys into groups that would rotate through five stations: an obstacle course, a documentary about the history of the CHAOS program, simulated battles that were basically video games, written tests, and combat class.

"Remember that you're being graded on everything today," Lohr said before he dismissed them, "and I'm not just talking about the obvious. How you act and what you say will tell us a lot about you, and trust me, we'll be watching. You're dismissed."

Lohr walked down a flight of stairs connected to the stage before approaching Colt and his team, which included Romero, Fletcher, Lawson, and DiMaggio. "It must be your lucky day, because you get to start with me."

He led the boys down a series of corridors before they passed into a hallway that was basically an acrylic tube that looked like it cut through some kind of lake. There was a strange green glow coming from the murky water, and exotic fish unlike anything Colt had ever seen swam all around them.

"This is our aquatic center," Lohr said. "The tank holds over six million gallons of water, with more than ten thousand speci-mens from twelve different planets."

The tube eventually opened up into a viewing theater where a wall of glass at least thirty feet high and a hundred feet wide offered a spectacular panorama. A forest of plants swayed in the current as an enormous sea creature swam by. It looked prehis-toric, with bulging eyes, a gaping mouth, and black scales lined with fluorescent markings.

"What is that thing?" Colt asked.

Romero shrugged. "Beats me."

Lohr allowed the boys to drink in the splendor of the strange underwater world, but not for long. "We have to keep moving," he said before disappearing through a set of double doors at the far end of the room.

Colt stopped to tie his boot. By the time he was finished, he was the only person left in the theater. He was about to leave when something caught his eye. At first he thought it was someone in scuba gear, like the people who vacuum out the aquarium beds at Sea World. He was wrong.

A boy, or at least what Colt thought was a boy, swam cau-tiously to the glass. He wasn't wearing goggles, a regulator, or an oxygen tank. Instead, a set of gills on his neck opened and closed as he stared at Colt with his head tilted to the side. His black eyes were enormous, and his skin was an undulating pattern of greens and blues. The tentacles on top of his head reminded Colt of dreadlocks, and the boy's hands and feet were webbed.

Don't be frightened. The voice had spoken inside Colt's head.

Too late for that. Colt backed away from the glass, heart pounding. "Did *you* say that?"

The creature nodded as the doors to the passageway opened.

"What are you doing?" Romero asked.

Colt turned back to the tank, but the boy was gone. "Where did he go?"

"Who?"

"The kid in the tank."

"We don't have time to mess around," Romero said. "Come on, we have to go."

By the time they caught up with the others, Lohr was already leading the boys through a series of stretching exercises. "Did you get lost?" the lieutenant asked. His tone was no longer friendly.

"Something like that," Colt said.

"Take off your boots and get in here."

Romero was already in his bare feet and had fallen in line before Colt untied his first lace. There were no windows in the room. The walls were covered with padding, and the floor was basically made out of rubber with a giant circle in the middle. Colt joined the rest of the group in time to loosen his hamstrings a bit, but that was about it.

"All right, everyone line up against the wall," Lohr said. "We know you're smart and that you can do a bunch of push-ups and sit-ups, but let's see how good you are at hand-to-hand combat. Has anyone taken boxing classes?"

Romero raised his hand.

"How about martial arts?"

Fletcher joined Romero.

"Have any of you even been in a fight before?"

The boys just looked at each other.

"Video games have made this world soft," Lohr said, shaking his head. "All right, Romero and McAlister, front and center."

"I wanted to spar against McAlister," Fletcher said.

Lohr turned to him with a raised eyebrow. "What makes you think you have what it takes?"

"I'm not too worried."

"We'll see," Lohr said as Romero ran out to the center of the circle.

Colt just stood there.

"What are you waiting for?" Lohr asked.

Colt lowered his eyes and walked over to stand next to Romero. The size difference was almost laughable, but Lohr didn't seem to care.

"Now face each other."

"Are you really going to make us fight?" Colt asked.

"It's called sparring," Lohr said.

"Don't we get gloves?"

"If you're half as good as everyone thinks you are, you won't need them."

Colt looked over to Romero, who was already in a fighting stance. His left foot was forward, his right fist cocked, but it was his eyes that held Colt's attention. They were intense. It was as though a raging bull had replaced the affable boy Colt had met in the locker room that morning.

Colt's only fighting experience was wrestling with his brothers, and they had never thrown a punch. If he had to fight, all he wanted to do was survive without getting a black eye or having a tooth knocked out.

"Are you ready?" Lohr said, turning to Romero.

He nodded.

"What about you?"

"I guess," Colt said.

"Then let's go."

The moment that Lohr stepped back, Romero pounced. He took two long strides before jumping in the air, then brought his fist back before punching. If Colt hadn't moved out of the way, it would have connected with his chest. Instead, Colt sidestepped and pushed Romero in the back. The momentum took the larger boy outside of the circle and onto his knees.

Lohr blew his whistle. "Not bad," he said.

Romero looked angry. His nostrils were flaring as he knelt on the ground. He closed his eyes, then popped back to his feet and stomped back to his starting spot.

:: CHAPTER 4 ::

Colt's heart was fluttering from the adrenaline surge as he stood across from Romero. He had no idea how he'd avoided getting his head knocked off, much less how he'd succeeded in shoving Romero to the ground. It was an invigorating sensation, but from the look in Romero's eye, Colt knew he was in trouble.

"Again," Lohr said once the boys were in position.

Romero took his time. His head hung low behind raised fists as he bobbed from side to side. "It's nothing personal, McAlister."

Colt's breathing was shallow and his palms were sweating as he waited for Romero to strike. He didn't have to wait long. Romero threw a jab with his right hand, forcing Colt to dip out of the way. As Colt stood back up, Romero threw another jab that grazed Colt's cheek. He followed it with an uppercut that connected with Colt's stomach.

The boys watching gasped as Colt's feet left the floor from the force of the impact. Colt could feel the wind rush out of his lungs before he hit the mat. He lay there, writhing and gasping for air. When he finally opened his eyes, Romero was standing over him. The larger boy offered his hand before helping Colt to his feet.

"Are you okay?" Romero asked, the rage replaced by concern.

"I think so." Colt's cheek was throbbing, and his stomach hurt so much that he wanted to throw up.

"You're not supposed to stand there like a punching bag," Lohr said. "What would you do if one of your brothers tried to take your head off?"

Colt looked over to see the Sasquatch standing with his arms crossed as though he was disappointed. He wanted to tell Lohr that he hadn't asked to come here in the first place, but instead he stumbled back to the center of the circle with his arm over his stomach.

"Don't you think he's had enough?" Romero asked.

Lohr growled like a dog protecting his dinner. "Until your father tells me otherwise, I'm in charge of the combat school."

"Whatever you say." Romero turned to Colt. "You need to cover up, okay?" he whispered.

Colt nodded and tried to mirror the stance Romero had taken. He balled his hands into fists and held them up to protect his face.

"Take a wider stance," Romero said. "That's where your power comes from. Besides, it'll make it harder to throw you down."

"Like this?"

Romero shook his head. "Loosen up a bit. You know, like a spring or something. You can't react if you're bunched up like that."

"Go!" Lohr said.

Romero kicked with his right foot. He had aimed for Colt's ear, but Colt slid to the ground and caught Romero's left ankle between his feet. He rolled over, and the motion made Romero buckle. He fell on his face, but Colt wasn't done. He slammed the back of Romero's head with his fist. Something cracked; then Romero groaned.

"You still want that shot?" Lohr asked as he looked at Fletcher.

"I'm sorry," Colt said, kneeling over Romero. He thought about taking off his shirt to wipe up the blood, but he didn't get a chance.

"He'll be fine," Lohr said as he picked Romero up by his arm. The Sasquatch knelt to inspect the boy's nose. "It's broken all right. Nice work, McAlister."

"Wait, I didn't mean to do that," Colt said.

"Romero was careless and he paid for it," Lohr said. "Now who's next?"

As Colt followed Romero to the wall, Lohr motioned for Fletcher and Lawson to take their place in the circle. Both looked nervous, but the Sasquatch didn't seem to care. At the same time, something that looked like an oversized toaster on wheels sped across the mat. Like a street cleaner, it had bristles under its belly. It swept away the pool of blood before rolling back to its alcove in the wall.

"Look, you have to believe me. I'm really sorry."

"Stop apologizing," Romero said. His voice sounded strange as he pinched the bridge of his nose with his thumb and fore-finger to try and stop the bleeding. "Injuries are part of training. Besides, that was a nice move. Think you can teach me how to do it?"

"I'm not sure," Colt said. "It just kind of happened."

After combat training, Lohr sent Romero to the infirmary, where the doctor set his nose before covering it with a splint and some bandage tape. By the time Romero caught up with the rest of the group at the obstacle course, there were black circles under his eyes, though his dark skin masked most of it.

"It's kind of cool, huh?" Romero asked.

"Yeah, I guess," Colt said with raised eyebrows. "If you want to look like a raccoon."

"Your cheek doesn't look much better."

"Trust me, it hurts worse than it looks."

"You haven't seen yourself in the mirror, have you?"

"Not yet."

"I didn't think so."

Despite his injury, Romero was able to coast through the obstacle course with the best time of the day. Colt wasn't far behind. After their rotation, the team was escorted back to the amphitheater to take a timed test. Most of the questions were multiple choice, but a few at the end were in essay format.

The questions bordered on the bizarre, and some were just crazy. One asked whether or not Colt believed that the conversion to digital television would allow the government to put two-way televisions in everyone's home. That way they could spy on every house in the United States. Another wondered if Colt believed that Princess Diana was killed because she discovered that a shape-shifting alien had assassinated the Prime Minister of Great Britain and was seated in his place. Colt finished just before the bell rang, even though he wasn't sure how. His hand hurt from all the writing.

"When do we get to play video games?" Colt asked as he walked to the mess hall with Romero. The last thing he wanted to do during summer vacation was take any more tests.

"After the movie."

"Don't you mean documentary?"

"It's not what you think," Romero said. "The screen is eight stories tall and the resolution is so amazing that it feels like you're right there."

"How many times have you seen it?"

Romero shrugged. "I've been coming here since I was six, and I figure I've seen it at least ten times each summer, so what's that?"

"Have you been through all this before?"

"The tests? Nah," Romero said. "At least not as a potential cadet. This time it counts."

They were the last group to arrive at the mess hall, which looked a lot like the cafeteria at Colt's school. For the most part, everyone sat at long tables with the rest of their team members. The instructors sat together in the back of the room.

"Don't get used to this," Romero said, stuffing half a cheese-burger into his mouth.

"What do you mean?"

Romero didn't wait to swallow before he answered. "They don't normally serve this kind of food. I mean, I don't remember the last time we had banana pudding or chocolate milk. Most of the time we get chicken and vegetables, and for breakfast it's lumpy oatmeal with raisins. Sometimes they give you powdered eggs and overcooked sausage. I don't think a dog would eat it."

"You could always have a protein bar."

"They don't let you bring anything into the academy."

"So do you want to be a CHAOS agent when you grow up?"

Romero shrugged. "It's not like I have a choice."

"I wonder why my brothers never told me about this place."

"You're not allowed to talk about it, even with your family," Romero said. "Besides, before you leave they give you a shot of something that wipes your memory."

Colt frowned. "Why?"

"Before today, what's the first thing that came to mind when you heard someone was a Bigfoot hunter?"

"I don't know. I guess I would have thought they were crazy."

"Exactly," Romero said. "If everyone knew the truth—that there really were monsters in their closets and under their beds, there'd be a widespread panic. That's why we keep it a secret."

"Makes sense." Colt looked around at the other boys in the mess hall. There were a couple impromptu wrestling matches going on, and some guys were having a belching contest at the next table.

Romero followed his gaze and smiled. "Would you trust any of these guys with the world's deadliest secrets?"

:: CHAPTER 5 ::

When lunch was over, Colt's team went to a movie theater that was big enough to seat five hundred people. Instead of spreading out to take advantage of the space, the boys crowded together in the back so they could get a good view of the enormous screen.

"What, no popcorn?" Colt asked.

"Hey, Lohr," Romero said. "McAlister wants to know if you'll get us some snacks. I like lots of butter on my popcorn."

Colt's eyes shot wide. He looked at Romero, then Lohr, and finally back to Romero. "I was just messing around. Now he's going to kill me."

"Relax. Once you get past the smell and that scowl, Lohr's just an oversized puppy dog," Romero said.

Lohr shook his head before walking down the stairs. Then he disappeared out the door.

The lights dimmed.

"Get ready," Romero said. "I've seen this dozens of times, and it's still amazing."

The screen flicked to life and then the music poured out of

a sound system that was better than any rock concert. It started out with a narrator talking over black-and-white footage of the Second World War. Colt recognized President Roosevelt, General MacArthur, and General Eisenhower, who would later become the president of the United States. Then they showed footage of the first CHAOS agents training for the war. Colt thought he saw his grandpa in a scene where they were teaching them how to fly in jet packs, but he wasn't sure.

After that there was some footage shot by Nazi video crews. There were robots, wolf men, aliens, and supersoldiers—the perfect human specimens, bred to eradicate their opposition.

Colt thought the most exciting part of the movie was the exploration sequence at the end. There was footage from some of the planets that were connected to Earth by gateways. In the first shot, the camera panned over the vast forests of Lohr's home planet, Nemus. Colt felt like he was flying in a helicopter looking down at the trees. Strange birds, like herons only ten times larger, coasted over the treetops as a waterfall splashed in the background.

Next came Yarix, where the surface temperatures reached more than two hundred degrees Fahrenheit. Strange creatures with hides of burning fire roamed the desert wastelands like packs of wolves.

The final sequence was from a water planet called Undar, where the combined landmass of all the continents was smaller than Australia. They showed amazing undersea creatures and entire cities that spread across the ocean floor like a great metropolis.

Colt jabbed Romero in the ribs with his elbow. "That looks like the kid I saw this morning."

"In the fish tank?"

"Yeah."

"Are you sure? I've seen a lot of weird stuff here—I'm talking fish that could swallow a school bus—but not any Undarians," Romero said.

"He talked to me."

"What?"

"I don't know how, but I heard his voice in my head."

"Was that before or after I hit you?"

"I'm serious," Colt said. "You heard the narrator; they use telepathy."

Romero shrugged. "I guess it's possible."

When the movie was over, Colt's team was brought to a large room where every inch of wall space was covered with video screens. Everyone was given what looked like night vision goggles, as well as a controller with a series of buttons, thumb sticks, and triggers. The overhead lights dimmed and the screens flared to life. As Colt turned slowly in a circle, he felt like he was actually in the middle of a post-apocalyptic world.

Vines had crept over the rubble of a city that had been obliterated by a devastating war. It reminded Colt of New York City, but the signs were written in some kind of alien script. The closest language he could think of was Japanese, but it wasn't. It didn't even look human.

There were three moons hanging in the sky, their glow caught in the haze of ash that clung to the air. Colt wasn't sure if they were piping in scents, but his nose was filled with the stench of a dying campfire.

"Your mission is to make it to the gateway at the end of the street," their instructor said.

"That's it?" Fletcher asked.

Colt wasn't sure if the instructor was smiling or sneering. "Talk to me when it's over."

Each boy had been assigned an avatar that looked a lot like him. Colt's was a sniper with a jet pack, and Romero was a gunner on the back of an armored vehicle that actually hovered over the street instead of using tires or tread. Lawson was riding inside something called an ABS, which stood for Armored Battle Suit. It looked a bit like a ten-foot-tall robot, but its chest was actually a cockpit where the soldier manned the controls.

"This is Gathmara," Romero said as Colt walked beside his vehicle. "You know, the planet with those shape-shifting aliens."

"Have you played this scenario before?"

"The computer never runs the same simulation twice."

"Incoming!" DiMaggio warned.

Colt heard the missile before he saw it. It screamed overhead, narrowly missing the ABS before exploding into a high-rise. Bricks, steel, and glass flew everywhere as a blast of heat burst in the darkened sky. Then the ground started to shake, in both the game and in real life. Colt watched as one of the kids fell down. So did his avatar on the screen.

"How did they do that?" Colt asked.

"It's called four-dimensional gaming," Romero said. "The floor is actually a hydraulic platform."

"That's crazy."

"Look out!" Romero pressed both triggers on his controller, releasing energy bolts from the cannon on the back of the armored vehicle.

Lizard men with six arms scattered amid the rubble as Fletcher and DiMaggio burst into the sky with their jet packs.

:: CHAPTER 6 ::

Like the written test, their video game scenario was timed. Not that it mattered. Their entire team was eliminated with more than twenty minutes left. Lawson and his ABS was the first to go. He never got the hang of the weapons system, which meant that their team had lost its big gun early. After that, everything fell apart.

Romero was the last one left, but Colt wasn't surprised. He was the only one who'd played the game before.

"Can we do another scenario?" DiMaggio asked.

"Not today," the instructor said. "It's time to hit the showers."

The boys had to turn in their goggles and controllers before they were taken back to the locker room. After a quick shower, Colt changed back into his street clothes, but not before opening and reopening his locker five or six times, just for fun.

"So what do you think?" Romero asked.

"It was fun."

"It gets tougher."

Colt shrugged.

"It's a twelve-month program—and I'm talking no vacation— so you wouldn't be able to surf," Romero said.

"I've surfed my whole life. Besides, as long as they let us play that video game, I wouldn't care."

Romero smiled. "It's definitely part of the training."

"Then I hope I make it."

"I don't think you have anything to worry about."

"How will we know?" Fletcher asked.

"Know what?" Romero said.

"If we made it into the academy."

"You'll get an invitation, but I wouldn't hold my breath if I were you."

"What's that supposed to mean?" Fletcher said, his brows furrowing as he flared his nostrils. He took a step toward Romero, but Romero didn't flinch.

"Don't take it personally," Romero said. "Not many of us are going to make it. I don't even know if I will."

"Yeah, right," DiMaggio said. "Your dad is the director of CHAOS. There's no way you won't make the cut."

"Stuff like that doesn't matter," Romero said. "You either have what it takes or you don't."

"So now what?" Colt asked as he slipped on his shoes.

"You dump your uniform in that hamper, get your shot, and go home."

"Are you sure we're not going to remember any of this?"

"Nothing."

"Then what was the point?" Fletcher asked.

"Today wasn't about having fun and building memories that will last a lifetime," Romero said. "Think of it like a county fair. They parade us around like we're prize hogs. Then they pick the best, give us blue ribbons, and hope we turn out to be the kind of soldiers who can save the world from big ugly monsters like Lohr."

Colt nodded, though he didn't fully understand, and from the looks on their faces the other boys didn't get it either. Instead of pressing with more questions, Colt said his good-byes and made his way to the door.

Before he could leave the locker room, he was stopped by a medical robot that injected him in the arm with a burning liquid. Colt did his best to try and remember everything that he'd experienced over the course of the day, but by the time he walked out the front door, his memory was already starting to blur.

"So how was it?" Dad asked as Colt stepped into the rental car.

"It was fun, I guess." Colt yawned.

"What did you do?"

"I don't know." He frowned. "I mean, I think we played some kind of video game, and I sort of remember a movie, but . . ." He yawned again. "I'm not sure. The rest is fuzzy."

"They must have kept you busy."

"Yeah."

"What happened to your cheek?"

"My cheek?" Colt reached up and felt a bump. It was tender.

"I'm sure the swelling will go down by morning. Just try to hide it from your mother. You know how she gets about that kind of thing."

"No problem," Colt said after yawning once more. "Do you think we can go back to the hotel? I'm kind of tired."

"I can arrange that."

||||||||||||||||||||||||||||||||

Colt woke up the next morning with a headache. The swelling on his cheek had gone down, but there was a bruise and it was painful.

"Good morning," Mom said when he wandered out of the bedroom he had been sharing with three of his brothers.

"What time is it?"

"Almost noon."

"Where is everybody?"

"They went to the baseball game."

"Why didn't they wake me up?"

"We tried, but you wouldn't budge."

"Do we have any food? I'm starving."

"Your brothers ate the last of the eggs and bacon," his mother said. "Since we're heading back tomorrow, I didn't get any more groceries, so all we have left are a few powdered doughnuts and some cold pizza."

"That's a start."

As Colt devoured the eclectic breakfast, his mother plied him with questions about the camp—starting with the bruise on his cheek. Colt couldn't remember any details—not about the bruise, any activities, or even what he'd had for lunch.

"Maybe you got a slight case of amnesia when you bumped your head," his mother said.

"I don't know, maybe," Colt said between bites of pizza. Then he slurped down half a glass of fruit punch. He was too tired to care about his lost memories. All he wanted to do was eat his breakfast and go back to bed.

:: CHAPTER 7 ::

olt had turned sixteen just before they left for Washington, D.C. His parents had given him an old Toyota Land Cruiser pickup as a gift. The red paint was fading and the interior was ripped and frayed, but Colt thought it was perfect. Of the eight McAlister brothers, he was the last still at home, and since both of his parents worked, nobody was ever around to give him a ride. That Land Cruiser meant freedom.

He was about to start his sophomore year at Scripps Ranch High School in San Diego. With summer winding down, Colt wanted to make the most of his vacation, so he was up before the sun on his last free Friday morning. He changed into his board shorts, a T-shirt, and some flip-flops. Then he threw on an old Padres cap before making a quick protein shake and heading out to the garage. His wet suit was already in the front seat and his surfboard was loaded in the back.

Colt had wanted to go to Black's Beach to avoid the tourists, but some of his friends were heading over to Solana Beach for the day, so he decided to meet them there. They'd at least have a few hours before the crowds showed up, and by then Colt would be too tired to surf more anyway.

There were only a few other cars when Colt pulled up, but he didn't see his buddy, Tyler's old woody station wagon. Colt parked on the side of the road before slipping into his wet suit. He didn't feel like waiting. Besides, for all he knew, Tyler and the rest of his friends were still sleeping. Colt waxed his board, and a few minutes later he was paddling out into the surf.

Once he was out in the open water, he stopped to watch the sunrise. It was serene, sitting there straddling his board as the waves swayed gently beneath him. A seagull flew overhead, and in the distance he could see a sailboat cutting through the water.

Colt took a deep breath and lay down on his board. The cold water lapped over the sides, spraying his face. He could taste the salt on his lips as his arms paddled against the strong current. Then he spotted a wave and Colt paddled harder. He steered back around to face the shore. When the first of the swell lifted the back of his board, he gripped the sides before rising to one knee. Then he popped up, catching his balance with his arms.

With his long bangs whipping against his forehead, Colt walked back and forth on his board, enjoying the ride as the water raged around him. The wave died too soon, and as it did Colt lowered himself on his board before paddling back out.

On his second run, Colt shot up to the crest of the wave, riding sideways before dipping back down. He shifted his weight and twisted his front foot to angle back to the top. That time he caught air and grabbed the tip of his board to get a bigger lift.

After the ride ended, Colt looked to the shore, hoping to spot Tyler. There were people on the beach, but from that far away he couldn't be sure if Tyler was there or not. Colt decided to try for another wave. If he didn't see Tyler or the others at the end of the ride, he'd go to shore and give them a wake-up call.

As Colt paddled out, he thought he saw a dark patch in the water ahead. He grabbed his board before dipping down and a wave crashed over him. When he came back up, whatever it was had gone. Shark attacks were rare, especially in San Diego, but that was part of the risk. Two years before, a great white had killed a man who was training with friends for a triathlon. The ocean was the sharks' domain, and sometimes nature struck back.

Colt continued to paddle. He could hear someone shouting, so he looked to the left and then to the right, but the nearest surfer was at least fifty yards away. He craned his neck to see tiny silhouettes waving from shore. He couldn't tell what they were saying, but he figured it was his friends. Colt waved back.

A large swell had snuck up on him, slamming him into the nose of his surfboard. He choked on the salt water as his board corkscrewed, flipping him under. He shot back out, gasping for breath as he whipped his head back and forth.

The water calmed and Colt managed to turn his board over before sliding back on top. Once he caught his breath, he lay back down and paddled toward another big wave. The people on shore were still shouting. Strange. Then, for a moment, Colt thought that he could see the dark patch again. He blinked, and it disappeared.

Colt turned around to paddle as the wave approached. Distracted by the thought of a great white lurking, Colt nearly lost his balance. He crouched, his legs wide as he cut across the wave. The spray splattered against his face when he turned to watch the swell. The water roared as it formed a pipeline that swallowed Colt, but he didn't fall. He smiled as he pressed his left hand against the wave to keep from getting sucked under.

That's when he felt the bump. His board hit something, and the nose pitched hard to the left. It crashed into the wave as Colt felt something slap his foot. He had just enough time to see a tentacle, thick as a fireman's hose that wrapped around his ankle before it pulled Colt off of his surfboard.

As he fell, Colt's head slammed against the board. He disappeared under the surf as the line that tethered him to his surfboard snapped. His ears started ringing as he struggled to retain consciousness. He tried to open his eyes, but all he could see was a mass of bubbles coming from below.

More of the powerful tentacles shot up. They latched onto his wrists, waist, and neck. Colt wiggled and writhed; he tried to break free, but the tentacles were too strong. The harder he fought, the more oxygen he spent. His lungs were burning and he could feel his mind slipping into darkness.

Then he saw the creature. It was some kind of squid, or maybe an octopus, except it had a human body. The fleshy crown of its head looked like a deflated bagpipe. Its yellow eyes glowed in the murky water, and eight tentacles writhed from the bridge of its nose like a living beard.

Colt kicked. It didn't matter. He pulled with his arms, but he couldn't break free. The tentacles pulled him closer. The creature reached for Colt. In a moment of clarity, Colt was certain he'd seen it before—in one of his father's comic books. This couldn't be real.

Maybe he was dreaming. There was no way a monster like that existed. Its shoulders were covered in bony protrusions and there were fins jutting from its forearms. Colt dug his thumbs into the creature's eyes, and the tentacles released.

Colt brought his knees to his chest before kicking out. The

force hit the monster in the head. As it fell into the deep, Colt swam toward what he hoped was the surface. That far under, there was no way to tell up from down or left from right. His lungs were on fire and his head was pounding from the pressure. Then he broke the surface, where the air had never tasted sweeter.

His eyes darted as he looked for his surfboard, which wasn't far. Colt kicked toward it as panic surged. He could somehow feel the monster tracking him below the water, and he tried to push the thought from his mind. All that mattered was getting his board. He had to get to shore.

Once he hit the sand, strong hands grabbed him. Someone was helping him out of the water. Blood poured from the gash where his head had hit the board and his wet suit was torn where the tentacles had latched on.

"Are you okay?" someone asked. It didn't sound like Tyler.

"Yeah, I think so." Colt tried to sit up, but the motion made him dizzy.

"Just relax. The ambulance is on the way."

"I don't need an ambulance," Colt said. Someone applied a towel to the cut on his head. "I'm fine, really."

"What happened?"

"I'm not sure. I mean, something grabbed me, but . . ." Colt wasn't about to tell them that a fish man with tentacles for a beard had attacked him. It wasn't real. It couldn't be real. There had to be a logical explanation, but Colt was having a difficult time concentrating. His head was pounding, and he felt light-headed.

Colt opened his eyes. A man in a wet suit was kneeling over him, his heavy brows furrowed. There were gray patches in his dark beard and his hair was pulled back into a ponytail. Colt didn't recognize him.

"I must have gotten tangled up in seaweed," Colt finally said.

"Since when does seaweed do that to a wet suit?"

Colt looked down to see welts forming on his skin where the tentacles had latched on. He pulled the towel away from his head. Whatever color it had been, it was crimson now.

:: CHAPTER 8 ::

As he sat in the waiting room at an urgent care facility, Colt wondered how he was going to explain this to his parents. The gash on his head was one thing, but he was worried about the welts. Blaming them on the seaweed was a thin excuse, but who was going to believe that a sea monster had attacked him?

Once he'd been discharged, Colt was happy to come home to an empty house. It gave him some time to formulate a plan and his first step was to search the Internet. Were there any giant squids in San Diego? It only took a few seconds to find an article. Thousands of giant squid had invaded the coast over the last few years.

In Mexico, the squid were called red devils. They could reach five feet long, weigh a hundred pounds, and there were lots of documented cases where the squid had attacked humans. With their sharp beaks and toothy tentacles, they could do serious damage.

Maybe he wasn't going crazy after all. It must have been one of those squid that grabbed him. The rest was a hallucination. Lack of oxygen could do that. It was the only thing that made sense.

Colt took some aspirin before making himself a turkey sandwich on wheat. Then he lay down on the couch to watch an old movie. He didn't make it to the first commercial before he fell asleep.

When he woke up to the sound of the doorbell, it was dark outside. Disoriented, Colt tried to straighten his hair before turning on a lamp. He looked over at the clock and realized that he had missed dinner. Most of the lights were still off, which meant that his parents weren't home yet.

It was Friday, so Colt figured they'd met up for dinner after work. They had a favorite restaurant in the Gaslamp Quarter, where there was live jazz on Friday nights. He just hoped they would remember to order him something to go.

He yawned before stumbling to the front door. Out of habit, he looked through the peephole—and saw a uniformed officer from the San Diego Police Department standing there. Colt's mind started to race. What did he do? Forget to pay a parking ticket? You couldn't get arrested for something like that, right?

Colt took a deep breath before running his fingers through his hair. He was only wearing board shorts, but there was nothing he could do about that now. He opened the door.

"Good evening. My name is Sergeant Scott," the officer said. He didn't offer his hand. His voice was professional, and he was flicking what looked like two driver's licenses against each other. "What happened to your head?"

Colt's hand went to the gauze that covered his forehead. "I hit it on my surfboard this morning."

The officer frowned. For a moment Colt was worried that he was there to ask him about sea monsters.

"Is this the residence of Roger and Mary McAlister?"

"Yeah," Colt said. "Is something wrong?"

"How do you know them?"

"They're my parents."

"I'm sorry to have to tell you this, son," Sergeant Scott said. "They were in an accident."

"Are they okay?"

The officer paused. "It was a head-on collision. I'm afraid they didn't make it."

Colt tilted his head in confusion. His mouth had gone dry, and it felt as though his ears were full of water. His hands started to itch. "Wait, are you sure you have the right house?"

"I'm afraid so." Sergeant Scott handed Colt the licenses.

There was no mistaking the pictures. "What happened?"

"The accident is still under investigation, but it looks like they were hit by a drunk driver."

"Maybe somebody stole my dad's car," Colt said. His parents couldn't be dead. It didn't make sense. "I mean, my mom always leaves her purse in the car. My dad must have left his wallet. Are you sure it was them?"

Before Sergeant Scott could respond, Colt pulled out his phone and called his father's cell. With each ring, his heart beat faster. It went to voice mail. Colt disconnected before hitting redial, but he ended up with the same result.

Colt struggled with the touch pad. His fingers wouldn't hit the right buttons. The phone slipped from his hands before hitting the tile. The battery skittered across the floor, sending Colt to his hands and knees, where he scrambled to put the phone back together.

"Just give me a minute." Colt called his dad a few more times, but nobody picked up. His hands started to shake.

The officer walked into the foyer to kneel by Colt. "I know this isn't easy, son."

Colt felt his chest constrict. "Let me just try my mom's phone. I'm sure she'll pick up, she always does." Once again the call went to voice mail. Colt looked up at the officer, his eyes brimming with tears. "You're sure it was them?"

Sergeant Scott nodded. "How old are you, son?"

The question hardly registered. "Um . . . I just turned sixteen."

"Do you have any older brothers or sisters?"

Colt wiped the streaking tear from his cheek before he turned his attention back to the driver's licenses. "Yeah. Brothers, but they don't live here anymore."

"Somewhere in town?"

Colt shook his head.

"What about grandparents?"

"My grandpa lives in Arizona."

"Do you have his phone number?"

"Yeah, it's in here somewhere," Colt said, scrolling through the numbers in his phone. When it landed on his grandfather's number, Colt pushed Send and handed it to the officer.

He stood there dumbfounded as Sergeant Scott spoke to his grandpa. Colt knew they were talking, but he didn't hear a word of the conversation. Breathing was supposed to be automatic, but Colt had to force himself to inhale and then exhale. It felt like someone had just hit him in the chest with a sledgehammer.

Sergeant Scott placed his hand on Colt's shoulder. "Your grandfather is going to try and catch an early flight tomorrow morning. Is there someplace I can take you until he gets here? A friend's house? Maybe a neighbor?"

"Yeah, I guess so, but I need to get dressed. Can I pack a bag first?"

"Of course, son. Take your time."

Colt was in a fog as he walked back to his bedroom. He turned on his television and clicked through the local stations looking for news of the accident, but all he could find was coverage about UFO sightings near the Naval Amphibious Base in Coronado.

He fired up his laptop. Moments later he was typing the names of his parents into a search engine. Then he added the words *fatal* and *accident*.

Click.

He read the first entry three times before it sank in.

Drunk Driver Arrested after Fatal Accident in San Diego

Aug 29 . . . Journalist Mary McAlister and her husband sustained fatal injuries after a suspected drunk driver struck their vehicle head-on . . .

:: CHAPTER 9 ::

Over the next few days, all seven of Colt's brothers flew in for the funeral with their wives and children. It didn't take long before the McAlister house was transformed into what felt like a campground. Come nightfall, every inch of floor space was covered with sleeping bags, blankets, and pillows. They had even set up tents in the backyard, but there still wasn't enough room to hold everyone. Some of the overflow ended up staying with neighbors, while others wound up at hotels. Colt, however, got to sleep in his own bed.

That would have been a welcome relief, if only he could fall asleep. Instead he would lie there imagining the horrors of the accident. The pickup truck was going so fast when it struck his parents their car flipped over three times before it burst into flames. According to the coroner's report, they were killed on impact. Colt could only hope that was true.

He didn't remember much about the funeral. The church sanctuary was nearly full, but Colt kept to himself in the front row, and he snuck out the side door when it was over. He wasn't in the mood to hear how sorry everyone felt for him. It wasn't that he didn't appreciate the gesture, he just wasn't ready to say good-bye to his parents yet, and all the well-wishing made it seem so final.

After the graveside service, everyone headed to the McAlister house. One of the neighbors owned a restaurant, and he insisted on catering. Volunteers from the church served the food, leaving Colt and his brothers the time they needed to grieve. Colt disappeared to his bedroom.

"There you are," Colt heard someone say. He turned around and saw a girl standing in his bedroom doorway.

"Oh, hi, Dani."

"What are you doing in here?" Danielle Salazar asked. Her skin was the color of terra-cotta, and her dark hair hung straight with bangs swept to one side.

"I guess I needed a break," Colt said. He was standing next to the telescope his parents had given him for Christmas.

"I brought you some food," she said, holding out a plate with a club sandwich, potato salad, and two pickle spears. "Your brother told me you haven't been eating very much."

"Which one?"

"Clive."

"It figures."

"Why do you say that?"

"He's the oldest, so he thinks the rest of us are his responsibility now."

"That's sweet."

"I guess."

Danielle and Colt were born only a few days apart, but despite the similarity in age, he still thought of her as the little sister that he never had. Their parents had grown up together in a suburb outside of Phoenix. The McAlisters moved away after they got married, but the families remained close.

Danielle set the plate down on Colt's nightstand. "You know, I don't think I've ever seen you in a suit before. You look handsome."

"Don't get used to it." He reached up and loosened his tie before lifting it over his head. "My grandpa had to tie the knot. Hopefully I'll never have to wear one again."

"How are you doing?"

Colt smiled, though the expression was empty. "You know, it's weird, but I still have a hard time accepting that they're gone," he said. "I'm only sixteen and I just buried my parents. I mean, yesterday Clive and my grandpa met with a real estate agent. They're putting the house on the market Monday morning."

"What are you going to do?"

"Clive wants me to move to Virginia with his family. Clayton and Clark said I could come and stay with them, but Clayton lives in Berlin, and Clark's wife just had their fifth kid last month. They don't need another one."

"I'm sure they'd all love to have you."

"Maybe," Colt said. "My parents left me a bunch of money, so I was thinking about getting an apartment down by the beach, but I'm too young to sign the lease. I just wish I could stay here."

"What about your grandpa?"

"I went to breakfast with him this morning. He thinks I should move in with him. I can handle Arizona for a week or two in the summer, but year-round? I don't know. Maybe it wouldn't be so bad."

"He has a swimming pool."

"I don't think it's big enough for my surfboard."

Danielle laughed. "Probably not, but we'd practically be neighbors."

"I guess that's a plus."

"You guess?"

"It'll help, anyway," Colt said with a half smile. "My grandpa is going to stay in town until we get everything settled with the house. We have to figure out what to put in storage and how to ship the rest of it to my brothers. Then we're going to rent a truck and drive my stuff out to his place."

"So you've already made up your mind? You're going to Arizona?"

"It's not like I have much of a choice."

Danielle's face lit up with a smile. "I can't believe we're going to be at the same school."

"Me either," Colt said. He grabbed a pickle from the plate. "How long are you guys in town for?"

"School already started, so we have to head back tomorrow night."

"Maybe we can go to the beach or something."

"I'd like that," Danielle said. "By the way, what happened to your head?"

Colt reached up to touch his bandage. He had been hoping that his bangs would cover most of it up, but it wasn't working. "I fell on my surfboard."

"What about the rash on your neck?"

"There was a patch of seaweed."

"Seaweed?"

"I was kind of groggy after I hit my head, but yeah. I think so anyway." A pack of his nieces and nephews chased each other down the hallway outside his room. "Look, I don't really feel like going back out there right now. How would you feel about killing some zombies?"

"Wait, did you get Zombie Extermination Squad?"

"Maybe."

"I thought it just came out last night."

"Since I couldn't sleep, I sort of went to the store and picked up a copy."

"At midnight?"

"The line wasn't very long." Colt turned on the television that hung over his desk. Then he handed Danielle a video game controller.

"Have you played it yet?"

"Only four or five hours."

"And you went to breakfast with your grandpa? Did you even sleep?"

"Sleep is overrated. Besides, if I don't save the world from the zombie infestation, who will?"

:: CHAPTER 10 ::

Danielle was a quick study, and before long they were both able to log into the online world where they joined the tens of thousands of other zombie exterminators. The two of them lost track of time as they hunted zombies through the streets of a city ravaged by nuclear war.

Three hours later Danielle's mom came looking for her. "We have to head out now," Mrs. Salazar said.

"Okay, I'll be there in a minute," Danielle said. She logged her character out of the game before turning to Colt. "Were you serious about going to the beach tomorrow?"

"Of course."

"Want to try and teach me to surf again?"

"Are you sure you're up for it?"

"I'm stubborn like that," Danielle said. Then she stood on her tiptoes to kiss Colt on the cheek before hugging him tightly. "Call me if you need anything, okay?"

||||||||||||||||||||||||||||||||||||

Colt changed into a pair of shorts and a T-shirt before wandering back to the reception. Nearly everyone had left by the time he found the dessert, but there were still a few stragglers. He scooped a bit of cherry cobbler onto a paper plate and popped it into the microwave. A couple of his sisters-in-law were wandering through the house with trash bags, picking up after their guests, while his nieces and nephews were gathered around the television watching *Finding Nemo*.

Colt decided to eat his cobbler on the patio next to the pool. It was a warm August day, but there was a breeze that rushed through the palm fronds and hibiscus. The pool was littered with rafts and beach balls from all the kids, and wet towels hung from most of the lawn chairs. Colt found a quiet corner next to the fire pit. He picked at the cobbler's crust, skipped the cherries, and watched a hummingbird flutter from flower to flower before flying off.

"You read the police report, right?" Colt heard someone say. He craned his neck to see his brother Clive standing with Grandpa McAlister and a man Colt didn't recognize. "The guy who hit them had red eyes. He wasn't drunk, he was an operative."

"We can't prove it," the stranger said. He was an older man, though not as old as Grandpa, wearing a dark suit with an American flag pinned to the lapel. His white hair was neatly trimmed, his cuff links shiny, and from the look of his tan, he probably spent a lot of time on the golf course. "Besides, why would Trident go after your father now? He's been retired for ten years."

Colt perked up at the mention of Trident. That didn't make any sense. His parents were accidentally killed by a drunk driver, not murdered by a bunch of old guys in expensive suits. Sure, there were fringe rumors that Trident wanted to take over the world, but even if they were true, why bother with his parents? It's not like Roger and Mary McAlister were corporate spies or anything.

"The agency still gave him a lot of business," Clive said before turning to his grandfather. "Tell me I'm not the only one who sees it. They were murdered."

There it was, plain as could be. Clive actually thinks they were murdered. Colt's chest constricted and his palms began to sweat.

"You might be right," Grandpa said. Though he was eighty-five years old, Murdoch McAlister still looked like an Olympic athlete. His chest filled out his shirt, his waist was trim, and he hardly had a wrinkle. If Colt didn't know better, he would have sworn that his grandfather had found the fountain of youth.

"So what are we going to do about it?" Clive said. His jaw was clenched and his eyes intense as he stood with tightened fists.

Grandpa McAlister shrugged. "Don't look at me."

Clive turned to the man in the suit. "With all due respect, Senator Bishop, I can't ignore the facts."

"I was at the hospital the day your father was born," the senator said. He placed his hand on Clive's shoulder. "When he was old enough, he worked at my ranch in Prescott during the summers. In fact, he stayed in our home. What I'm trying to say is that you have my full support, but we have to go through the proper channels. The agency isn't in vogue right now. The president continues to press for budget cuts, and programs like ours are first on the chopping block."

"It doesn't make sense," Clive said. "Something is happening. Trident must have found another gateway."

"That's a possibility," Senator Bishop said, "but we have to be careful how we approach this. Do you know how much money Trident executives gave to the president's campaign? The fundraiser dinner that their CEO held raised over a million dollars alone."

"They're smart," Grandpa McAlister said. "We stopped them on the battlefield, so they turned to politics and industry."

"But their biotech division is in your backyard," Clive said to the senator.

"What do you want us to do, raid their offices?" the senator asked. "It's not the Wild West anymore."

Colt had finished with his cobbler. He stood up, but his chair scraped the pavement. The senator turned to look at him. So did his grandfather and his brother.

"I didn't see you there," Grandpa McAlister said. His smile looked forced.

"Hey, Grandpa."

"Have you met Senator Bishop?"

"No, sir." Colt set his plate back down before walking over to shake the senator's hand.

"You have your mother's eyes," the senator said. "How old are you, son?"

"Sixteen."

The senator frowned and turned to McAlister. "Did he take part in the training program?"

McAlister shook his head. "Not yet; he just had a birthday. He should be there in a couple of years, though."

"This is the one, right?"

"That's what they say. Now, is there any more of that cobbler left?"

:: CHAPTER 11 ::

I t had been two weeks since Colt moved from San Diego to live
with his grandfather in Arizona, but he hadn't unpacked much
of anything. Settling in would make this new life feel permanent.

It wasn't that he didn't appreciate what his grandfather had
done. After all, at his age, it was no small sacrifice to invite a teen-
ager to live under his roof. Grandpa McAlister had always been
a private man, and after a career of service in the United States
Army, he had an eye for particulars. Everything in his house had
a place, and he didn't appreciate it when things weren't put back
where they belonged.

Grandma Dottie had lost her battle with cancer nearly a decade
ago, and since then Grandpa spent most of his time puttering
around his yard or working in the garage. When he wasn't doing
that, he liked to play cards with his war buddies from the VFW.

It was early in the morning and Colt was about to hit the snooze
button for a third time, but at the last minute he decided to snatch
the alarm clock from his nightstand and throw it across the room.
If it had been one of those cheap plastic models with a digital display, the clock would have exploded. Unfortunately it had a metal

casing. Instead of shattering, it sank into the drywall, where it left a large hole before it fell to the ground. The alarm was still clanging.

Colt sat up, squinting as rays of sunlight squeezed through the slats in the blinds. After three restless hours of sleep, he wasn't ready to face the day. His hair looked like tangled stalks of wheat after a windstorm, and he wasn't sure any amount of mouthwash would get the stale taste out of his mouth.

He kicked free from his sheets and then slid out of bed before navigating through the cardboard boxes that were stacked haphazardly around his room. When he finally reached the clock, he considered hitting it with the baseball bat that was leaning against the wall. Instead, he reached down to shut it off, then set the clock on the top of his dresser.

His phone rang.

"It's too early," Colt said after checking the caller ID.

"Good morning to you too," Danielle said.

Colt didn't respond.

"Are you ready?" she asked.

"Seriously?"

"I'll be there in ten minutes."

"I still have to shower."

"You're joking, right?"

"I haven't been in a joking mood lately."

"Hurry, okay?"

"I'll do my best."

Colt's Land Cruiser was still in San Diego, so Danielle offered to take him to school. He took a quick shower, but finding clean clothes wasn't going to be easy. He surveyed the massive pile of clothes spread across his bedroom floor. Every shirt he picked up smelled like it had been sitting in a garbage Dumpster, but he finally settled on a pair of board shorts, a faded T-shirt, and a pair of leather flip-flops. He hoped a quick spray of cologne would be enough to cover the musty smell.

His mom had always taken care of his laundry in the past, and though Colt wasn't going to admit it to anyone, she had made his bed every morning as well. Colt just figured it was one of the benefits of being the baby in the family, and he didn't mind milking it. It hadn't taken long to realize that Grandpa McAlister wasn't going to be coddling him the same way.

Colt grabbed his backpack, along with an energy bar and a bottle of water, before heading out to the front porch. As he opened the door, he recoiled. It wasn't even eight in the morning, but the September sun was insanely intense. Dry heat or not, Arizona was going to take some getting used to.

It wasn't long before he felt beads of sweat sliding down his backbone. After five minutes of hovering under the shade of an awning, he was about to head back inside. Finally Danielle pulled up to the curb in an old Ford Thunderbird with whitewall tires and fins on the back.

"You're kidding, right?" she asked through the open window.

"What are you talking about?"

"You look like a beach bum. Did you even take a shower, or is the whole homeless thing popular in San Diego right now?"

"Of course I took a shower. I even wore deodorant and brushed my teeth."

Danielle rolled her brown eyes. "That's a relief. Get in. We're running late."

"When's it supposed to cool off?"

"It doesn't," Danielle said as Colt sat down and strapped into his seat belt. "You might as well get used to it."

"What about air-conditioning?" Colt asked as he reached over to try and crank it up.

"Sorry, it's not working."

"Great."

"You could always walk."

"No, thanks."

"So are you ready for this?"

Colt shrugged. "I guess so."

"Look, I know this has been a nightmare for you, but I'm going to be with you every step of the way. You know, kind of like a guardian angel."

Colt broke into what almost looked like a smile. "Thanks."

"I got you something," Danielle said and reached beneath her seat to grab a small package.

Colt hesitated, but then he opened the paper until he could see some kind of book bound in a suede cover. There was no title, and as he thumbed through it, he couldn't find any words. "Wait a minute, is this a diary?"

"It's a journal," Danielle said as she pulled up to a stop sign. "If you aren't going to talk about what's going on inside that head of yours with anybody, then you need to find another outlet. Either that or you're going to end up in an institution."

"It's just that . . . I don't know. What I want is a distraction so I don't have to think about it all the time. I don't see how a diary is going to help. Besides, the only people who write in diaries are girls with secret crushes."

"Don't be like that," Danielle said. Her eyes narrowed slightly. She was the only person in Colt's life who refused to treat him like a victim.

"Like what?"

"All wrapped up in stupid preconceptions. You're better than that," she said. "Besides, did you know that Theodore Roosevelt, Thomas Jefferson, Benjamin Franklin, Ralph Waldo Emerson, and Winston Churchill kept journals?"

"Thomas Jefferson had a wig, and Benjamin Franklin wore knickers," Colt said. "That should tell you something."

"I'm sure they'd say the same thing about bleached blond hair and board shorts."

"I don't bleach my hair."

"You're impossible, do you know that?"

"Thank you."

"It wasn't a compliment."

Colt felt the beginnings of a smile curl at the edge of his lips. "Look, I appreciate what you're trying to do, but what if somebody finds it?"

"So what?"

Colt sighed. "You aren't going to let this go, are you?"

"Of course not," Danielle said. "Why don't you turn it into a music journal? That way you can write down all of the songs you write. You still play the guitar, right?"

Colt ran his hand over the soft cover. Then he unzipped his backpack and slid the journal inside.

"So does that mean you're going to give it a try?" she asked.

"Only if you don't rub it in."

With a satisfied smile, Danielle eased into the intersection.

"I can't make any promises, but I'll do my best."

:: CHAPTER 12 ::

They listened to the radio as Danielle drove through streets lined with stucco homes painted various shades of white, beige, and brown. Each was covered in a red tile roof, and instead of grass, most of the lawns were filled with gravel and cacti.

"Did you hear about this?" Danielle asked as she reached down to turn the volume up.

"Just when you thought that the world couldn't get any crazier . . ." the disc jockey said through the speakers. "And no, this isn't another UFO sighting. Apparently a rancher in Argyle, Texas, claims that he's caught Bigfoot.

"According to Earl Thomas, he had set out traps to catch what he thought was a bear, but what he found the next morning was something right out of a horror movie. If you haven't seen the video yet, you can find it on our website."

"Can you believe that?" Danielle asked, as the station went to commercial.

"It's probably some viral marketing campaign for a movie."

"I don't know, there's a lot of weird stuff going on lately. My dad is even freaking out. He started talking about buying a gun after those lights showed up over South Mountain again."

"I bet it's just a weather balloon."

"Maybe," Danielle said. "Do you remember that time I thought there were monsters living in my closet?"

Colt nodded. "I think so. Wasn't that over a spring break?"

"We were ten years old, and you were visiting your grandparents. After I told you about it, you filled a wagon with scrap lumber and pulled it to my house so you could board up my closet door."

"Didn't you get in trouble for that?"

"I didn't care," she said. "That was the first good night's sleep I had in weeks."

Colt smiled. "And that's why you got me the journal. You think it's going to help me sleep, is that it?"

"I hope so."

Danielle pulled her car into the parking lot at Chandler High. The campus looked more like an Ivy League university than a high school in the middle of a desert. A perfectly manicured lawn led to a series of stone buildings that were lined with pillars.

"The office is just up those steps," she said, pointing to the main building. "Ms. Skoglund told me that she'd be waiting for you."

"Who's that?"

"Trust me, you'll know when you see her."

Colt felt vulnerable as he opened the car door. For some reason, he was reminded of his first day at kindergarten. His mother had walked him to his room, but before she left, she turned one last time to blow him a kiss.

"Are you okay?" Danielle asked. She placed her hand gently on Colt's forearm.

He stirred, blinking as the daydream faded. "Yeah, sorry." He wasn't sure how long he'd been sitting there.

"I hope we have at least one class together," she said as Colt slammed the door and stepped onto the sidewalk. "If not, I'll see you at lunch."

Ms. Skoglund was a plump woman with stylish red glasses perched on the end of her nose. Her blonde hair was pulled back and twisted into something akin to peacock feathers, with bangs that were cropped and streaked with pink.

As Colt walked up to the counter, she was typing something into the computer, so he cleared his throat to get her attention.

"Oh, I'm so sorry," Ms. Skoglund said, looking up. "You must be our transfer student from San Diego. I was so sorry to hear about what happened to your parents."

"Thanks," Colt said.

"It was such a tragedy." She paused to stare at him for what Colt thought was an uncomfortably long moment. "Now I know the schools in San Diego haven't started up yet," she finally said. "But we've been in session for nearly a month, so you're going to be a little behind. If you need anything, I want you to come and see me."

Ms. Skoglund's wrists tinkled like chimes from all her bracelets as she shuffled through a stack of papers. "Now where did I put your schedule?"

Colt waited as she walked over to a set of filing cabinets, only to return to a nest of papers on her desk. "Ah, here we go," she finally said, pulling out a slip of paper that had been tucked beneath the attendance folder. "I knew it was around here somewhere."

As Colt reviewed his schedule, the office door opened and a tall kid with an easy smile walked through. He was wearing faded blue jeans and a cream-colored T-shirt that accentuated his dark skin. It was snug, showing off his physique. Colt wanted to roll his eyes, but he didn't.

"Look what the cat dragged in," Ms. Skoglund said. "Were you waylaid by all your female admirers?"

"It's nothing like that," the boy said. "Besides, you know I only have eyes for you."

"Sure you do," Mrs. Skoglund said. "I mean, why bother with one of those skinny little things your age when you can go for someone who's trying to lose another thirty pounds before her twenty-year class reunion next summer? That makes sense."

"If you lost thirty pounds, you'd be a skeleton."

"That's why they call him Romeo," Ms. Skoglund said to Colt. "His real name is Oswaldo."

"You can just call me Oz," he said, extending his hand. "I don't usually tell people my real name. I mean, Oswaldo? What were my parents thinking?"

"Sorry," Ms. Skoglund said as Colt offered a half smile.

"I'm Colt."

"Yeah, I know," Oz said.

Colt thought that was an odd response, considering they'd just met. He was about to ask how Oz knew him, but Ms. Skoglund spoke first. "Didn't you say that you knew Colt's grandfather?"

"I've met him once or twice."

Colt had a nagging feeling that the larger boy was hiding something, he just wasn't sure what it was.

"As you can see by his bulging muscles, Romeo here spends more time in the weight room than he does on his homework."

"Ouch," Oz said, putting his hand on his heart in melodramatic fashion that Colt found slightly nauseating.

"Anyway, apart from being the object of desire for most of the girls on campus, he's actually a sweetheart. Since the two of you have the same first-period class, I thought it would be nice for Oz to show you around today."

"We better get going," Oz said. "Mr. Pfeffer freaks out when people are late."

"That's an understatement." Ms. Skoglund rolled her eyes. "He's so wound up that . . . well, never mind. Just let me know if he gives you any lip."

||||||||||||||||||||||||||||||||

"So how do you know my grandpa?" Colt asked as he followed Oz through the hallways.

"My dad served in the same company when he was in the army."

"Wait a minute . . . how old is your dad?"

Oz laughed. "It wasn't at the same time, but when my father was coming up through the ranks, he was in the same company that your grandfather fought in during World War II."

"You already know more about my grandpa's service record than I do," Colt said.

"Really? What about his nickname?"

"Sorry."

"I was told everyone called him the Phantom Flyer."

"As in the comic book?"

"It's crazy, right? Did you ever read it?"

Colt paused. People who read comic books typically didn't rise to the top of the popularity chart, and they definitely didn't look like Oz. "My dad had some," he said with a shrug. "I might have had a few of the action figures."

"Are you serious? I had all of that stuff. What about the Phantom Flyer Airship?"

Colt nodded.

"You had to have the Yeti cave with the blaster cannons."

"Yeah, I got it for my sixth birthday," Colt said, unaware of the growing enthusiasm in his voice. Maybe Oz wasn't so bad after all. "After we went to the first Phantom Flyer movie, my parents took me to pick it up at the toy store."

"So you know about the rumor, right?"

"What rumor?"

Oz stopped to gauge Colt's sincerity. "Your dad never told you that the Phantom Flyer was based on your grandpa?"

Colt's eyes narrowed. "Are you serious?"

"Of course I am. Think about it . . . the Flyer's real name is Malachai McAdams. Sound like anybody you know?"

"Wait, you're saying my grandfather fought against Nazi supersoldiers and robots while he flew around in a jet pack?"

"Like I said, it's just a rumor."

Colt wanted to ask more questions, but he was distracted by laughter. When he looked around to see who it was, he wished he'd taken Danielle's advice and worn something a little nicer.

Three girls were standing in a cluster talking, but Colt only noticed the one in the middle. Her hazel eyes were playful, and her blonde hair fell down her back like golden waves from the ocean. She wore a denim jacket over a brown dress, and her cowboy boots pulled it all together.

Oz looked back to make sure that Colt was keeping up. "Are

you coming, or are you planning on standing there and staring at Lily Westcott all day?"

Colt's eyes shot wide. He didn't mean to be so obvious. If Oz had noticed, he was afraid that she had too. "What are you talking about?"

Lily caught his gaze and smiled before her friends pulled her into a classroom.

Oz shook his head. "You're in luck, McAlister. She's in our class."

:: CHAPTER 13 ::

olt's new history teacher was squatting in front of his laptop as he tried to sync it with a projector that had a Trident Technology logo on it. They were everywhere. His shirttail had pulled out from his pants, revealing more of Mr. Pfeffer's backside than Colt had hoped to see.

"One of these days computers are going to rise up and enslave us all," Mr. Pfeffer said to no one in particular. "I know most of the sheep in this world believe all these little gizmos have made our lives easier, but we're setting ourselves up. What was wrong with filmstrips, anyway? They always worked when you needed them."

"Mr. Pfeffer?" Colt said.

"Can't you see that I'm busy?"

"Be nice, Mr. Pfeffer," Oz said as he took his seat. "It's his first day."

"What?" The teacher turned to find Colt looking down at him. "Oh, I'm sorry. I forgot we were getting a new student today. Welcome to the glories of World History."

"Thanks," Colt said.

Mr. Pfeffer stood up, then motioned for Colt to hand him his schedule. The history teacher was tall, with narrow shoulders, a doughy midsection, and a face shaped like a kernel of corn—square on the top and pointed at the chin. His hair, at least what was left of it, was parted down the middle, and he wore glasses that were at least ten years out of date.

"It looks like everything is in order. Why don't you take a seat over there." Mr. Pfeffer pointed to the only empty desk in the room. It was between Oz and Lily.

Colt hesitated as he made eye contact with her. She smiled, then Colt saw one of the other girls start to laugh.

"By the way," Colt said to Mr. Pfeffer, "all you need to do is hit this button." He reached down to select a different input setting and the projector flared to life, displaying Mr. Pfeffer's desktop on the whiteboard.

"That was dangerous," Oz said as Colt took his seat.

"What?"

"Mr. Pfeffer doesn't like it when people show him up."

"I was just trying to help."

"Now who here would like to tell Master McAlister what we've been studying?" Mr. Pfeffer said. "Come on, people, this isn't a difficult question . . . no? Okay, then perhaps we should take a pop quiz."

Every student, save Colt, raised a hand.

"That's better," the teacher said. "What about you, Master Savage? I'd love to hear your response. Of course you'll have to spit your gum out first."

A thin boy with messy hair retrieved an enormous wad of gum from the inside of his cheek before whipping it across the room. It fell perfectly into the wastebasket. Then he sat back, kicking a pair of black boots on the chair in front of him. "World War II, sir."

"How enlightening," Mr. Pfeffer said. "No wonder your parents named you Aristotle."

"Thanks."

Mr. Pfeffer rolled his eyes and then clicked a button on his remote control. Suddenly an image of Japanese fighter planes showed on the whiteboard. "Today we will discuss Pearl Harbor."

As the teacher started his lecture, Colt pulled out a notebook and a pen. He intended to take notes, but Mr. Pfeffer got sidetracked. He started discussing the attack that launched the United States into the war, but he ended up spending most of the class talking about a family vacation that he took when he was seven years old.

Colt let his mind drift as the history teacher droned. He started thinking about his own family vacation in Maui. Colt and his dad took surfing lessons, and their whole family went snorkeling and saw a school of dolphins.

"What about you, Master McAlister?"

As Colt came out of his daydream, everyone was looking at him. Lily Westcott leaned over in her chair, trying to look discreet. "He wants to know if you have any family members who served during World War II."

Lily's voice had a melodic quality that made it sound like she was singing, even when she whispered. If that weren't distracting enough, she smelled like orange blossoms, and it was intoxicating. Caught off guard, Colt suddenly lost the power of speech. He looked at her dumbly, and Lily just smiled in return. She was either oblivious to how awkward he felt or kind enough to ignore it.

"Oh . . . ah, yeah," Colt said. "From what my dad says, my

grandfather was part of a special unit that was supposed to assassinate Hitler."

It was obvious that Mr. Pfeffer didn't know what to say. He finally settled on "Seriously?"

Colt shrugged, as though being related to an assassin was an everyday occurrence. "That's what my dad said, anyway."

Mr. Pfeffer walked over to his desk and scratched a note in his lesson planner. "Do you think he'd be willing to come in and talk to our class about his experiences?"

"I could ask him, but I don't know. He's never really talked about what happened."

"I understand," Mr. Pfeffer said. "But if you'd be willing to gauge his interest, I would be in your debt."

"Yeah, sure," Colt said. "I'll see what I can do."

"Excellent. Now on to the fun," Mr. Pfeffer said. "Let's talk about our class project."

There was a series of groans as Colt turned to Lily. "Thanks."

"Don't mention it," Lily said. "I know how hard it is to concentrate when he starts talking about his childhood memories."

"Does he do that a lot?"

Lily laughed, though quietly. "Yeah, you could say that."

They both turned their attention back to Mr. Pfeffer as he reviewed the semester's big assignment. "Each of you will write an essay about an important event during the Second World War," he said, handing the specifications to everyone on red sheets of paper. "I will have to approve the subject, of course, but you might select a battle, a political figure, or even a top secret unit that was assigned to kill Adolf Hitler."

Colt did his best to avoid eye contact as Mr. Pfeffer turned to look at him.

"Wait a minute, this—"

"I'm sorry, Aristotle, but I didn't see you raise your hand," Mr. Pfeffer said.

Aristotle rolled his eyes, but he complied.

"How can I help you?" Mr. Pfeffer said, now that Aristotle had his hand in the air.

"This is actually going to be 50 percent of our grade?"

Mr. Pfeffer smiled. "Think of it this way: you won't have to worry as much about tomorrow's test, because even if you fail, you can make up for it. Just write an incredible essay. Besides, you haven't even heard the best part."

The class was quiet as they waited for more bad news.

"I'll be collecting your work and publishing it as a book."

"When do we get paid?" Aristotle said.

"That's the beauty of it," Mr. Pfeffer said. "We'll be donating any proceeds to help homeless veterans."

"Is that a joke or something?"

"No, it is most certainly not a joke."

The bell rang, and without waiting to be dismissed, every student in the class packed up and filed out of the room. Colt tried to time it so that he would walk out the door with Lily, but he was cut off.

"So how many German officers did he assassinate?" a pudgy boy wearing a Chewbacca T-shirt wanted to know.

"What was that?" Colt asked. He'd been watching Lily walk out the door and didn't hear the question.

"I just wanted to know how many people your grandfather assassinated."

"What kind of question is that, Farkus?" Oz said, getting between Colt and the growing crowd.

"It's okay," Colt said. "To tell you the truth, I don't know. I mean, I asked him once, but he wouldn't say anything."

"Can you imagine listing yourself as an assassin on a business card?" Farkus said to a boy standing next to him.

"Assassins don't carry business cards," Oz said. Then he ushered Colt through the door and into the hall.

:: CHAPTER 14 ::

The rest of the morning was mundane compared to World History. Colt had hoped that either Danielle or Oz would be in another class with him, but in a school with more than two thousand students, he knew the odds weren't good.

"There you are," Oz said as Colt left his fourth-period algebra class with a load of homework. "What are you doing for lunch?"

"I should probably stay in here and try to finish some of these assignments. All this math is killing me."

"Why would you be thinking about homework when Chandler High's five-star cafeteria is awaiting?"

"I'm actually supposed to meet someone."

Oz smiled. "A lady friend? I don't know why I'm surprised. Every girl on campus is talking about you."

"Why does it sound creepy when you say it like that?"

"What's her name?"

"Danielle."

"It's not ringing a bell."

"Salazar?"

"The girl who drives that old Thunderbird?"

Colt nodded.

"Here I thought you only had eyes for Lily."

"It's not like that," Colt said. "We're just friends."

"Danielle's a little different, but I like her eyes. She's cute."

"I guess," Colt said with a shrug. "I've known her since we were kids. She's like a sister."

"I'm sure Lily will be relieved."

"I was thinking," Colt said, ready to change the subject, "are you sure we've never met before?"

"Why?"

"It's just that . . . I don't know, you seem familiar."

Oz wrapped his arm around Colt's shoulder. "Why don't we hunt down Danielle and grab some food before the bell rings? I had a killer workout this morning and I'm starving."

|||||||||||||||||||||||||||||||||||

The food at the cafeteria was anything but gourmet—not that Colt expected any different. For the most part everything was deep-fried, canned, or loaded with saturated fat. Colt wasn't exactly a health food nut, but when he passed by mashed potatoes covered in what looked like radioactive gravy he nearly lost his appetite.

"So what's going to happen to the guy who killed your parents?" Oz asked as he grabbed two chicken sandwiches off of the rack, placing them next to a gigantic chef salad loaded down with turkey, ham, and lots of chopped eggs.

Colt might have been offended by that question had it come from anyone else, but for some reason, Oz was able to get away with it. His direct manner of speech was actually refreshing. Colt had never met anyone who said what was on his mind without worrying about whether or not he was going to offend somebody.

"I'm not sure," Colt said. "He's supposed to go through some kind of psychiatric evaluation. His blood alcohol level was nearly twice the legal limit at the time of the crash, but he claims he hadn't been drinking."

"I bet the cops hear that all the time."

"I guess," Colt said, contemplating whether or not he should try one of the hamburgers. "He'd just come from an appointment with his doctor, and the doctor said he wasn't drunk. In fact, he didn't even smell any alcohol."

"What's wrong?"

"What do you mean?"

"You're kind of fidgety."

Colt couldn't say what he was thinking—that Uriah Bloc, the guy who killed his parents, probably worked for Trident Industries. And that Colt's brother and a United States Senator thought Colt's parents were murdered. He was pretty sure people who believed that kind of stuff ended up in padded rooms wearing straight jackets.

"I've been looking all over for you," Danielle said, interrupting as she approached the boys in the food line. "I thought we were going to eat together."

"We are," Colt replied. "Oz wanted to join us."

"I hope that's okay," Oz said. He flashed a smile that would give any movie star a run for his money.

"Yeah, sure," Danielle said, looking up at Oz through her long eyelashes.

Danielle's eyes had always been her best feature, and she knew how to use them to her advantage. That's why Colt thought the whole shy act was a smoke screen. Danielle was trying to keep Oz off guard before she lured him in.

"Good, because lunch is on me today," Oz said.

"In that case, I'll get a hamburger and a corn dog," Colt said.

"Knock yourself out," Oz said, "but I thought everybody in California ate avocado and bean sprouts. Isn't all that grease going to kill you?"

"If I'm going to die, I might as well go big," Colt said, adding an order of onion rings to his tray.

Danielle excused herself to go back and grab a salad before she met the boys at the cashier. After Oz paid for everything with his father's credit card, they headed over to grab a table next to the wall.

"I never see you in the cafeteria," Danielle said.

Oz shrugged. "I usually go to the gym and run on the treadmill, but I promised Ms. Skoglund that I'd stick with McAlister, so here I am. What about you?"

"Mr. Bradford gave me a key to the computer lab, so I generally eat in there."

"Why?" Oz asked, before taking a gigantic bite out of a chicken sandwich.

"I don't know," Danielle said, shrugging. "I guess I'm one of those techie needs. I'll surf the net or play video games."

"Wait a minute," Oz said, nearly choking. "You play video games? How about Orion's Revenge 3: Rise of the Dog Star?"

"It was okay, but I like Zombie Extermination Squad better."

"She's pretty good at it," Colt said.

"What do you mean 'pretty good'?" Danielle asked. "Last night I broke into the top one hundred, and that's a global ranking, thank you very much."

"You're not making this up, are you?" Oz said, stopping before he took another bite of his sandwich.

"Why would I?" Danielle asked. "Can't girls play video games too?"

"It's just that I've never met a girl like you who's actually a gamer, that's all."

Danielle furrowed her brows. "And what kind of girl am I?"

Oz took that bite. "I didn't mean anything by it," he said, revealing lumps of his sandwich with each word. "Let's put it this way. When I think of computer geeks, I don't think about girls who look like you, that's all."

"I guess that I'll take that as a compliment," Danielle said, before turning to Colt. "What about you?"

"Are you trying to rub it in because I'm not ranked yet?"

"I already know that you're a terrible zombie exterminator," Danielle said. "I wanted to know how your day is going."

"It's okay, I guess."

"He has a crush on Lily Westcott," Oz said, causing Colt to choke on the corn dog.

"Get in line," Danielle said. "She's the most beautiful girl in our school."

"It depends," Oz said. "Everybody has different taste."

Colt watched as Danielle and Oz smiled at one another. "It doesn't matter," he said, "because I don't have a crush on her."

"Give me a break," Danielle said. "Your neck is bright red. I've never seen you blush like that before."

"I'm not blushing," Colt said. He lifted the collar of his T-shirt to cover his neck.

"You're definitely blushing," Oz said.

"Don't look now, but I think Colt's little crush is staring at him," Danielle said.

Colt took the bait. He slinked his neck around to see if

Danielle was lying, and as soon as he did, his eyes locked with Lily's. She smiled and waved as the girl sitting on her right whispered something in her ear. Colt nodded in her general direction, realizing almost immediately how ridiculous that must have looked. Why hadn't he just waved to her like a normal person?

Lily turned her focus back to her friends, but Colt's eyes lingered. He watched a guy walk over to kiss her on the cheek and sit down in the empty chair on her left.

"That's Graham St. John," Danielle said as Colt turned back around. "In case you couldn't tell, he's Lily's boyfriend."

"Yeah, I kind of got that." Colt hoped the disappointment wasn't evident.

He managed to avoid staring at Lily for the rest of lunch, at least directly. He glanced at her out of the corner of his eye on two separate occasions, and each time he was certain that Graham caught him gawking.

"If it's any consolation," Danielle said as she watched Colt wince, "Graham is a senior, and he's heading to Idaho State on a football scholarship next year. Everybody knows that long-distance relationships never last."

"What are you talking about?" Colt said as a phone started ringing. He patted his pockets. "Whose phone is that?"

"It's not mine," Oz said.

"Me either," Danielle said.

"That doesn't sound like my ringtone." But it was coming from Colt's backpack. He unzipped a small pouch on the front and pulled out a phone that was heavier than most handhelds, with a shiny black case and a simple touch display that flashed blue each time it rang.

"Aren't you going to answer it?" Danielle asked.

"It's not my phone."

"Well, it's in your backpack," Oz said. "So if it's not yours, whose is it?"

"There's only one way to find out." Danielle reached over and hit the Send button.

Colt stared at the phone until she pushed it to his ear. "Um . . . hello?"

"Is this Colt McAlister?" The voice was creepy, as though masked by sound equipment.

"Yeah," was all Colt could manage.

"Please listen carefully. Your parents weren't killed in a random act of violence."

"Who is this?"

"Your mother was writing an investigative story about an organization that preferred anonymity. She was about to go public, so they assassinated her."

"If this is some kind of joke—"

"I'm afraid it's not a joke, and I am willing to prove my claim. You will receive a text message later today with instructions on what to do next. If you ignore the message, you will never hear from me again."

CHAPTER 15

Who was that?" Danielle asked.

Colt turned to her, his face drained of any color. "I'm not sure."

"Well, what did he say?"

"That he knows who murdered my parents."

"Can I see the phone?" Danielle asked. She turned it over in her hands a few times, considering it like a master jeweler looking at a diamond. Then she removed the battery before putting it all back together. "Did you leave your backpack sitting around?"

"I've had it with me all day," Colt said. "Before that it was sitting in a box in my bedroom. I just got it out this morning."

"What about the caller ID?" Oz asked.

"It was a blocked call," Colt said.

"It's one of those prepaid phones that you can't trace," Danielle said. "I bet whoever called you has one just like it. It's too bad we don't have the number because we could probably trace the signal to a cell tower."

Oz looked at Danielle. "How do you know about that kind of stuff?"

"She's a hacker," Colt said.

"No, I'm not." Danielle glanced around the lunchroom to make sure that nobody was looking. "I just watch a lot of movies, that's all."

"Now she's a hacker and a liar," Colt said.

The bell rang, announcing that lunch was over. Colt put the phone back in the pouch. "I guess I'll have to wait and see if I get a text."

|||||||||||||||||||||||||||||||||||||

Even though there were only three classes remaining, time crawled. Colt kept looking into the pouch in his backpack to see if the text had come through. The teacher in charge of his study hall nearly confiscated the phone, but he let Colt off with a warning since it was his first day.

Danielle was clearly upset when she dropped Colt off at his grandpa's house after school. "I have a bad feeling about that phone," she told him.

"I'll be fine," Colt said. "Besides, what's the worst that could happen?"

"Just be careful. Okay?"

"I promise."

Danielle drove off, and Colt found his grandfather in the garage working on a 1946 Chevy pickup. It was over one hundred degrees in the shade, but Murdoch McAlister was still wearing his jumpsuit. All he had to cool himself was an oscillating fan and a glass of lemonade and the ice was long gone.

"Hey, Gramps."

"You're home already?" Grandpa McAlister said, his voice echoing from under the hood.

"It's almost four o'clock."

Grandpa McAlister lifted his head so he could see the clock that was hanging on the wall. "I guess it is," he said. "So how was your first day? Did you make any new friends?"

Colt smiled. He wanted to point out that he wasn't in kindergarten any longer, but he decided to give his grandpa a break. "A couple," he said. "A kid told me that he knew you . . . or at least his father did."

Grandpa McAlister nodded. "Was that the Romero boy? His father was the best soldier I've ever seen."

"Really? Oz said that you were the legend."

"*Pfft*," Grandpa McAlister said—the sound he used when he thought somebody was talking nonsense. "I was no more a legend than the man in the moon. I was just lucky enough to survive, that's all."

"Have you been out here all day?"

His grandfather shut the hood to the truck and wiped the grease from his hands onto a blue towel. "A couple of hours or so, I suppose," he said. "I was helping the Broeks put in some fence posts to keep their horses from running away."

"Are you sure you're eighty-five?"

"As far as I'm concerned, you're only as old as you act. That's why I like to roll up my sleeves and put in a good day's work. It keeps you young and your back strong. Which reminds me, I need to take my pills."

"So what's for dinner tonight?" Colt asked.

"I'm afraid you're on your own. There're some cold cuts in the meat drawer and potpies in the freezer, but it's poker night and I have people depending on me."

"That sounds pretty serious," Colt said.

"If I'm not there, who's going to take all their money?" Grandpa McAlister said with a wink.

"Then you better get cleaned up. I wouldn't want you to leave grease prints on the cards. They'll think you're marking the aces."

"By the way," Grandpa McAlister said. "I found a box of your father's things, so I put it in your bedroom . . . not that you'll be able to find it in that mess."

At the mention of his father, Colt felt his throat tighten. "Sorry about that," he finally said. "I'll pick everything up tonight."

"There's no rush."

Colt went through the door to the kitchen and grabbed a couple slices of cold pizza before heading back to his bedroom where he found a box filled with his dad's old Phantom Flyer comic books. The pages were starting to yellow, and most of the covers were ripped or bent, but his dad had never bought comic books as an investment.

Before long Colt found a Phantom Flyer ring and patch that were part of a mail-in offer from the Phantom Flyer radio show. Without thinking, he placed the ring on his finger, wondering if his dad used to run around the house pretending to fight Nazis and space aliens.

As Colt paged through the comics, he thought about all the times that Dad used to read them to him before Colt went to bed. Then there was the year that Mom made him a Phantom Flyer costume for Halloween. It took almost a month of shopping at thrift and army surplus stores. Even then, she had to enlist an old college roommate to help. Ellie Salinger was a costume designer in Hollywood, and Mom talked her into sewing a replica of the Phantom Flyer's leather mask.

After Colt paged through the comics, he decided it was finally time to put his things away. His first order of business was to wrap some of his grandmother's old ceramic figurines in hand towels before placing them in a now empty cardboard box. Then he attacked the massive pile of clothes on the floor. Once a load of whites was churning in the washing machine, he turned back to the boxes, figuring he'd rather clean than do his algebra homework.

"I'm heading out now," Grandpa McAlister said, stopping by Colt's bedroom before leaving. "Do you want me to put anything in the oven for you?"

"I'll grab something later."

"Don't say I didn't offer."

"Thanks, Grandpa. For everything."

"I'm expecting you to carry your weight around here, so don't get ahead of yourself."

"No, sir. I won't."

"Besides, don't you have a lot of schoolwork to catch up on?"

"I'll stay on top of things."

With that, Grandpa McAlister headed to his car. Colt decided to stack a few more boxes in the closet before standing back to survey his progress. "Not bad."

An hour later he was ready to wander into the kitchen to scrounge for dinner when the phone in his backpack started to beep. It was the text. Colt could feel his heart pounding. He thought about ignoring it, but that wasn't an option. If his parents had truly been murdered, Colt needed to know who did it.

Slowly, carefully, he reached over to unzip the pouch. A flashing light showed that there was a text waiting. He took the phone in his hand before punching the button to call it up. The message was brief: **A car is waiting for you outside.**

:: CHAPTER 16 ::

Colt peered through the blinds of his bedroom window to find a sedan waiting in the street. It looked like one of the cars used to shuttle traveling executives back and forth to wherever they need to go.

He slipped out the front door, careful to make sure that it locked behind him. His palms started to sweat and his skin was itchy, but he willed himself to walk across the lawn. The driver got out of the car, and Colt felt short of breath. There was no turning back now.

The driver had olive skin and dark stubble that covered his head as well as his cheeks, chin, and upper lip. He was dressed in a black suit with a crisp white shirt and a black tie. Colt couldn't see his eyes behind the sunglasses.

"Good evening, Master McAlister," the driver said in a British accent as he opened the door.

Colt hesitated. He looked back at the house before turning to the driver, wondering if he should have left a note for his grandpa. At least, Colt thought, he had his cell phone in case something went wrong.

After a deep breath, he slipped into the backseat. The door slammed shut with a finality that made Colt feel like a corpse getting sealed inside a coffin. As his eyes adjusted, the driver started the car. That's when Colt realized he wasn't alone. Someone—or something—was seated next to him.

Though it seemed impossible, Colt was certain that there was a robot dressed in a dark suit identical to the one the driver was wearing. The robot had a shiny metal hide and glowing eyes that reminded Colt of two flashlights. There was a slit in place of a mouth, and it had five mechanical fingers on each hand.

It turned its head to regard Colt, who moved as far away from the machine as he could without jumping out the window. Its eyes flashed bright before dimming to a dull glow. Then it turned away without a word.

"Is that a . . . ?"

"Robot?" Even though the driver was wearing sunglasses, Colt could tell he was looking at him through the rearview mirror. "You're looking at a prototype of the latest P-RC unit." Colt must have looked confused, because the driver continued to explain. "You know, a Private Robotic Combat unit? It's part bodyguard and part tank, with an advanced artificial intelligence system that would make you think it was alive. You can even program it to cook like a gourmet chef or walk your dog."

"Where did you get it?"

"Not at the local hardware store, if that's what you're asking. It has retractable hands that turn into plasma cannons."

It wasn't long before they ended up on the freeway heading westbound toward Phoenix. Traffic was light as they cruised at the speed limit, never straying so much as a single mile per hour over or under.

"What's your name?" Colt asked as the desert landscape blurred outside his window.

"You can call me Salaam."

"Where're you from?"

"I was born in Jordan, but I grew up in London. What about you?"

"I just moved here from San Diego."

"It's bloody hot, isn't it?"

"You could say that," Colt said. "So do you know where we're going?"

"I'd better, since I'm the one who's driving," Salaam answered, flashing an infectious smile.

"You know what I mean." Colt sat back. His breathing was getting back to normal, and the tension in his chest was gone.

"Sorry, but I'm not at liberty to say," Salaam said as he merged the car onto Interstate 10. "You'll know soon enough."

It wasn't long before they exited on the ramp that led to Sky Harbor Airport. Salaam steered them through construction and roadblocks, passing all the terminals before he turned into a private drive.

"We're not flying anywhere, are we?" Colt asked.

"I'm just the driver," Salaam said as he pulled up to a gate.

Colt watched as the robot's eyes flared three times. The gate opened up, and Salaam drove toward a small hangar that looked like a giant tin shed with a concave roof. The door slid up, and he parked next to an armored truck.

"This way, please," Salaam said after getting out to open Colt's door. He led Colt past a row of vehicles that looked like hybrids between motorcycles and fighter jets.

"What are those?" Colt asked as the robot followed.

"Think of them as military-grade ultralights," Salaam said.

He led Colt to a door at the far end of the room before placing his hand on a biometric scanner imbedded in the wall. There was a series of clicks after a light turned green, and the door swung open.

"Please," Salaam said. He motioned for Colt to go inside what looked like the remains of an office. The walls were empty, and the only thing left on the desk was a lamp. Filing cabinet drawers were cocked open, with manila folders and an assortment of paperwork littering the floor.

"Wait, are you the guy who sent me the message about my parents?" Colt asked.

"No, he wasn't," a voice said as the door shut behind him.

When Colt turned around, Salaam was gone. In his place was an older man with silver hair, drooping shoulders, and bags under his bloodshot eyes. "Please, take a seat," he said, then walked around to the other side of the desk where he collapsed into a swivel chair. "I apologize for the mysterious conditions of our meeting, but I have to take certain precautions."

"Where's Salaam?"

"Just outside the door."

"Who are you?"

"My name is Albert Van Cleve."

"Then you're the guy who contacted me?"

Van Cleve nodded.

"How did you know my mom?"

"We were working together on an important article."

"So you're a reporter?"

"I'm the lead research scientist for a company called Trident Biotech."

Colt had heard the name. "You make biochips, right?"

"My team developed a technology that improves the quality of life for people who suffer from things like epilepsy, Parkinson's, and even paralysis," Van Cleve said as he pulled a metal disk out of his coat pocket. He set it on the desk and pressed a button. A vibrant holographic image of one of the microchips flickered to life over his desk without the use of a monitor.

"I contacted your mother because those same biochips are being used as part of an illegal mind-control program. You see, during the Second World War, scientists from Trident worked with the Nazis to plant receivers into the cerebral cortex of prisoners."

As he spoke, Van Cleve touched the image of the biochip with his fingertips. Then he motioned as though he were wiping it away. It was replaced by an X-ray of someone's head and spine, and Colt could see where the biochip was attached. Tendrils had snaked from the chip and into the patient's spinal column like a mechanical parasite. It looked painful.

"The implant gave them control over those poor people in the same way a child would steer a remote control car."

"Then my brother was right?"

"Excuse me?"

"I heard my brother say that the guy who killed my parents was a Trident operative."

"That's partially true," Van Cleve said. "As you would assume, the practice of controlling people in this manner is highly illegal, and the board of directors would prefer that their little secret not get out. When they got word that your mother was going to publish the article about their indiscretions, they decided to eliminate her."

"Wait—they were going after my mother?"

"I'm afraid so," Van Cleve said. "I'm sorry to say that your father was collateral damage."

Colt sat back in his chair and looked at Van Cleve. Then he shook his head. "If you were feeding her the information, why didn't they kill you too?"

"I'm only alive because they aren't sure who your mother's informant was. Once they figure it out—and they will—my life will be forfeit."

:: **CHAPTER 17** ::

D o you really expect me to believe any of this?" Colt stood up. "I mean, you're telling me that one of the biggest companies in the world hired assassins to kill my mom because she was going to write an article about them? Come on!"

"Perhaps this video will help explain why the technology is so dangerous." Once again Van Cleve lifted his hand to the image before wiping it away. He selected a small icon, and the image of a boy no older than ten showed on the display. Van Cleve tapped the image once, and a video started to play.

The boy was standing in a gymnasium as a nurse checked his blood pressure, then his heart rate. Once she finished, Colt watched as an image of Van Cleve walked into view. He was holding a small device that looked a bit like a phone. After he entered a combination onto the touch screen, the boy's back stiffened and his eyes started to glow with a red light.

"We call these people the Cursed," Van Cleve explained as he watched the video with Colt. "Once they're activated, they're victims of our whims."

"*Very good,*" Colt heard Van Cleve say on the video. "*Now I'd like for you to run to the wall and back.*"

The boy did as he was told.

"Excellent. Do it again, please. Only this time, I'd like for you to run backward."

Again the boy followed instructions. Van Cleve continued to put him through a series of tests, asking him to climb ladders, jump over obstacles, and run through tires that were lying on the hardwood floor.

The scene jumped to show the boy standing next to a window. The cameraman panned down to show that they were ten stories above a busy street. Then he pulled back to show Van Cleve standing next to the boy, whose eyes were still red.

"I'd like for you to climb up and stand on the ledge, if you wouldn't mind," Van Cleve said.

Without hesitation, the boy walked up a step stool and placed his feet on the windowsill. Van Cleve reached down to enter another combination into the device that had activated the remote mechanism inside the boy's head. Once Van Cleve hit Enter, the boy's posture slumped. His arms shot out so he could brace himself from a fall, then his knees started to buckle.

A nurse ran over to catch the boy by his shirttail before she helped him back down to the step stool. *"What happened?"* the boy asked. His eyes were no longer red. Instead, they were filled with panic.

"Tell me, son," Van Cleve said. *"What is the last thing that you remember?"*

The boy looked confused. *"I . . . I don't really know."*

Van Cleve paused the video before turning his attention back to Colt. "As you can see, we are able to force the microchip recipients to do our bidding, and they don't remember any of it. I could have made that young man jump, and he would have without pause."

"What's the point?"

"Think about it," Van Cleve said. "Politicians, law enforcement officials, military leaders, the executives who guide our competitors . . . we control thousands of people around the globe. They do whatever we tell them without question."

Colt sat there a moment, trying to let it all sink in. "The guy who killed my parents had a biochip, didn't he?"

Van Cleve nodded. "He received the implant to stabalize his seizures."

"Then it's your fault," Colt said. "My parents are dead because of you. I mean, if you created the technology, then you're just as guilty as the person who sent that guy to kill my parents."

Van Cleve sighed before running a hand through his wispy hair. "I'm afraid you're right," he said. "I sold my soul to advance science, but in the end it wasn't worth it. Too many innocent lives have been lost, including your parents'. I have to find a way to make amends."

"It's a little late, don't you think?"

"For your parents, yes," Van Cleve said, "but there are thousands with those biochips . . . thousands who are mere puppets in the hands of Trident."

"Why me?" Colt said. "I mean, why not take this to the police, or to another reporter?"

There was an explosion.

"They're here!" Van Cleve said.

"Who?"

"Trident assassins."

Another explosion struck, this time closer. The ground shook, throwing Colt from his chair. He rolled across the floor and slammed into the wall.

:: CHAPTER 18 ::

There was a flash of green light before the door shattered into countless pieces. Colt ducked, taking the brunt of the wooden shards on his back. After everything stopped shaking, he looked over to see Van Cleve slumped against one of the filing cabinets. His face was bleeding from all the cuts.

Salaam rushed in and knelt next to Van Cleve. The robot was there as well, standing protectively over both men. Its hands were gone, and in their place were two cannons held at the ready. A tall figure swept into the room, dressed in deep gray with a ski mask, night vision goggles, and a jacket with a Trident logo on the shoulder.

Colt could hear a humming sound as the robot's cannons flared to life. The barrels started to crackle with energy as two blasts erupted. Each struck the masked intruder in the chest. Like honey spreading over toast, the energy expanded until it encompassed his entire body. Then, in a flash of light, the man disappeared. Colt scrambled to his feet as he tried to process what had just happened, figuring the guy had been atomized.

"Go," Van Cleve said. His eyes were barely open and his voice was weak.

As the ceiling gave way, two more Trident assassins repelled down through the debris. The robot hit one of them with a plasma charge, but the second landed and shouldered the rifle strapped to his back. His first shot released a concussive wave of energy that knocked the robot against the wall.

The assassin took aim at Van Cleve, but Salaam was quicker. He leapt at the masked man, grabbing his wrist. The assassin's shot hit the ceiling, which buckled under the impact. Chunks of plaster and wood fell, creating a cloud of dust.

"Quickly," Van Cleve said between coughs. He reached into his pocket and tossed Colt a key. "It's out back . . . use the window."

Colt unlatched the hinges and threw the window open, then he turned back to look at Van Cleve.

"I'll be fine," Van Cleve said with a frail smile. He coughed once more. "Go and find your mother's files. It's the only way you'll be able to bring her killers to justice."

As Colt placed his leg through the window, two more assassins entered the room. The first kicked Salaam in the ribs before turning his attention to Colt. "Get the kid."

The second assassin took aim, but Colt slid out of the window before the shot was fired. As he landed, his breathing was shallow and his eyes wide. He tried to form a coherent thought, but none of this made sense.

Colt ran, but his feet got tangled up. He fell, scrambling forward on his hands and knees. A shot exploded in the ground a few feet away, forming a crater in the asphalt. Colt lay still, his hands covering the back of his head. Then, after two more shots, he forced himself to stand.

He looked for a car, but all he could see was one of the armored ultralights. That couldn't have been what Van Cleve meant, could it? He paused to look at the key, but another shot brought him out of his haze. Colt bolted, running to the left, then right, and left again, hoping the erratic motion would make him a difficult target. Another plasma bolt erupted. He felt the heat from the blast before it exploded against a No Parking sign.

There was a blur of motion from his periphery, followed by a loud pop. Colt turned in time to see a canister shooting toward him. It exploded, releasing a net that spun through the air. Colt dove to the ground, rolling over his shoulder before regaining his feet. The net passed overhead and he kept running.

He could see more Trident assassins jumping out of the shadows to give chase. The ultralight was only a few paces away.

"Blow it up!" Colt heard someone shout.

He risked another glance over his shoulder. One of the assassins was taking aim. Colt watched as the man's finger pulled the trigger. The bolt raced toward him, but it flew over his shoulder, missing both Colt and the ultralight.

Someone shouted. Colt turned to see the wall of the office building explode in a flash of blue light. Trident assassins were thrown through the air as Salaam's robot emerged from the dust and debris. Its eyes were glowing and its arms waving as bolts of energy erupted from the end of its arms.

Colt grabbed the handlebars and threw his right leg over the body of the ultralight. It felt like he was sitting on his dad's Harley Davidson, except there was a complicated set of gauges on top of the gas tank, not to mention a set of wings and a propeller attached to the back.

Colt looked for someplace to insert the key, but he couldn't find anything. There was, however, a helmet. He put it on and attached the chin strap. Then Colt started flipping switches and pressing buttons. Still nothing happened.

There was another explosion behind him, and a plasma bolt struck one of the ultralight's wings. Colt could see a scorch mark, but the damage looked cosmetic. He ran his fingers along the sides of the ultralight, and that's when he found the ignition.

Another plasma bolt struck the ground a few feet away, throwing chunks of asphalt against the machine as Colt fumbled with the key. It slid into the ignition slot, and Colt twisted as the machine roared to life. So did the heads-up display inside the visor of his helmet.

"No way," Colt said. He was smiling as a digital map with a series of numbers and gauges showing power levels, shield capacity, and more shone inside the visor. Colt cranked the throttle and his head snapped as the engine engaged. Before he knew what was happening, he was racing down the narrow runway.

It wasn't long before he felt the front tire lift. Moments later he was flying as bolts of energy erupted in the air around him. Caught between elation and fear, Colt looked down to see explosions of light as the assassins focused their attention on the robot.

Colt turned to the front in time to see a light pole. He dipped his shoulder to the left, and the motorcycle followed. He skirted the pole, but when he pulled back to the right, he overcompensated and the ultralight started to corkscrew. Colt felt dizzy. His stomach lurched as he pulled hard to the left, trying to straighten out. His jaw was clenched, and the veins in his neck were popping out.

Colt leaned his body as far to the left as he could, pulling the handlebars in hopes that they would follow. They did, but Colt was heading toward an RV on the interstate. He leaned back, pulling on the controls. The nose of the ultralight lifted, then Colt revved the accelerator. It shot into the air, but not before the tires skimmed the top of the RV.

Colt exhaled as he rose into the night sky. His hands were shaking and his mouth was dry. The display readings inside the visor showed that he had already hit seventy knots and he was at fifty-seven feet in the air and climbing.

Colt heard the jet packs before he saw them. Moments later two Trident assassins stormed into view. Heat blasts shot out from the engines strapped to their backs, and each carried a rifle.

According to the readings, Colt had topped out at about a hundred knots, and it didn't look like the ultralight was able to go any faster. He pulled back on the handlebars and the flying machine climbed another thirty feet, but the assassins kept pace.

Colt had no idea how to use the weapons system. Instead, he bore hard right. The surprised assassin tried to dodge out of the way before the ultralight crashed into him, but the sudden motion sent him into a tailspin. His rifle fell from his hands and Colt watched as the man landed with a thud on the desert surface.

The second assassin kept his distance as he fired a series of plasma bolts. Colt responded by pulling back on the handlebars. The ultralight shot straight up before looping backward. The plasma bolts missed, and now the assassin was in Colt's sights. A light started to flash on the display inside Colt's helmet. Then, as though the ultralight could read his mind, bolts of light erupted from the barrels beneath the wings.

The man in the jet pack swerved this way and that, but one of the discharges caught a hose that was attached to his jet pack, and it started to smoke. The assassin pulled up. He had to land before his fuel ran out.

Colt knew he wasn't safe yet. It wouldn't be hard for the

Trident assassin to radio Colt's position to the rest of his team. He'd been lucky with these two, but he wasn't sure how he would do against a whole squad. He started thinking about a good place to land—somewhere that would give him enough cover to slip into the shadows without anyone seeing where he went.

Minutes later he was approaching a municipal airport that was only a few miles from Grandpa McAlister's house. Since most of the traffic came from hobbyist aviators, Colt figured there wouldn't be much going on.

All he had to do was hold on to the handlebars, and the ultra-light guided itself to a smooth touchdown. Colt drove it around the tarmac until he found what he hoped was a good place to park. He settled on a spot behind a large hangar on the far side of the airport.

Just as he was about to dismount, Colt heard a loud click, followed by the sound of hydraulics. He turned to watch the wings of the ultralight fold once, twice, and again until they no longer looked like wings. If anything, they had turned into some kind of storage compartments.

"This is unreal," Colt said as he sat on a fully operational motorcycle, trying to digest what he had just seen. "Nobody is going to believe it."

:: CHAPTER 19 ::

Colt drove through the streets, not sure what to do. The only person he could think to call was Danielle. As soon as the thought popped into his head, a keypad appeared on the heads-up display. When he pictured the number, it started dialing. How was this even possible? Then the phone rang.

"Hello?" Danielle said.

"Hey, it's me."

"It sounds like you're in the middle of a windstorm."

"I need you to meet me."

"Now?"

"I'm in a lot of trouble, Dani."

"Why don't you come over here? I'm already in my pajamas. Besides, my parents haven't seen you yet. They're starting to think you have something against them."

"I can't . . . not now, anyway."

"You met the creepy guy who called you today, didn't you?" Colt didn't reply.

"That's what I thought. Where are you?"

Twenty minutes later Danielle met Colt at a pizza place

down the street from the airport. She was wearing a baseball cap with her ponytail hanging out the back. Colt could tell that she was agitated, but when he finished describing everything that happened, she just sat there.

"Will you say something?" he asked.

"Like what? Congratulations on almost getting yourself killed? I mean, you just told me that you flew here on some kind of winged motorcycle while masked men in jet packs tried to shoot you with ray guns. Forgive me if I don't do cartwheels through the restaurant while I try to decide if you've lost your mind."

"Trust me, I was there and still can't believe it."

"Are you going to call the police?"

"What would I tell them?"

"How about that a crazy person is stalking you? Or, I don't know, maybe you could tell them that one of the largest companies in the world is trying to turn all of us into mindless slaves."

"If you don't believe me, why would they? Besides, they're already getting a bunch of calls about flying saucers and alien invasions. I'll just be another nut job."

"Why don't you just show them the motorcycle?"

"Not yet."

"What do you mean, 'not yet'?" Danielle said, not bothering to hide her agitation.

"I can't risk it," Colt said. "At least not until we find my mom's files. I mean, what am I supposed to say? That all those crazy conspiracies about Trident watching us are true? Would you believe me?"

Danielle sighed. "Maybe not. But what about your mom's laptop?"

"I didn't see it at the house," Colt said. "She must have left it in her office. Either that or it was in the car when they got hit."

"Did she back her files up?"

Colt shrugged.

"That's where I'd start," Danielle said. "I bet she had an external hard drive, or maybe she backed them up online."

"How would I find that out?"

"Call her editor."

"What, and just ask him where my mom's backup files are? He's going to think something is up."

"Tell him you're looking for family photos."

"Then I'd just be lying."

"Well, if she *was* backing up photos, wouldn't you want them?"

"I guess."

"Then there you are," Danielle said. "Just make sure you use that untraceable phone."

"Why?"

"Because the guys who were after your mom probably bugged your lines."

Colt sighed.

"What's wrong?"

"I didn't think about that."

"That they were going to bug your house?"

"No, that they'd know where I live," Colt said.

"Then we better find your mom's files before Trident sends some of their remote control assassins after you."

After Colt paid for the pizza and drinks, they stopped by Danielle's house to grab some old sheets so Colt could cover up the armored ultralight.

"Pink?" Colt asked when Danielle walked out of the garage.

"What do you want? It's all I have."

A few minutes later they were at the airport. Danielle watched as Colt parked the motorcycle behind one of the hangars before he covered it with the pink sheets.

"Think it'll last until the morning?" Colt asked once he finished.

"Your guess is as good as mine," Danielle said. "Although I don't know why you won't park it in your grandpa's garage."

"What am I supposed to tell him? That I bought a motorcycle on a whim? Besides, what if the wings unfold again?"

"I guess you're right," Danielle said. Her eyes kept roving back and forth, then to her rearview mirror. "Can we leave now?"

The ride home was nerve-racking. Colt thought he saw people with glowing red eyes in every car that they passed, and each time an airplane flew overhead, he was convinced that it was a Trident assassin in a jet pack ready to swoop down on top of them.

"Are you sure you're going to be okay?" Danielle asked after she pulled into Grandpa McAlister's driveway.

"Of course," Colt said. He flashed a smile, but it felt hollow.

Grandpa McAlister wasn't back from playing cards yet, so Colt went through the house to flip on all the lights. He did a quick scan to see if he could find any hidden cameras that Trident secret operatives might have planted, but he didn't see any. "I think I'm losing my mind."

It had been a long time since he'd been scared of the dark, but under the circumstances he didn't care. Once he was satisfied that all the doors and windows were locked, he decided to search the Internet for articles about mind control programs even though he had plenty of homework. There wasn't much that he didn't already know.

Next he plugged Albert Van Cleve's name into a search engine, but outside of stories about his work in biochip technology, Colt couldn't find anything. Then he tried to search for the armored ultralights, but there was nothing.

Finally his phone buzzed. It was a text message from Danielle:

The guy who hit your parents . . . Uriah Bloc . . . he didn't work for Trident, but he was definitely implanted with a Trident chip.

It wasn't much, but it was a start.

Colt put his head on his pillow. Then he started reviewing the events of the night, trying to decipher fact from fiction, and before long he fell into a fitful sleep where masked men with rifles chased him through the night sky.

:: **CHAPTER 20** ::

M r. Pfeffer's classroom was empty when Colt walked in the next morning. He decided to take advantage of the quiet by finishing three of his algebra assignments, but someone walked in. Colt stiffened, then looked over his shoulder to see if it was one of the Trident assassins.

"Check you out, McAlister. Is that an authentic Phantom Flyer fan club ring?"

Colt looked down to realize the ring was still on his finger. "You scared me," he said. He removed the ring and stuffed it into his front pocket, but his eyes never left Oz. Something wasn't sitting right, and Colt couldn't place what it was. He still felt as though Oz was keeping something from him, and he was determined to figure out what it was.

"Why hide a piece of Americana like that?" Oz said. "Let me see it."

Colt took the ring back out and handed it to Oz. "My grandpa brought it out last night," he said. "I guess it used to be my dad's."

"You could only get these through the radio show. Does he still have the Agents of CHAOS patch?"

Colt nodded.

"I've wanted one of these things since I was a kid," Oz said and handed the ring back to Colt, who quickly shoved it back into his pocket.

"How did everything go last night?" Oz said.

Colt turned away from Oz to focus on his algebra book.

"You got the text, didn't you?"

Colt nodded. Telling Danielle was one thing, but he'd just met Oz. Trust took longer than a day to build.

"Are you going to make me beg?"

"I don't know," Colt said, shrugging. "The guy seemed kind of crazy."

"You should have called me for backup," Oz said. "You never go into a situation blind, especially when you don't know who you're meeting."

"You're probably right," Colt said. He closed his algebra book.

"Are you okay, McAlister?"

"Yeah, I'm fine. Just waiting for the caffeine to kick in."

"You better hope it happens soon," Oz said as the first bell rang. "Pfeffer's lectures are enough to put anybody to sleep."

The classroom started to fill up, but Lily's desk remained empty. Then, just as the second bell rang, she slid into her seat and stuffed her backpack under her desk. "Good, I beat him," she said to no one in particular.

Mr. Pfeffer walked into the classroom carrying his battered briefcase. "Let's get down to brass tacks, shall we?" he said, looking harried. "I've always thought that Tuesday was a good day for a test. What about you?"

The entire class moaned.

"Relax, it's multiple choice."

Since it was only his second day, Colt didn't have to take the test. He sat there looking at the other students, wondering if any of them had been implanted with a Trident biochip. Parkinson's was rare in young people, but doubtless there was at least one kid at Chandler High who suffered from epileptic seizures.

Oz was the first to finish the test. He walked to the front of the room with confident strides and handed it to the teacher. "Number twelve almost tripped me up, but I saw where you were going," he said. "And the bonus question? Genius. Nicely done, Pfeffer."

Colt could see that Mr. Pfeffer didn't know how to respond. It looked like he wasn't sure if Oz was mocking him or giving him an actual compliment.

The rest of the class wasn't as confident when they handed in their tests, including Lily. When it was over, Mr. Pfeffer launched into a lecture about American industry during the War and how it helped pull the country out of the Great Depression.

"You really need to work on your game, McAlister," Oz said in a whisper when he caught Colt staring at Lily. "Maybe the girls in San Diego appreciate the whole stalker vibe you're giving off, but around here you need to play it cool."

"Do you always talk that loud?" Colt asked, nervous as he watched Lily out of the corner of his eye, hoping she hadn't heard.

The moment the dismissal bell rang, the classroom was filled with the sound of shuffling paper and books being slammed shut.

"Look, why don't I just introduce you to her? It'll be a good icebreaker," Oz said.

"Don't—"

Lily was stuffing her textbook into her backpack when Oz called out to her. "Has anybody officially introduced you to Colt yet?"

"No, not officially."

"Then, Lily Westcott, I'd like you to meet our resident surfer dude and my fellow Phantom Flyer super fan, Colt McAlister."

Colt's eyes shot wide.

"Go ahead, show her your official Phantom Flyer fan club ring," Oz said. "That thing is a classic."

Colt wondered if it would be more embarrassing to run away or just stand there. "It's nothing," he said, mumbling as he kicked at the floor.

"Look at you all shy," Oz said, scruffing Colt's thick mop of hair. "Go ahead. Show her the ring."

Colt took the ring out of his pocket, figuring it was best to get it over with.

"I've never seen anything like it," Lily said, her tone polite.

"It was his dad's," Oz said.

"I guess that does make it special."

As his face flushed, Colt shoved the ring back into his pocket, but just as he was about to slip into the current of students flowing down the hall, Oz grabbed him around the shoulders.

"Colt, I want you to meet the next pop country sensation, Lily Westcott."

Lily slapped Oz playfully on the shoulder. "Why do you get such a kick out of embarrassing people?"

"What are you talking about?"

"You're like an overgrown six-year-old. Do you know that?"

"I've heard that once or twice."

"Are we done? I need to get to Spanish," Colt said. Then one of the phones in his backpack started to vibrate.

"Well, are you going to get it?" Oz asked.

"I'm sure it's nothing."

"You never know."

Colt slipped his backpack off of his shoulder and opened the pouch. It wasn't his phone. Someone had sent him a text message on Van Cleve's untraceable phone. Colt tried to be discreet as he read both words. **You're next.**

"What's wrong?" Oz asked.

"Nothing."

"Then let me see it."

Colt dropped the phone into the pouch before zipping it back up. "Seriously, it's no big deal."

Oz was standing there with a scowl. For a moment Colt thought that he was going to try and rip the backpack away from him.

"Am I missing something?" Lily asked.

"No," Colt said.

"Don't try and be a hero, McAlister," Oz said, ignoring Lily.

"I don't know what he's talking about," Colt said.

Oz shook his head. "Look, I have to pick something up in the office, but I'm supposed to babysit the little guy. Do you think you could walk him to Spanish?"

"I know where—"

Oz placed his large hand over Colt's mouth. "I was talking to Lily."

"Yeah, sure," Lily said. "The choir room isn't too far away from there."

"Perfect. I'll see you later," Oz said. "Then you're going to show me that text." With that, Oz took off down the hall, but he had one last tidbit to add. "I almost forgot . . . Colt isn't just a comic book nerd. Danielle told me that he plays the guitar too . . . Oh, and he surfs. I guess chicks in California dig that kind of thing. That's why his hair looks like a mop."

:: CHAPTER 21 ::

Maybe, Colt thought, if he just stood there, Lily would eventually walk away.

"I'm sorry about that," he finally said, hoping he wasn't blushing. "I know how to get to Spanish."

"Don't worry about it," Lily said. "We're used to Oz and his sense of humor. Besides, if we're both heading that way, we might as well walk together."

"It depends," Colt said as they started down the hall. "Do you promise not to tell anyone about my Phantom Flyer ring?"

Lily laughed. "I'll do my best," she said. "If it's any consolation, my bedroom is filled with My Little Ponies."

"Really? Mine too."

They both laughed this time, but as Colt walked beside her he wondered if he remembered to wear deodorant and whether or not there was anything hanging from his nose.

"So how long have you been playing guitar?"

"I don't know." Colt shrugged. "I think I was about eight before I could finally form a chord. My dad bought me one of those acoustics they make for little kids, but I'm not very good."

"I bet you're just being modest."

"What about you?" Colt asked. "If you're going to be the next big thing in country music, you must play."

"Just enough so it looks like I know what I'm doing," Lily said. "I'm really a singer."

"Let's hear it."

"Right here in the hallway?"

"Why not?" Colt said. "I mean, if you're going to play to stadiums full of screaming fans, you should be able to sing here."

"Oz doesn't know what he's talking about," Lily said. "I'd love to be a singer, but I doubt it's going to happen."

"Now you're the one who's being modest."

"How do you know?"

"I can tell."

"Is that so?" Lily looked at him with her eyebrows raised. "So what do you think about Chandler High so far?"

"It's okay, I guess," Colt said as he brushed his hand casually under his nose, just in case something was hanging. "I thought there would be more cowboys."

"Does that mean everyone in San Diego wears board shorts and bikinis to school?"

"Pretty much."

Lily smiled. "Then I'm glad I live here. That would be embarrassing."

"You get used to it," Colt said with another shrug. "The guy who taught shop used to wear a Speedo and construction boots."

Lily laughed. "That's disgusting."

"You should have seen how much hair he had on his back."

"Okay, now I'm not going to be able to eat my lunch."

"Sorry," Colt said. "Have you ever been to San Diego?"

"I was just there last weekend."

"Seriously?"

"My parents own a condo on Imperial Beach, so we go there a lot. I love falling asleep to the sound of the waves. I bet you miss it."

"A little."

Lily lowered her eyes. "Look, I know that you're probably tired of hearing this, but I'm really sorry about your parents."

"Thanks," Colt said. "They say everything happens for a reason, but I don't know. It feels so random." He paused, his mind drifting to some forgotten memory. "It still doesn't seem real. I mean, I keep thinking that I'm going to wake up and everything will go back to the way it was."

He turned to Lily and saw that her eyes were red. "I'm sorry," he said. "I have no idea why I said any of that."

"Don't apologize."

"It's weird, but I haven't even been able to talk to my own brothers about what happened, and here I go blabbing to a stranger."

"I understand . . . more than you know, actually."

Out of the corner of his eye, Colt saw someone moving toward them. His chest constricted as he envisioned another Trident assassin. He was about to step in front of Lily, but when he recognized Graham St. John, he relaxed—a little. Guys with beautiful girlfriends could be territorial, and Colt had enough problems at the moment. He didn't need to start a rivalry with one of the most popular guys in the school.

"Hey, Lily," Graham said, reaching down to kiss her on the cheek.

"Have you met Colt McAlister yet?" she asked. She gave a quick wipe to her eyes.

"My name's Graham," he said.

His smile appeared genuine as he extended his hand. Not what Colt expected.

"Welcome to Chandler High."

"Um, Lily was just showing me where the Spanish room was," Colt said. "I mean, I know where it is and everything, it's just that Oz . . . you know Oz . . . ?"

"Yeah, I've been trying to get him to play football since he was in seventh grade. Can you imagine what a quarterback would think if he saw Oz lined up, ready to knock his head off?"

Colt didn't hear a word. He was too worried that Graham thought he was trying to hit on Lily. "Oz is supposed to show me around this week, but he had to go somewhere. I guess he figured Lily was heading this way, so he asked her to take me to my class."

Graham put his arm around Lily. "You're in good hands," he said. "Look, I don't mean to be rude, but I'm going to be late. I just wanted to stop by and introduce myself."

"No problem," Colt said.

"Are we still on for lunch?" Graham asked.

Lily nodded. "I'll see you in a bit."

"He seems like a really nice guy," Colt said as Graham disappeared into the crowd.

"Yeah. He is."

Colt felt a pang of jealousy, which he knew was ridiculous. He wasn't sure why he was so smitten by Lily. Sure, she was beautiful, but so were half the girls in San Diego. It didn't make any sense. Then again, nothing in his life made sense at the moment.

:: CHAPTER 22 ::

G'randpa McAlister owned a piece of property near the
Superstition Mountains on the outskirts of town. It amounted
to a little over ten acres of raw desert in the middle of
nowhere. Outside of coyotes and wild hogs called javelina, nobody
but Grandpa McAlister knew where it was.

The only building on the property was an oversized tin shed,
which Colt thought would be a perfect place to hide the ultralight. The only problem was that he'd need a ride home once he
dropped it off, and it wasn't like he could ask his grandpa.

Danielle agreed to help, but given the circumstances, she
wasn't excited about driving out to the middle of the desert—
especially at night. Still, it wasn't like Colt could ride a flying
motorcycle in the middle of the day, so they didn't have much of
a choice.

"I can't believe it was still there," Colt said as they drove back
toward town.

"That makes two of us."

"Can I ask you something?"

"Sure."

"What do you think about Oz?"

Danielle looked at Colt sideways. "He's okay, I guess. Why? Did he ask about me?"

"That's not what I'm talking about," Colt said. "I mean, it kind of seems like he's keeping something from me, and I'm not sure what it is."

"Why would he do that?"

"Beats me," Colt said. "He knows something, though, and I have a feeling it's important."

"About what?"

"Everything that's going on."

"So you think he's in on it or something?"

"Not exactly."

"Then what's the problem?"

Colt sighed as he looked at the gas gauge. "By the way, you're almost on empty. I think there's a gas station just off the next exit. Why don't you pull over and I'll fill it up."

"You don't have to do that."

"Come on, Dani. You've been my chauffeur ever since I got here. It's the least I can do."

"When are you supposed to get your car?"

"I'm not sure," Colt said. "I was hoping to fly to San Diego over the weekend and drive it back, but my grandpa thinks we should wait."

"Why?"

"You'd have to ask him." Colt paused. "You know, maybe buying a motorcycle isn't so crazy. I have enough money saved up. I could just tell Grandpa that I got a good deal on it. I wonder what kind of gas an armored ultralight would take. Jet fuel?"

"Did you forget about the wings?"

"Yeah, I guess that would be a problem."

"By the way," Danielle said as she turned on her blinker to exit the highway, "I was looking at the Trident Biotech website today, and according to their latest press release, they just signed contracts with three different countries to provide RFID tags for their soldiers."

"What are those?"

"You know, radio frequency identification tags. People use them to track things with radio waves. They're going to embed them in the soldiers' skin. That way all a doctor would have to do is scan the chip to access a soldier's name and medical records."

"That's freaky."

"China is even considering it. They have something like three and a half million active soldiers and another million on reserve."

"So you think Trident is going to try and turn the Chinese army into remote control slaves?"

"Why not?"

"How would they control that many people at the same time?"

"They wouldn't have to," Danielle said. "All they'd need is to control a few key generals, and everyone else would fall in line. It's brilliant, really."

"I didn't think about that."

"That's why you have me," Danielle said as she pulled up to a gas pump. "Will you fill it up while I pay?"

"Only if you take this," Colt said, handing her some money.

"I told you I don't need it. My parents pay for gas."

"It doesn't matter. They shouldn't have to pay for me."

"Fine," Danielle said. "It's too late to argue. I just want to go home, take a bath, and go to bed."

"Will you get me a hot dog or something? I'm starving."

"From a gas station? Do you know how long those things have been sitting there?"

"I forgot to eat dinner."

As Colt waited for Danielle to pay, he decided to wash her windshield. At the same time, a pickup truck pulled into the gas station with a barking dog in the back. Colt watched as the driver, a large man with a scraggly beard, parked by the air and water station. He turned off the engine and shut off his headlights, but he didn't get out.

Colt turned his attention to the windshield, scrubbing all the dead bugs that were cemented to the glass. When he finished with the squeegee, he glanced over at the truck to find the man staring at him.

"I got you one of those disgusting hot dogs," Danielle said as she walked back to the car. "I hope you like onions and jalapeños."

"Do I have a choice?"

"Nope."

"Then onions and jalapeños it is." Colt looked over Danielle's shoulder. The truck was still there, but the man was gone.

"What's wrong?"

"Nothing," Colt said.

"I know you better than that."

"I'm jumpy, that's all. I keep seeing red eyes everywhere I look. Just don't tell anybody, okay?"

"Fine, but I know what you mean," Danielle said. "I was convinced that my chemistry teacher was trying to poison me during an experiment today."

Colt cracked the bottle of water that Danielle had given him and took a swig. "I'm going to use the rest room."

"Hurry up. I don't like being out here in the middle of nowhere by myself."

"I'll be back before the tank is full."

Colt wandered inside the gas station to get the key for the rest room. He glanced around for the man from the pickup but didn't see him. Colt went back outside, where he followed the stench of rotting urine until he found the men's room.

After he unlocked the door, Colt pulled his collar over his nose to keep from gagging. The only light came from a flickering bulb that hung above a mirror and there was so much graffiti etched into the surface that Colt couldn't see his reflection.

He finished quickly, but the water wouldn't turn on. "Great," he said to no one in particular. Then Van Cleve's phone started to vibrate again. Colt pulled it out of his back pocket to find another text message: **You can't hide from us. We're watching.**

Colt felt his mouth go dry as his heart started to pound. He stuffed the phone back into his pocket but when he opened the door, he found the man from the pickup standing there. The guy was over six feet tall with a wide belly and broad shoulders. According to the patch over the left breast pocket of his work shirt, his name was Jimbo, and Jimbo's eyes were glowing red. He didn't look overly friendly, either.

"I guess you need the key," Colt said, handing it over.

The man didn't move.

"I'll just leave it here." Colt hung the key on the doorknob, but when he turned to leave, Jimbo grabbed him by the arm.

"What are you doing?" Colt asked as he tried to break away.

Jimbo was expressionless as he reached into his pocket and pulled out a syringe filled with blue liquid. Colt tried to pry the man's fingers away, but he couldn't. Panic set in. He shot both of his palms into Jimbo's chest. The large man stumbled backward, but he didn't let go.

Once Jimbo regained his balance, he raised the syringe, ready to plunge it into Colt's neck. He swung but Colt dodged to the side before bringing his shoulder into Jimbo's sternum. Jimbo cocked his arm to bring the needle down on Colt once more, but Colt lifted his head to hit Jimbo in the jaw before bringing his elbow down on the man's collarbone.

Colt heard a sickening crack, but Jimbo didn't react. His eyes continued to glow as he tried again to plunge the syringe into Colt's neck. Colt sidestepped. Then he took the door handle and yanked, crushing Jimbo's hand between the door and the jamb. Jimbo dropped the syringe, but he was still holding on to Colt's arm.

Without thinking, Colt brought his knee up into Jimbo's kidney. Jimbo winced and let go, allowing Colt to pull away. He could see Jimbo's keys hanging from a clip on his belt loop. Colt grabbed them and threw the keys over a wall and into the desert. Then he ran to Danielle's car.

"What's wrong?"

"Just get in!"

Danielle narrowed her eyes.

"I'm serious." Colt looked over his shoulder to see Jimbo coming toward them. He was limping, but he was moving fast enough.

"What happened?" Danielle asked again.

"Will you just get in the car?" Colt was agitated as he slid into the passenger's seat, slammed the door shut, and locked it.

Danielle fumbled for her keys.

"Hurry up!"

"I'm trying." The keys slipped out of her hand and onto the floor just as Jimbo reached the car.

"Are you kidding me?"

"That's not helping," Danielle said with a shriek. She was bent down, her hands roving through the shadows as she looked for her keys.

"Dani, look out!"

Her window was open, and Jimbo reached inside to grab her. His chin was bleeding, and his right arm hung loosely at his side. Danielle screamed as the dog barked in the background.

"Here," Colt said. He found the key and slid it into the ignition. The engine roared to life. Danielle threw the car into drive and pressed down on the gas pedal. They shot toward the gas station with enough force that Jimbo had to let go.

Danielle slammed on the brakes before the car rammed into the curb of the sidewalk. Then she threw the Thunderbird into reverse and hit the gas. She narrowly missed Jimbo before she hit the brakes again so she could put the car into drive. Smoke kicked out as the tires spun. The old Thunderbird roared as Danielle sped toward the exit.

"Please tell me that didn't just happen," she said once they were safely on the highway. Colt could see that she was shaking.

"Dani, I'm so sorry."

"How did they find you so fast?"

"I don't know." Colt knew that he should tell her about the text messages, but he didn't want to scare her any more than he had already. Besides, he wasn't sure how they found the number. The best he could come up with was that they'd gotten it from Van Cleve's phone.

"We need your mom's files," Danielle said. "This has to end."

CHAPTER 23

Do you want to come in?" Colt asked. They had been sitting in Grandpa McAlister's driveway for ten minutes, neither saying a word.

Danielle exhaled. "I'll be okay."

"Look, why don't I drive home with you. You only live a couple blocks away, so I can just walk back."

"That's sweet," Danielle said, "but I'll be fine."

"I wish I hadn't dragged you into this."

"You didn't drag me into anything," Danielle said. "And as soon as we track those files down, we're going to nail these guys."

"By the way, I left a voice mail with my mom's editor this afternoon, but he hasn't called back yet."

"A good reporter never leaves a voice mail," Danielle said. "You need to keep calling until he answers his phone."

"I'll try again in the morning."

"Good."

"Are you sure you're going to be okay?"

"Stop treating me like I'm helpless."

"Will you at least call me when you get home?"

Danielle rolled her eyes. "Fine."

|||||||||||||||||||||||||||||||||||||

Colt hadn't heard from his mom's editor, Jonah White, and he wasn't going to anytime soon. Jonah's assistant told Colt that he was on vacation and wouldn't be back until next week. At least, Colt thought, there hadn't been any more threatening text messages or strangers with red eyes.

As the final bell rang on Friday afternoon, Colt rushed to his locker to grab the books he'd need for his homework assignments over the weekend. Then he met up with Danielle so she could give him a ride back to Grandpa McAlister's house.

"You realize everyone on campus is starting to think you're a couple," Oz said from his Jeep.

"Are you jealous?" Danielle asked.

"That's not my style," Oz said before reaching over to open his passenger door. "Hop in."

"We have things to do."

"Come on," Oz said. "I have a special treat for McAlister. He's going to love it."

Danielle looked to Colt. "It's up to you."

"Only if you come with us."

Danielle puffed her cheeks before she exhaled. "I want to finish my homework so I have the weekend free and clear."

"We won't be gone long. I promise," Oz said.

"Fine," Danielle said, and threw her backpack at Oz. Then she opened the back door and hopped in, leaving the front seat for Colt. "Where are we going, anyway?"

"You aren't going to make me ruin the surprise, are you?" Oz said as Colt climbed in.

"Let's just get this over with."

It wasn't long before they turned into the parking lot of a tired strip mall that was in need of a face-lift. Many of the storefronts were empty. Signs hung in the windows noting that space was available, and from the looks of the neighborhood they were going to stay available for a long time to come.

"I don't get it," Danielle said as she looked around. Outside of some fast food restaurants, a sandwich shop, and a pizza place with a bunch of old carnival rides inside, there wasn't much else.

"You see, don't you, McAlister?"

There, near the end of the lonely row where it shared a wall with a check cashing business, was a small shop with a sign overhead reading GREG'S COMICS.

Colt perked up. "I haven't been to a comic book shop in months."

Danielle rolled her eyes. "This was your big surprise?"

"Don't be so quick to judge," Oz said. He pulled the parking brake before getting out of the Jeep. "This place has the best selection in the entire state . . . maybe even west of the Mississippi."

With the exception of a bearded man behind the counter who was eating Thai food out of a Styrofoam carton, the store was empty. It wasn't a big space, but it had everything a collector would want. There were vintage toys in glass display cases, unopened action figures pinned to the wall, and row after row of long white boxes stuffed with comic books.

"I used to come here when I was a kid," Oz said. "I'd sit on the floor rummaging through the fifty-cent boxes for hours while I daydreamed about saving the world."

"That sounds familiar," Danielle said. "Colt used to run around in a ski mask with swimming goggles, pretending he was the Phantom Flyer. It didn't matter if it was a hundred and ten degrees outside, he was determined to defeat evil."

"Which reminds me," Oz said. "Hey, Howard, do you have that box you told me about?"

"As a matter of fact, I do." Howard wiped his beard with a napkin before disappearing into the back room. It wasn't long before he returned with a short box filled with comic books in plastic sheaths. "It's strange, but there's been a resurgence with the Phantom Flyer lately. It must be all that garbage in the news about an alien invasion."

"What, you don't believe in aliens?" Oz asked.

"Are you serious?"

"I don't know—a lot of weird stuff has been happening. What do you think about those lights over South Mountain?"

"It's probably the military jerking us around like they always do." Howard set the box down in front of Oz and Colt.

"Thanks," Oz said. Then he angled the box so Colt could thumb through the contents. "Go ahead."

"Are you kidding me?" Colt said as he looked at the first cover. "Freedom Comics number 32? That's the first appearance of the Phantom Flyer."

"I told you Howard has everything."

"Wait a minute. Isn't this place called *Greg's* Comics?" Danielle asked.

"It's a long story," Oz said.

"This had to come out in what? The 1940s?" Colt said.

"December 1942," Howard said. "That issue in your hands is cherry too. You won't find many like it anymore."

Colt held the comic book with reverence, drinking in every detail before he carefully placed it back in the box.

"The issue was so popular that the publisher decided to give the Phantom Flyer his own title," Howard said.

"*Phantom Flyer and the Agents of CHAOS*," Colt said. The next one that he pulled out was the first issue. The cover showed the Phantom Flyer bursting into the sky with his signature jet pack. He was holding an American flag that streamed in the wind as dozens of Nazi soldiers lay unconscious on the ground below. The caption read *I Will Fear No Evil*.

Colt was too entranced to notice a man with short-cropped hair walk into the store. He was wearing baggy jeans and a shirt that read MY OTHER CAR IS THE MILLENNIUM FALCON.

"Hey, Robert," Oz said as the man took off his backpack and set it behind the counter.

Robert offered a friendly wave. "Haven't seen you in a while."

"School's been killing me," Oz said with a shrug. "I should start making it back in on Wednesdays, though. How full is my box?"

"Let's take a look," Robert said. He turned to a row of boxes that held all the subscriptions and pulled out a thick stack of comic books to hand to Oz. "Here you go."

"Nice."

"I have to run some errands," Howard said. "Just give that box to Robert when you're done. I don't let just anyone see the good stuff."

CHAPTER 24

A h, another Phantom fan, I see," Robert said as he assumed the seat behind the cash register.

"Yeah, my dad used to have some issues," Colt said. "I haven't seen many of these, though. They're incredible."

"I commissioned a few Phantom Flyer sketches at the San Diego con a few weeks ago," Robert said. "If you're coming back, I'll bring them in next week so you can take a look."

"That'd be great."

"I'm pretty sure we have some of the action figures in the back. Just let me know what you want to see, and I'll grab them for you."

Colt flipped through the stack until he came to an issue titled *Beware the Cursed.* The cover showed a pack of snarling men in tattered U. S. Army uniforms. Their eyes were glowing red as they circled around the Phantom Flyer with a ghosted image of Adolf Hitler in the background.

"Where did you find this?" Danielle asked.

"The secret stash in the back room."

She lowered her voice to a whisper. "Didn't Van Cleve

mention that Trident helped the Nazis develop mind control technology?"

Colt nodded.

"I wonder . . ." she said, looking up at the ceiling as she pondered. "If the Nazis had secret projects, I bet we did too. I mean, there were plenty of American industrialists who could've made all kinds of crazy inventions."

"I suppose," Colt said. "What are you thinking?"

"I bet the gadget that the Phantom Flyer used to defeat the Cursed really exists. Maybe we could find one."

"Maybe," Colt said. He slipped his fingers under the strip of tape that Howard had used to seal the protective bag.

Danielle peered over his shoulder as Colt thumbed through the comic. Nazi scientists were placing what looked like mechanical squids on the necks of captured American soldiers. The squid would plunge tentacles into the back of the soldier's head as the GI screamed.

"That's disgusting," Danielle said.

When Colt turned the page they could see that the eyes of those soldiers were glowing red. The Nazis transmitted an order that forced the captured GIs to attack American paratroopers holed up in the city of Bastogne.

The effect was devastating, because the paratroopers didn't know if they should fight back or retreat. After all, the men attacking them were fellow Americans. It was bedlam, but in the end the Phantom Flyer and his Agents of CHAOS were able to scramble the signal and release the captured GIs.

"Look at that," Danielle said, pointing to a panel where the Phantom Flyer had removed his mask. "That looks like your grandpa."

Colt studied the image. There were similarities, but Colt had a hard time believing that it was his grandpa. "Have you been talking to Oz or something?"

"No. Why?"

"He said the same thing."

"You never know."

While Colt tried to imagine his grandfather flying around in a jet pack, Oz was on the other side of the store going through his stack of new comics. None of them saw Robert's posture grow stiff or his eyes flare with a red light. Like a marionette controlled by a puppeteer, he reached stiffly to unzip his backpack.

As Robert dumped the contents on the countertop, dozens of iron spheres rolled across the glass, tinkling as they went. They were about the size of golf balls, and once they stopped, eight jointed legs unfolded from each body. Then red lights, like a cluster of eyes, flared to life.

Danielle was the first to notice the mechanical spiders. "What are those?"

"Injector drones," Colt said, his face lighting up. "No way! Where did you get those?" Robert didn't answer, but Colt hardly noticed. "Baron Iron Cross used them to poison the Phantom Flyer in issue 74."

"It was actually 73," Oz said. "74 was where the Phantom Flyer teamed up with the Star-Spangled Patriot to defeat Torrax, Destroyer of Worlds."

"For the two most eligible bachelors on campus, you guys are geeks," Danielle said. "I wonder what—" She stopped talking when the first drone started to move. It crawled down the front of the display case, its metal legs tapping on the glass with each step.

Others followed. One climbed on top of the register. Another skittered up Robert's arm before it climbed over his face and onto the top of his head.

"We need to get out of here," Colt said, taking Danielle by the arm.

The drones were too fast. They were already clinging to the walls and ceiling, shooting wire webbing that crisscrossed through the store. In seconds, the front door was covered with the strange material, cutting off any hope of escape.

"Don't move," Oz said. One of the drones had climbed onto Danielle's shirt and another was on her shoe. "The front legs are like needles, and they're filled with poison."

Colt looked down to see two drones inching up his pant leg. A third was directly above, creeping across the ceiling. It stopped before lowering itself with the strange webbing until it was inches from Colt's face. Poison seeped from the pointed tips of the drone's legs.

Colt grabbed the webbing from the spider hanging in front of him. He whipped it across the room, where it smashed against the wall. The lights behind its eyes faded as it twitched on the floor and then stopped moving.

"Look out!" Oz said.

The man behind the counter was taking aim at Danielle with a pistol that looked like a ray gun. Oz jumped over a table and tackled her. They fell to the ground as Robert pulled the trigger, releasing a pulse of energy that obliterated a shelf loaded with comic books.

"Come on, Robert, I don't want to hurt you," Oz said as paper covered in colorful panels fell like a ticker tape parade.

Robert pulled the trigger again and more comics exploded.

"Don't say I didn't warn you!" Oz threw the table to the side, took two steps, and launched over the glass counter to tackle Robert. A remote device went spinning across the floor in one direction, the plasma pistol in another. The drones started falling to the floor around the shop, their lights fading.

"What happened?" Danielle asked.

"Robert just tried to kill us with those drones, that's what," Oz said as he struggled to keep Robert pinned to the ground.

Colt found some duct tape, and between the three of them, they were able to secure Robert to a chair in the office. Then Oz collected all the drones and locked them in a cooler that he took from the back of his Jeep.

"What are we supposed to do now?" Danielle asked.

"We can worry about that in a minute," Oz said. "First I want to know why those things were after you two."

"What makes you think they were after us?" Danielle asked.

"Because they were locked to your genetic signatures," Oz said. "They didn't even know I was in the building."

Danielle turned to look at Colt. "We might as well tell him."

Colt still wasn't sure if he could trust Oz—not wholly anyway. He seemed like a good enough guy, but Colt still felt convinced that Oz was somehow a part of everything that was happening.

"Any day, McAlister," Oz said.

Colt looked at Danielle, who nodded. "This is going to sound crazy."

"Try me," Oz said.

"We think someone from Trident Biotech murdered my parents, and now they're after me . . . well, us."

Oz didn't flinch. "Why?"

"Because my mom was working on a story about a mind

control program that Trident is running. They didn't want it to go to print, so they killed her." Colt paused, waiting to see if Oz was going to react. He didn't, so Colt went on to describe everything that had happened, from Albert Van Cleve to his run-in with Jimbo at the gas station.

"That's quite a story," Oz said. "Have you told anyone else?"

Colt shook his head. "Who'd believe us?"

"You might be surprised."

"What about you?" Danielle asked.

"I believe you, but that's not saying much," Oz said. "I was the last kid in third grade who thought Santa was real."

"That's not what I meant."

"Fair enough," Oz said. "But this has to stay between us or I'm going to get in a lot of trouble, okay?"

Colt felt vindicated, if only a little. He was right. Oz did have something to do with it.

Danielle raised an eyebrow. "It depends."

Oz flashed a smile. "Then I guess I'll have to trust you," he said. "My dad is the director of something called CHAOS."

"The Central Headquarters Against the Occult and Supernatural?" Colt's eyes were wide. That's not what he'd expected, but it was better than the alternative. At least Oz wasn't part of the organization that murdered Colt's parents. "As in *Phantom Flyer and the Agents of CHAOS*? Are you serious?"

"I thought you might be impressed," Oz said. "We've had this conversation before, though. Not that you'd remember."

Colt frowned. "What are you talking about?"

"I told you about my dad when we were at the CHAOS Military Academy last summer."

"The what?" Colt was incredulous.

Oz didn't seem bothered by the skepticism. "If you don't believe me, ask your grandpa."

Colt looked at Danielle, but she just shrugged. He turned back to Oz. "Are you messing with me or something, because if you are, it isn't funny."

"Your family went on vacation to Washington, D.C., a few weeks before school started, right?"

Colt nodded.

"And one of those mornings, your dad dropped you off at a military school?"

The spark of a memory flashed in Colt's mind, but it didn't catch, leaving him confused.

"Well, he did," Oz said. "That's where I met you. In fact, you broke my nose."

"How?" Danielle asked, stifling a laugh.

"What's that supposed to mean?" Colt was frowning at her.

"It's just that . . . I don't know," she said, stammering. "Look at you two. I mean, if anyone was going to get his nose broken—"

"Fine, I get it."

"It's true," Oz said. "We were sparring, and you took me out. The only reason you don't remember anything is because they gave you a serum that buried your memories."

"Let's pretend what you're saying is true," Colt said.

"It is."

"Fine," Colt said, wanting to keep the conversation hypothetical. "Then why me? I mean, why was I at a CHAOS military academy?"

Colt stood there waiting for Oz to tell him this was all a joke.

"Every summer CHAOS flies in a bunch of us to see if we

have what it takes to become agents," Colt said. "We were part of this year's batch of candidates."

"So I might get to be an actual CHAOS agent?" Colt said as the corners of his lips started to break into a smile.

"From what my dad tells me, you have a pretty good shot," Oz said. "But you can't tell anyone. Most people don't even know CHAOS exists, and it has to stay that way."

Pushing aside his disbelief for the moment, Colt peppered Oz with as many questions as came to mind. Did soldiers in the CHAOS program really fly in jet packs? Did the Nazis actually build UFOs using alien technology? Were Yetis real, and could they speak? What about the Undarian Coliseum, where alien races were supposed to send their greatest warriors to fight in hand-to-hand combat?

Oz stood there, amused. "Slow down, McAlister," he said. "I can't give away all my secrets."

"But—"

"You could torture me with Katharian slugs and it wouldn't help."

"Could you two stop geeking out, or am I the only one who realizes that someone just tried to kill us with poisonous spiders?" Danielle asked.

"Injector drones," Colt said.

"Whatever." Danielle's eyes flared. "We almost died, and you two want to sit here and act like a couple of nerds at a Phantom Flyer convention. Have you lost your minds?"

Colt looked at Oz. They were both smiling.

"You weren't kidding, were you?" Colt said. "My grandpa really was the Phantom Flyer."

"I told you, McAlister. No more questions. If you want an answer, you're going to have to ask him yourself."

"So what are we going to do about this place?" Colt asked, turning to look at the wrecked comic shop.

"CHAOS has cleanup crews for this kind of thing." Oz pulled out his phone. "It'll be back to normal before the sun goes down."

CHAPTER 25

I don't think I can do this," Colt said as Danielle pulled her car into the driveway. "My grandpa doesn't like to talk about what happened during the War."

The last time Colt had felt this nervous was when he played a Lost Boy in *Peter Pan* in grade school. He only had two lines, but he forgot them and ran off the stage in a panic.

"You'll be fine," Danielle said, trying to hide her smile. "Just think of him as your grandpa, not the famous soldier from World War II who inspired a radio show, comic books, toys, a television show, a movie, and a new video game that's coming out next summer."

"Wait . . . are you serious? There's going to be a video game?"

"You realize that by asking that, you're in jeopardy of losing your status as a card-carrying member of the Phantom Flyer fan club, right?"

"Come on, Dani. Be serious."

"If you don't believe me, look it up."

"Trust me, I will."

"You're just stalling."

Colt closed his eyes, took a deep breath, and exhaled slowly.

"You're pathetic, do you know that?" she said. "This is the same man who wears that goofy hat and drives one of those little motorized cars in the Fourth of July parade every year. Why are you such a wreck?"

"I guess you're right," Colt said as he grabbed the door handle.

"Of course I'm right."

"Just be careful. Oz said those drones were programmed to go after both of us."

"Don't worry about me," she said. "I'll be fine."

When Colt got out of the car he noticed a sedan parked in the street. It had government plates, but that didn't mean much. There was no way to tell who had a Trident biochip planted in his head and who didn't. His grandfather's Cadillac was in the driveway, which was strange. Everything on that car was original, and Grandpa McAlister never let it sit out in the sun like that. He was paranoid about the paint oxidizing. Grandpa must have been in a hurry.

As he walked up the front steps, Colt was careful not to make a noise. He placed his hand on the doorknob and slowly twisted it before pushing the door open just a crack. He could hear his grandfather talking with two men, but they were back in the kitchen, so the conversation was muffled.

Colt slipped off his shoes before sneaking into the front room, down the hall, and into the laundry room. From the crack between the hinges, he could see his grandfather seated at the kitchen table. Colt recognized Senator Bishop from his parents' funeral, but he didn't know the other man, who had skin the color of the night sky and a clean-shaven head. There were two stars fixed to the shoulders of his suit coat, a cluster of colorful medals pinned over his left breast pocket, and the name WALKER pinned over the right. Colt was relieved to see that none of them had red eyes.

"Everyone in this room knows that Santiago Romero is one tough son of a gun," the man named Walker said. "And I understand that we're partially responsible—"

"Partially?" Grandpa McAlister said. "It was your decision to privatize the CHAOS program and put him in charge. Now that he doesn't want to be your puppet anymore, you want to get rid of him? What did you expect? Romero is a soldier, not a politician."

"I'd like to sit here and tell you that you're wrong, but I can't," Senator Bishop said. "We made a mistake, and it's cost us. All we can do now is move forward and pray that we make better decisions . . . and that's why we're here."

Grandpa McAlister pinched the bridge of his nose and shook his head. "I'm retired, Senator."

"But your grandsons aren't," General Walker said.

Colt watched as his grandpa shifted in his chair. His eyes grew heavy, then he sighed. "I told Roger not to let them join the military."

"We've been conducting evaluations to find Romero's successor for more than a year," Walker continued. "We've narrowed our search to a handful of candidates, but we'd like to interview one more to gauge his potential."

Colt couldn't believe what he was hearing. It had only been an hour since he learned that the CHAOS program even existed, and here one of his brothers might take over as director. That wasn't going to be good for his friendship with Oz.

"I know this much," McAlister said. "The twins aren't on your list, and I doubt that Curtis is ready. I could make a case for the others, but why don't we cut to the chase? Which grandson are you going to lead to the slaughter? Clive? Christian?"

"We'd like to think that this appointment is a privilege, McAlister," the senator said. "But I understand your concerns. The CHAOS program isn't for the weak of heart."

"Who is it, Sam?"

"The person with the highest aptitude scores in the history of the program."

"Please tell me that was a joke," Grandpa said. "Colt just turned sixteen."

||||||||||||||||||||||||||||||||||||

"You can come out now," Grandpa said after the other two men had left.

Colt emerged from the laundry room with his head bowed like a puppy expecting a scolding. "Grandpa, I . . ."

"It's okay," McAlister said. "You were bound to find out sooner or later. You remember Senator Bishop?"

Colt nodded.

"He's the chairman of the Senate Committee on Homeland Security. The tall one was Major General Robert T. Walker of the United States Army. Apparently you've made quite an impression on them."

"Why me? I mean, they can't be serious . . . Do they really think that a sixteen-year-old should be the director of CHAOS?"

Grandpa McAlister walked to the kitchen to pour himself a cup of coffee. "You're too young to get involved in this mess."

"You didn't answer my question."

"Apparently so."

Colt sat down, and neither one of them spoke for a long while. "Why do they want to get rid of Oz's dad?" Colt finally asked.

"It's complicated, but you can bet that Lobo has his own opinions about how to run the program, and they aren't working."

"Lobo?"

"That's what the men called Romero. He's cunning and strong, like a wolf."

"You said you don't want me to get involved."

Grandpa McAlister nodded. "That's right."

"I think it's too late."

"How's that?"

Colt described the bizarre twist that his life had taken thanks to Albert Van Cleve's phone call.

"I don't know why I'm surprised," Grandpa said. He sat there staring at his coffee cup.

Colt didn't say a word.

"Did you know that I was your age when I enlisted?" Grandpa said.

"I thought that you had to be eighteen to join the army."

"Back then it didn't take much to forge documents. I was living in Sanborn, Iowa, and I ran around with a couple of guys named Dale and Hank. Dale's brother had already been through basic, and he was getting ready to ship over to London.

"We decided that we couldn't wait any longer, but the nearest recruiter was twenty miles away. He probably thought we were a band of idiots when we showed up on that old tractor, but by the time we left the office we were enlisted in the United States Army."

"You took a tractor?"

"If we'd tried to borrow a car, our parents would have known what we were up to."

"Weren't you scared?"

"We were too young and stupid to be scared," Grandpa said. "I suppose that's why we volunteered for an experimental unit. Well, that and the fact that they offered double the pay. A month later we were shipped off to the Military Intelligence Training Center at Camp Ritchie for something called the CHAOS program."

"So you really are the Phantom Flyer."

Grandpa McAlister laughed. "I'm no superhero, if that's what you're asking. But from what I've been told, the artist may have used my picture as a model for his drawings."

Colt sat there caught between euphoria, disbelief, and awe. "Did Dad know?"

"He joined the program after he graduated from the Naval Academy," McAlister said.

"Dad was a CHAOS agent?"

"For a time, but he got out at the first chance. It was the smartest thing he ever did."

"So everything that happened in the Phantom Flyer comics was real?"

Grandpa McAlister didn't say anything for a moment. "I suppose it's real enough, but they took liberties when it suited their needs."

"Did you wear a jet pack?"

"It's not as glorious as it sounds, but yes."

"I don't get it," Colt said. "If CHAOS was supposed to be classified, why did they make comic books about it?"

"It was all part of the propaganda machine," McAlister said.

"The revenue helped support the war effort, and President Roosevelt knew that a comic book would keep young men enthusiastic about the war. He was right. The Phantom Flyer became the face of the United States military to anyone who wasn't old enough to enlist yet."

"Or sneaky enough to forge his own documents."

"I suppose that's fair," Grandpa McAlister said with a wink.

Colt reached into his backpack and pulled out a comic book. It was the issue where soldiers with red eyes were swarmed around the Phantom Flyer. "Did you see anything like this?"

Grandpa McAlister turned the comic book facedown on the table with a shaking hand. "I prayed that my children would never face the horrors that we did, but it looks like we've come full circle." His voice faltered. "They've taken my son, and now they're coming after you."

|||||||||||||||||||||||||||||||||||||||||

Grandpa McAlister retreated to the backyard under the auspices of watering his plants, but Colt watched him pull out a handkerchief to wipe his eyes and blow his nose. Not wanting his grandfather to think that he was spying, Colt went to the refrigerator to pull out a root beer. It cracked open with a hiss, and the cold liquid burned as it went down his throat.

As he sat down at the kitchen table, Colt thought about his dad working as a CHAOS agent, and wondered whether he had ever fought against alien life forms or investigated Bigfoot sightings. Then his mind drifted to his mom. He wondered if she understood the dangers involved with investigating Trident, and if she did, why she thought it was important enough to put her life at risk. Colt wasn't sure anything was worth that.

When the phone rang, his heart started pounding. Then he realized it wasn't Van Cleve's phone. The ringtone was different, and besides, that phone's battery had died. Colt reached into his front pocket to check the display before he answered.

"Let me guess," Colt said. "You found a way to reprogram the injector drones."

"That's easy," Oz said. "I was thinking about sending one after Mr. Pfeffer. Not to kill him or anything, but I'd love to see what he would do if it crawled up his pant leg."

"You're cruel."

"His lectures are cruel."

"You have a point."

"What are you doing right now?"

"I should be doing my homework."

"Can you blow it off?"

"I guess, why? What's going on?"

"Meet me out front."

"You're already here?" Colt stood up.

"Why don't you come outside and check for yourself?"

When Colt opened the front door he found Oz standing at attention. His arms were stiff, his knees locked, and he was looking straight ahead. Then Colt saw his eyes. They were glowing red.

:: CHAPTER 26 ::

Colt nearly swallowed his tongue before he tried to slam the door shut, but Oz's arm shot out. The door flung back open, hitting Colt in the shoulder.

Colt tripped over himself as he tried to back away. The floor mat in the entryway slid out from under him as he tumbled to the ground.

"Got you!" Oz was laughing as he reached up to remove a tinted contact from one eye. "See? It's a fake."

Colt's breathing slowed a bit as he tried to wrap his mind around what had happened.

"I saw them at the drugstore and couldn't resist," Oz said.

"I'm going to kill you." Colt stood up and shoved Oz in the chest.

Oz laughed harder. "You really thought I was one of them?"

"I don't know," Colt said as he ran his hand through his hair. "What was I supposed to think?"

"Come on," Oz said as he removed the second contact.

Colt looked at him sideways.

"Look, McAlister. So far you've been lucky, but Trident isn't just watching you. They're coming after you, and they aren't going to stop until the job's done. Somebody has to teach you how to defend yourself before you end up six feet under. Besides, Lily would kill me if anything happened to you."

"She said that?"

"See, I knew you had a thing for her."

Colt shook his head and went to tell his grandpa that he was going over to Oz's house for a while.

The Romeros lived a few miles south of Chandler High. The city planners hadn't anticipated the population boom, so the streets were torn apart as construction crews widened the roads to keep up with all the new housing developments in the area.

"This isn't a house, it's a compound," Colt said as Oz pulled into his driveway. "I thought you said your dad was in the army."

"He was," Oz said as he clicked a button on the remote. The front gate opened. "A few years ago CHAOS branched out. Now it's a private agency, which means instead of answering to the president of the United States, my dad answers to a board of directors. It's not as glamorous, but it pays a lot better."

"I can see that."

The Romeros' drive was made out of brick pavers that led to an enormous Tuscan house constructed of stone and plaster. There was a fountain wreathed by colorful flowers just outside the front door, with stone archways that stretched across the length of the porch.

Colt watched as Oz lifted his hand to a sensor next to the door. It flashed green, and the front door clicked open.

"You have a biometric scanner at your house?"

"Doesn't everybody?" Oz smiled as he walked in. He threw his keys into a bowl that sat on a table in the foyer, then led Colt past rooms with opulent furnishings before he came to a set of double doors. Oz placed his hand on another sensor, and it lit green just like the first. He opened the door and flipped some switches. The lights hummed to life.

Inside was a full-fledged gymnasium complete with hoops, a hardwood floor, and the works. A glass wall separated the gym from a weight room that was better than any health club Colt had seen. There were free weights, stair steppers, treadmills, and elliptical machines.

"This is incredible," Colt said.

"Just wait." Oz walked across the gym to a door that looked like it led to a utility closet. Instead, it was a circular room with a wall covered in Venetian plaster. Twelve monitors stacked in three rows covered one section. One showed a busy cityscape where flying cars zipped along invisible highways, while another had images of a world with lakes of molten lava. Fire burned over the surface as strange creatures flew overhead. They looked like winged frogs covered in red scales.

"Are those screen savers?" Colt asked.

"They're windows into other worlds," Oz said. "See the one with the trees? That's Nemus."

"The planet Bigfoot is supposed to come from?"

"That's the one," Oz said as he continued the tour of the windows. "The underwater city is on Undar, and those ruins that look like they were swallowed by the jungle? That's Gathmara."

"Was there a nuclear war there or something?" Colt asked as he looked at the wreckage. Skyscrapers crawling with vines had been knocked over, while others were charred and riddled with gaping holes, the windows knocked out. The city, if that's what it still was, didn't look inhabitable, and yet there was movement in the streets as humanoids, some with two arms and some with six, walked beneath the shadows of destruction.

"Something like that," Oz said as he shut the door.

Colt lifted his hand to the moving images, trying to reach inside though he couldn't.

"They aren't portals," Oz said. "They're more like windows. We use them for surveillance so we can see what's happening in the other worlds."

"Oh." Colt watched as the ground inside the frame started to shake. Then a machine came into view as it lumbered down the street. It resembled a robot, but it was at least thirty feet tall and had six arms instead of two.

The exoskeleton of the machine looked like it was made from the scrap of decommissioned tanks. Camouflaged plating was thick with heavy rivets protruding like metal gooseflesh. A black cross outlined in white was painted on its dented breastplate, and the barrel from a gun turret on its shoulder scanned back and forth as though looking for a target.

There was a shout, followed by a trail of smoke that erupted from a window in one of the buildings. A missile screamed as it tore through the air. Then it slammed against the head of the machine.

"Whoa! Did you see that?" Colt asked as fire erupted in the frame.

CHAPTER 27

O z didn't seem concerned by Colt's panicked tone. Instead, he sat down at the table.

"Are you ignoring me or something?" Colt said. "There's a war going on inside this one." He watched another missile slam into the giant machine. When the smoke cleared it looked like the only damage it left was a scorch mark.

"What?" Oz said, reaching under the table. He looked up to catch a glimpse of the footage that had Colt worked up and smiled. "That's nothing."

"Nothing? Are you kidding me?"

The robot turned toward the building where the missiles were coming from. Then Colt watched as the gun turret adjusted before a rocket burst from the barrel. There was an eruption of light and smoke as it exploded against the wall. Brick was turned to dust as a cloud of debris fell to the street. The hole left by the rocket was bigger than a subway tunnel. Colt knew that whoever was inside those rooms was probably dead.

"That big thing? It's called a Vanquisher," Oz said as the machine bent down to pick up a car in one of its six hands. The

Vanquisher hurled it toward the gaping hole. "The Thule use them to round up refugees and terrorists."

"Terrorists?"

"Yeah—pretty much anyone who stands up against them. They've basically destroyed their planet trying to conquer every living creature. That's why they want to break through into our world. As far as they're concerned, Earth is prime real estate once they exterminate all the humans."

"That's not going to happen, though, right?" The idea of being exterminated was just shy of terrifying as far as Colt was concerned, but the Thule didn't have a way to cross over from their world to Earth—at least not yet—so there wasn't much to worry about. He hoped.

"It's already happening," Oz said.

That wasn't the response that Colt was looking for.

"What do you think all those lights over South Mountain are? And the stuff that's happening in San Diego? We're gearing up for war, McAlister. The Thule are everywhere, and there are more coming every day."

"I thought the gateway to Gathmara was shut down?"

"It was," Oz said. "Well, at least the one we could find. Small ones pop up all the time. Something wacky is going on."

"Like what?"

"Think of it this way. The membrane that separates our world from others is getting thin in spots, and if our teams don't catch where they rip, things slip through."

"I thought that's been happening forever. I mean, that's how stuff like the Loch Ness monster got here, right?"

"Yeah, except it's been happening more often. There're so many weak spots we can't keep up."

"Is there going to be an invasion?" Colt asked. From the way Oz looked at him, Colt thought he must have said something wrong.

"It's already started," Oz said. "Look, all of this is classified, so if you tell anyone, you're going to end up in a mental institution hopped up on so many drugs that you won't remember your own name . . . either that, or they'll send you to a work camp in Siberia for the rest of your life."

"Funny."

"I'm serious," Oz said. "Some of the gateways are still open. We have embassies on seven of the planets, and there are alien embassies here."

"In Arizona?"

Oz flipped a switch, and a panel opened, revealing a keyboard and a controller.

"New York," he said, and entered a code into the keypad. The tabletop flickered, and a three-dimensional hologram of a grassy field appeared.

After another series of commands, a tiny army of CHAOS agents appeared on the field next to Colt. They wore camouflaged battle suits with matching ski masks covered by helmets, goggles, and oxygen masks.

"What is that?" Colt asked, but Oz didn't answer. Some of the soldiers hovered over the long grass in jet packs, but most were ground troops. There were hover tanks, soldiers inside of armored battle suits, troop transports that walked on six mechanical legs instead of rolling on tires or treads, and a variety of other vehicles that Colt had never seen before.

There were even robots scattered among the troops. Some had hands that were flamethrowers, others had Gatling guns fixed to their shoulders, but all looked intimidating.

"How did you do that?" Colt asked.

"You remember the game Risk?"

"Yeah, I used to play it with my dad."

"It's kind of like that, only the game board has animated holograms instead of little plastic pieces."

"Wait, this is a game?"

Oz entered another code. The board flickered again, and a second army appeared on the other side of the table. A cluster of battleships shaped like manta rays hovered over armored land vehicles that looked like scorpions. They had treaded wheels in the place of their legs, and their claws opened up to shoot what looked like crackling balls of energy. Gigantic mechanical spiders crept through the tall grass, each with a turret that held a cannon on top of its thorax.

"What are those?" Colt asked, pointing to enormous robots that looked like binoculars on two legs.

"Trackers," Oz said. "The Thule used them during the war to hunt escapees from Nazi internment camps."

"What about those?" Colt pointed to a robot that was a bit taller than a man, with a wide chest and a narrow head.

"That's a Sentry, but people used to call them bunker busters. They were part of the first wave of any German attack. Their exoskeletons were as strong as tanks, but they were more mobile. Imagine sitting in a bunker with one of those coming at you with guns blazing."

"No, thanks," Colt said. He turned his attention to a squad of lizard men with six arms.

"Those, my friend, are the Thule." Oz stood up, but not before reaching over to touch one of the lizard men with his finger. He dragged it off the table and into the air. As he expanded his thumb and forefinger, the figure started to grow until it was bigger than Oz.

Somehow, a full-size Thule soldier was standing between Colt and Oz. If it weren't for the fact that the lizard man was slightly transparent, Colt would have assumed it was real. The monster's eyes glowed with an amber light, and its chest heaved up and down as though it were breathing. It had three sets of arms, each ending in black claws that could rip through human flesh. Its tail swished back and forth.

Oz walked back to the control panel. "Tell me what you know about the Thule," he said.

"Well, they can change shapes."

As Colt spoke, the Thule soldier flickered. A moment later Colt was looking at a holographic image of his grandfather. The image shimmered once more before it became Danielle, and finally it morphed back to its native lizard form.

"How can you tell if someone is a Thule or if they're human?" Oz asked.

"I don't know."

"You can't," Oz said. "Not unless you have a special sensor or you cut them open. They're like reptiles, so their core body temperature is lower than ours. They also bleed green." He entered another series of commands before the holographic image of the lizard man turned to face Colt. It crouched as though ready to attack. "Any idea how to fight one?"

Colt shook his head. He knew the alien wasn't real, but his heart was still beating fast.

"Their skin is kind of like a rhino's, but there are a few soft spots." As Oz spoke, circular lights lit up where the six arms met the thorax. There were also lights around its throat and eyes. "Are you ready?"

"For what?"

The monster leapt at Colt with arms wide. A pair of hands gripped Colt by his shoulders, a second set ripped at his stomach with its claws, while another tore at his face. He didn't feel anything, but he got the picture.

"That was pathetic," Oz said.

"I didn't know it was going to attack me."

"That's the point," Oz said with a frown. "You're never going to know, so get used to it."

The lizard man flickered, then disappeared. It surfaced on the other side of the room before attacking again. This time Colt was ready, but he didn't fare much better. The monster spun around, using its tail as a whip. It followed up by raking Colt across the face with a pair of claws, and then it bit down on his shoulder.

"Let me try," Oz said. He entered another code before walking over to push Colt out of the way. He waited for the Thule soldier to strike, and when it did, Oz sidestepped and struck the monster under one of its arms. A light flashed at the point of contact to show that it was a clean strike. Oz followed up with an elbow to its throat, and another light flashed.

He jumped as the monster tried to whip him with its tail. Then he struck twice more under its arms before another jab to the throat. The Thule soldier toppled to the ground.

"How did you do that?"

"Lots of practice," Oz said. "And that was only the first level." He walked over to the console and shut the program down.

"I thought we were going to play the game," Colt said as he watched the battlefield on the tabletop flicker and disappear.

"How are you supposed to beat an army of those things if you can't even beat one?"

"That's different."

"Not really," Oz said as he walked over to the door.

"Wait, that's it?"

"For today."

"So when's my next lesson?"

Oz smiled. "If I were you I'd sleep light, McAlister."

:: CHAPTER 28 ::

"What's Danielle up to tonight?" Oz said as he slid into the driver's seat of his Jeep.

"My mom's editor finally called me back. He told me where she used to back her files up, so Danielle is looking to see if she can find that Trident Biotech story."

"He had the password?"

"No, but my mom used the same password for everything, so Danielle got in on the first try."

"Are you going to see her tonight?"

"Maybe," Colt said. "Why?"

"I got a present for you two."

"What?"

"Check the glove compartment."

"Let me guess. You have a dozen injector drones waiting for me."

"Just open it."

Colt hesitated, but he eventually opened it. "We already have phones," he said as he pulled out two sleek models with silver cases and large touch screens.

"Not like this," Oz said. "I have a feeling Trident has been monitoring your calls and text messages, but they won't be able to with these. I already programmed my number into both of them. You should have Danielle's in yours, and she has your number. These are just for us, okay?"

<hr />

It was late afternoon as Danielle sat on her bed reading her bio-tech science book. Wolfgang, her Pomeranian, was sleeping by her side. Clumps of his black fur covered Danielle's bedspread, but she didn't care. He was like a security blanket. Whenever Wolfgang was around, Danielle felt safe.

Her laptop was sitting on her desk on the other side of the room. Colt had sent her a text with the web address for the site where his mom had backed up her files, and Danielle was able to log on. She had used a search function to find a folder titled *Trident*. It was filled with image files, videos, and text documents, but every time she tried to download them to her laptop, she got an error message. She called Colt.

"What about tech support?" he asked.

"I already tried. They said the files are definitely on their server. The guy had to send me to level two support because he'd never seen that error message before, but nobody could help me. I've tried downloading them all at once, then I tried them one at a time. Nothing's working."

"Did you restart your computer?"

"Along with my modem and my wireless router. I even called my ISP and had them check the connection. Everything should be fine. Let's hope it's something on their end."

"At least we know the files are there. Why don't you just try again in the morning?"

"I don't have much of a choice," Danielle said. "By the way, how did everything go with Oz today? Did he knock you around?"

"It wasn't too bad," Colt said. "Look, I have to go. My grandpa just got home, and I'm in charge of dinner tonight."

"I should get back to my homework. I'll see you in the morning."

After Danielle hung up, she had a difficult time concentrating on the chapter. Her eyes kept drifting from her book to the laptop, then up to the ceiling. She was half expecting a swarm of mechanical spiders to stream through the vent. Then Wolfgang jerked awake, lifting his head and cocking it to one side.

"What's wrong?"

As the dog barked, Danielle could feel her pulse rise. Her parents were at a Bible study, so except for Wolfgang and the fish in her aquarium, she was alone. She forced herself to slide off the bed and Wolfgang kept yapping.

"Shhh, it's okay, boy," she said in a whisper as she stroked his thick fur.

He wouldn't stop barking.

Danielle thought that she heard a noise coming from the kitchen . . . like someone rattling the doors. She picked Wolfgang up before walking over to the window, but all she could see was the swimming pool and the palm trees. Then a shadow moved across the water. Danielle froze.

Someone was back there, she was sure of it. She closed the plantation shutters, stuffed her biotech book into her backpack, and grabbed her keys. With Wolfgang still yapping in her arms, she was halfway down the hall before she remembered the laptop.

She raced back to grab the computer, and that's when she saw the silhouette of someone standing outside her bedroom window. It took all of her willpower not to scream, but Wolfgang made enough noise for both of them. She tried to grab his muzzle, but the dog pulled away and kept barking. Danielle set him on the bed long enough to slam the laptop shut and slide it into the main compartment in her backpack. "Let's go, boy."

Wolfgang jumped off the bed and followed her down the hall and out the front door to the driveway. Danielle fumbled with her car keys, trying to find the right one to place in the lock. Her hands were sweaty and her thoughts were scrambled. Since when had opening a car door become so difficult?

She could hear footsteps in the gravel. "Come on," she said, urging her fingers to cooperate. She slid the key into the lock and twisted, and heard the familiar pop of the mechanism unlocking.

"Get in," she said as she tossed the backpack into the passenger's seat.

Wolfgang kept barking.

"This isn't the time to play hero," she said and picked the dog up.

She pulled out of the driveway and slammed her foot on the gas. As the Thunderbird roared down the street, she exhaled.

It wasn't until she looked in the rearview mirror that she saw the exterminator's truck parked in front of their house. She rolled her eyes. Her parents had told her that he would be coming over to spray, but she'd forgotten . . .

Since she had everything she needed, Danielle decided to drive over to the Coffee Rush to finish her homework. Besides, at the moment she liked the idea of being in a public place with lots of people around.

She turned on the radio before reaching over to scratch Wolfgang behind the ears. "You're such a good protector," she said. "What would I do without you?"

As Danielle drove down the road, she noticed that a car had pulled up behind her. It had a long front end and wide wheel wells, and a Mercedes-Benz hood ornament sitting on top of the chrome grille.

She eased into the left turn lane before stopping at the light. The Mercedes did as well. She glanced in her rearview mirror to see a man with short blond hair and a strong jaw.

When the arrow turned green, Danielle shifted her attention to the road ahead. She pulled out and as soon as it was safe enough, she crossed over to the far right lane to see if the man in the Mercedes would follow. He did. She turned her blinker on before merging back to the left. So did the Mercedes. No matter what she did, he kept pace.

Danielle felt her heartrate increase. She pressed on the gas, and before she knew it her car was barreling down the road at seventy miles per hour. Wolfgang jumped into Danielle's lap looking for comfort. Startled, she accidentally jerked her steering wheel to the left. She tried to correct her trajectory, but she overcompensated and nearly crashed into a station wagon.

The Mercedes was right behind her.

Up ahead the light was turning yellow, but Danielle was going too fast to stop. She breathed deep, exhaled, and pressed the gas pedal to the floor. Her engine roared as she shot through the intersection. Behind, she could hear tires screech. The Mercedes narrowly missed a pickup with a horse trailer as the strange man followed her.

CHAPTER 29

The first day she had her driver's license, Danielle got a speeding ticket. Her parents had threatened to take her car if she ever got another one, but at that moment she was desperate for a policeman. As she sped through a school zone, she pulled at her seat belt to make sure it was cinched tight. Then she reached over and took Wolfgang in her arm, cradling him like a football.

The speedometer read eighty miles per hour now. Danielle looked in her rearview mirror again and gasped. The man was gone and in his place was some kind of lizard man, with green skin and a head that looked like a dragon's.

"This is crazy!"

Wolfgang barked. Danielle turned in time to see that she was heading toward a stop sign. She turned to the left at the last possible second and her hubcap scraped against the curb. She risked another glance at the Mercedes but the lizard was gone, replaced by the man.

"I'm losing my mind, Wolfie." She took a deep breath and then another before slamming on her brakes. The front end of her car dipped, and Danielle lurched toward the windshield, but the seat belt held tight. Her head snapped back into the headrest but some-how she managed to hang on to Wolfgang.

The man in the Mercedes was forced to brake as well. His car careened to the left until it was almost perpendicular to the Thunderbird. She watched as he turned his steering wheel to try and regain control. Then his car shot forward, narrowly missing the back end of Danielle's car before it darted across two lanes and into oncoming traffic.

He steered to the left, avoiding a collision with a cement truck, but he was going too fast. The Mercedes jumped the curb and smashed into a light pole. The front end crumpled. The horn blared, and steam rose from what used to be the engine.

Danielle took her foot off the gas. Her heart was pounding and her hands were shaking as she continued down the road. "I don't know how much longer I can take this," she said as Wolfgang tried to lick her cheek.

At this point coffee was only going to make her jittery, so she decided to get some ice cream instead. She drove around looking for a place to stop and then a few minutes later she was inside an ice-cream shop where they mix in the toppings on a marble counter.

Danielle ordered dark chocolate with chocolate cake and sprinkles. As the ice-cream chef blended everything together, she looked out the window to see Wolfgang with his nose pressed against the windshield. He barked when he saw her, and she waved back. She paid, took a quick bite, and then went back to her car.

When Danielle slid into the front seat, Wolfgang pounced. He wanted some of her ice cream but she forced him to sit still. Then she frowned. Something wasn't right.

She looked around the car, and then she knew. Her backpack

was missing. She set the ice cream on the dashboard before turning to look in the backseat. It wasn't there.

"Get down," she said, catching Wolfgang trying to get at her ice cream.

She checked beneath the passenger's seat and she sighed when she wrapped her hand around one of the straps of her backpack. It must have fallen when she hit the brakes. She unzipped the bag to see if the laptop had been damaged.

Her computer was gone.

||||||||||||||||||||||||||||||||||||

"I'm sorry," Danielle said when Colt answered the door. "I didn't know who else to call."

"What happened to the guy who was following you?"

"I don't know. I drove by to see the wreck on the way over here, but his car was gone. I didn't even see a police car or an ambulance. It's like it never happened."

"Maybe it's time for us to back off."

"We should at least try to download those files. Maybe it'll work from here. Can we use your computer?"

"Sure."

Colt's laptop was sitting on the kitchen table where he had been doing his homework after dinner. Danielle logged on to the website, but this time the Trident folder didn't come up after her search.

"What's wrong?"

"The files are gone," Danielle said. "They were there an hour ago. I saw them myself."

"Maybe there's a glitch in the system. You know, like a virus or something."

"I doubt it. Companies like that have all kinds of redundancy."

"What do you think happened?"

"Trident."

"How?"

"Who knows," Danielle said. "They probably own the company."

"And you think they took your laptop?"

"Who else would take it?"

"I'm sorry, Dani."

"Would you stop apologizing? None of this is your fault."

After Danielle went home, Colt told his grandpa about everything that had happened. Even though it was nearly eleven o'clock in Virginia, Grandpa called Senator Bishop at home. Not an hour later, two CHAOS agents showed up at his house in an unmarked sedan wearing fedoras.

Colt hadn't been expecting them to fly in on jet packs carrying laser guns, but as they walked up the drive he thought they looked more like accountants than elite agents who protected Earth against unseen dangers from other worlds.

When he opened the door, Colt did a double take. The man in front removed his hat and introduced himself as Agent Thomas E. Richmond. He had a wide brow, a receding hairline, and bags under his eyes. Colt guessed that he had been an athlete when he was younger, but now his stomach hung slightly over his belt buckle.

"How do you do, young man," Agent Richmond said with a southern accent that Colt couldn't place. "Is your grandfather home by any chance?"

Unfortunately Colt hadn't heard a word he said. He was too busy staring at Agent Richmond's companion. The robot was slightly taller than Richmond, and it stood there wearing a tan trench coat.

It was an odd choice for a September evening in Arizona, but the machine's chest was too wide for a shirt, and the ball joints that connected its legs to its hips wouldn't have allowed for pants.

Though this was the second robot Colt had seen, he was still mesmerized by its single eye. It sat square in the middle of a head that was shaped like a capsule that had been cut in half. Its arms looked like the corrugated tubing that connects a clothes dryer to the wall, and its hands weren't hands at all. They were large pinchers that reminded Colt of vise grips.

"Forgive me," Agent Richmond said. "I'd like to introduce my partner, Agent D3X."

"Good to see you," Grandpa McAlister said as he appeared from the hallway. He gently placed his hand on Colt's shoulder and nudged him to the side so the agents could come in.

"It's been too long," Agent Richmond said as he slipped past Colt.

Agent D3X followed, his movements surprisingly fluid considering the robot's size. Grandpa McAlister invited them both to take a seat on the couch before offering Agent Richmond a cup of coffee.

"Oh, no, thank you," Agent Richmond said before he sat down. "I have to tell you, I was real sorry to hear about Roger."

"I appreciate that," McAlister said.

"If we had known that Mary was investigating Trident . . ."

Grandpa McAlister raised his hand. "I know," he said, "but there's no need to spend time on something that can't be fixed, so let's focus on what we can do to protect my grandson."

"As far as we can tell, the two are connected."

"It was bound to happen sooner or later," Grandpa McAlister said. "Have they struck any of the gateways yet?"

Agent Richmond looked at Colt, then turned back to Grandpa McAlister. "There's not much I can say on the record."

"I understand."

"What I can tell you is that we got a report about a break-in," Richmond said, looking directly at Colt. "Someone stole your mother's computer from her office."

:: CHAPTER 30 ::

At the mention of his mom, Colt felt as though someone had reached through his chest and grabbed his heart. The world was a tolerable place to live as long as he didn't think about his parents, but the second either one of them came up— whether in casual conversation or in someone's well-intentioned but depressing condolences—Colt plummeted right back into a state of depression.

His eyes fell to the worn carpet. He sighed. "When?"

Agent Richmond studied Colt for a moment. His face had turned to something that almost showed warmth, but the kindness didn't last. "It happened this afternoon. You don't know anything about that?"

"No, sir."

"If you know something, son, this would be a good time to share it with me. You're already in a bit of pickle."

Colt shook his head.

Agent Richmond paused as though he was giving Colt time to reconsider.

"I think we can move on with questions now," Grandpa McAlister said.

Colt looked up in time to see Agent Richmond clench his jaw. His eyes narrowed, if only for a moment, but he didn't push the issue. The agent led him through a series of questions about his ordeal with Albert Van Cleve, followed by everything that had happened since. At times he would go back and ask for more details. Then he would skip ahead to the end, only to swing back somewhere in the middle.

Colt found Agent Richmond's ever-present smile distracting. Though the words the agent spoke were often kind, Colt found them to be insincere.

While Agent Richmond did most of the talking, Agent D3X simply stood there like some kind of industrial floor lamp, its single eye pulsing as though it were breathing.

"Tell me something," Agent Richmond said toward the end. "You claim that your backpack never left your sight, yet someone managed to unzip one of the compartments, plant an untraceable phone inside, and then zip it back up—all without your seeing a thing. How do you explain that?"

Colt looked to his grandfather, who simply nodded. "To tell you the truth, I'm not sure."

"I see," the agent said. "That same night you voluntarily got into a car without asking where they were taking you. Now don't you think that seems a bit . . . oh, I don't know. Let's call it daring?"

"I suppose so," Colt said, "but I wanted to find out what happened to my parents."

"And you'd never met Albert Van Cleve before?"

Colt shook his head.

"Had you read any articles about him? Seen him on television?"

"If I did, I don't remember," Colt said.

"And you have no idea where he is now?"

"No, sir."

"You know, I find it interesting that you'd never seen anything like a winged motorcycle before, and yet you were able to hop right on and fly away with not one but two Trident assassins shooting at you."

"Yes, sir," Colt said. "I can't explain how I did it. It just kind of happened."

"Seems that way, doesn't it?"

"Well, to be honest, I guess I've seen them in comic books."

Agent Richmond laughed. "Yes, indeed. Those crazy comic books."

"Is there anything else, Agent Richmond?" Grandpa McAlister asked as he stood up.

"Well, Colonel, I was thinking. If it's all right with you, I'd like to try and record a bit of your grandson's memories. I need to get a good look at this Albert Van Cleve to make sure Colt was talking to the real deal."

Colt watched his grandfather's eyes narrow for a moment.

"I suppose that would be all right," Grandpa said, though Colt wasn't quite certain what the man meant by recording memories. "But only from the phone call moving forward. I think anything else would be a bit premature at this point."

"That's sounds fair," Agent Richmond said. He rubbed his hands together. "Let's get started, shall we? Agent D3X, I believe it's your turn."

As the robot approached, Colt looked at it with wide eyes. He tried to reassure himself that his grandfather would never let Agent Richmond do anything that would harm him.

"Now just sit still, son," Agent Richmond said. "You're going to feel a little tingle, that's all. This won't take but a minute."

Colt watched as a pair of plates in the center of the robot's chest opened up like curtains on a stage. Inside was a screen that flared to life. At the same time, six long tentacles shot out from behind D3X's back. They slithered into place, and Colt could see tiny suction cups on their ends. Then, in perfect synchronicity, the arms struck. Colt didn't have time to duck out of the way, and the suction cups locked on to his forehead, temples, and the base of his skull.

"You're doing fine," Agent Richmond encouraged.

Colt didn't feel like he was doing fine. What he felt was a wave of panic as six needles inside those cups pierced his flesh simultaneously. His eyes darted as he looked for his grandpa to intervene, but Grandpa stood there with his hands in his pockets. Colt felt his eyes roll back and start to twitch.

He watched as his memories flashed in front of him. They were so fast that they barely registered, but he saw images of himself flying through the sky on the winged motorcycle, of Jimbo attacking him with the syringe, of Danielle crying when she told him that her computer had been stolen. There were even snippets of Colt smiling at Lily, which made Colt feel violated.

"That's it," Agent Richmond said.

Colt shook his head to clear his vision. The first thing he saw were the tentacles wrapping back around Agent D3X before they disappeared. The robot's chest closed back up as Agent Richmond stood. "I believe we're done for the night."

"Wait a minute . . . what about Dani?" Colt asked. He followed the agent to the door.

"Oh, don't you worry about her," Agent Richmond said. "We have someone looking after that pretty little girlfriend of yours."

"She's just a friend."

"That's what they all say, son." Agent Richmond placed a firm hand on Colt's shoulder. "Now if there's anything you need, you just let me know."

He pulled a business card out of his inside breast pocket and turned to Grandpa McAlister. "We'll be in touch as soon as we find out anything," he said. "In the meantime, we'll have some agents in the area. The school is pretty well covered, but I might stop by tomorrow to make sure everything is secure."

"I'd appreciate that," Grandpa said.

:: CHAPTER 31 ::

Colt wasn't sure which was more frightening: biochips that could turn everyday people into assassins at the flip of a switch, or robots that could record your memories to play them back at will.

Without realizing it, his fingers kept finding their way to the spots where the robot's tentacles had interfaced with his skin. Colt was certain that he would find some kind of coaxial cable outlet, but no matter how many times he tried, he couldn't find anything.

That night he lay in bed reading more of his father's Phantom Flyer comic books. He was hoping to find an issue with D3X, but he couldn't. Instead, the Agents of CHAOS battled shape-shifting Thule, and there was a strange adventure where the Phantom Flyer was stranded in a parallel world fighting an evil version of himself.

Eventually Colt drifted to sleep, where he was haunted by dreams of D3X chasing him through rain-slicked streets in the middle of the night. The robot's arms danced like cobras before lashing out, and each time they would narrowly miss him. The next morning Colt woke up sprawled out on the floor. His bed was torn apart, and there were comic books everywhere.

On the way to school, he told Danielle about Agent Richmond and the robot. Her biggest concern was whether or not D3X got any close-ups of her when her makeup was smudged.

"Seriously?" Colt said. "I didn't think that you cared about stuff like that."

Danielle shrugged. "I usually don't, but . . . oh, never mind."

"Did you see any guys in suits hanging out around your house last night?"

"No," Danielle said. "Do you think they're going to interview me too?"

"Maybe."

"I'm not sure how much longer I can keep this from my parents."

"I think my grandpa is going to take care of that," Colt said. Then he told Oz as much as he could before first period started.

"Richmond? I'm impressed," Oz said. "They only involve him on the big cases."

"Have you ever had a robot record your memories?" Colt asked.

"Nah," Oz said. "Not yet anyway. They usually save that for the courtroom. Not that they think you're a criminal or anything."

"You should have seen the way that Agent Richmond was looking at me," Colt said. "I mean, he asked me if I was going to sell Van Cleve's motorcycle. It's not like I'd be able to stick it in front of the house with a FOR SALE sign. Give me a break."

"I might have been interested."

"Maybe I'll let you take it for a ride."

"He let you keep it?"

Colt's eyes shot wide. "Wait . . . they know where it's at! Do you think they're going to take it?"

Oz shrugged. "I doubt it. People don't mess with your grandpa. Besides, Richmond isn't going to break into his storage facility for something like that. It's just an ultralight."

Not to Colt it wasn't. It was an amazing piece of technology straight from the future. Then again, compared to D3X, maybe it wasn't such a big deal. "I'm curious," he said. "Agent Richmond told me that they already have people watching our campus. Did you know about that?"

"They're all over the place."

"Wait, are you saying that some of the teachers are CHAOS agents?"

"I can't confirm or deny it," Oz said, but his head was nodding dramatically.

"Who?"

Oz pointed his eyes to Mr. Pfeffer, who was trying to pull the wedgie out of his backside with one hand while sipping coffee from the cup in his other.

"Yeah, right."

"I'm telling you, they're in deep cover," Oz said. "You wouldn't be able to pick them out if you tried."

"Ms. Skoglund?"

Oz raised his finger to his lips before looking to the left and then the right.

"Who else?"

"Let it go."

"Fine," Colt said. "But why our school?"

"My dad thinks people have a bounty on my head."

"Are you serious?"

"It makes sense," Oz said after a shrug. "I mean, my dad's the head of an agency that deals with the underbelly of at least a dozen worlds. If the bad guys can't get to him, they're going to try and hit the people next to him."

"Have you ever been attacked?"

"Not yet, but I'm hoping somebody will try one of these days. Why do you think I train so hard? I always have to be ready."

IIIIIIIIIIIIIIIIIIIIIIIIIIIIIIIIIIIIIIIIIII

Apparently the CHAOS agents assigned to protect him were doing their job, even though Colt had no idea who they were or where they were hiding. The rest of the week was surprisingly uneventful. Nobody tried to run Colt off the road, he wasn't shot at, and there were no more cryptic messages or memory extractions.

Mr. Pfeffer even approved Colt's proposal for his World War II essay. He wanted to write about propaganda, focusing on the Phantom Flyer in particular. Apparently Mr. Pfeffer was an avid fan.

Lily hadn't been in class for the last few days, which made the lectures even more unbearable than usual. Colt was relieved when Mr. Pfeffer decided to show a documentary about aerial combat during the War. As soon as the lights were shut off, Colt placed his elbows on the desk so he could rest his head in his hands. Then he fell asleep.

He was startled awake when the door opened in the middle of the movie, and Lily walked to the front of the room to hand Mr. Pfeffer a pass. The teacher pulled out a penlight to examine the authenticity of the signature, then directed her to take her seat.

"Did you miss me?" Lily whispered.

"I didn't even know you were gone," Colt said.

"That's enough chatter," Mr. Pfeffer said. His penlight was shining on Colt's face.

"Sorry," Colt mumbled.

After the movie Mr. Pfeffer turned on the lights. "Now then, it looks like we have a little extra time," he said. "Why don't we gauge how much those little minds of yours soaked in today. Please take out a pencil and a sheet of paper."

There was a collective moan. Oz raised his hand.

"Yes, Master Romero?"

"I was just thinking, are you still part of that UFO club?"

There was snickering.

Mr. Pfeffer frowned. "Are you mocking me?"

"No, it's nothing like that," Oz said.

"Then why do you ask?"

"You know how there were rumors about the Nazis working with aliens from outer space?"

"Yes, I'm familiar with the theory. They were called gray aliens."

"Well, I was wondering if you thought all these UFO sightings had anything to do with that."

Mr. Pfeffer scanned the room. His eyes were narrowed and his lips were pursed. "It's interesting you should mention it," he said after a long pause. "I was conversing with some friends about this very topic last night."

"Imagine the odds."

There was more snickering, though it was stifled.

"Indeed," Mr. Pfeffer said. "All I know is that this universe is a vast place, and I would imagine there are life forms on other planets. Did Hitler ally himself with extraterrestrials? Perhaps. Are they back to finish what they started? I believe it's a possibility."

"Are you serious?" a girl asked from the back of the room.

Mr. Pfeffer blushed. "I simply said it's a possibility. I didn't state that it was a fact."

"What about those lights over South Mountain?" Oz asked. "Didn't they show up again last night?"

"It was three o'clock this morning, to be precise," Mr. Pfeffer said. "As to what they are, I'm not sure. I can tell you this, though. They aren't weather balloons, and there is no manmade aircraft that can hover in place like that. So if it's not a UFO, I'm not sure what it is."

"What if it was those gray aliens?" Oz asked.

The bell rang, ending the conversation and any chance of a quiz.

Colt stuffed his book into his backpack and rushed to catch up with Lily. "So where were you?"

"I thought you didn't notice that I was gone."

"Maybe I noticed a little," Colt said.

"I was out hunting aliens with Mr. Pfeffer."

"That's what I thought."

Lily rolled her eyes. "You don't believe in that stuff, do you? I mean, life on other planets and all that nonsense?"

"Who knows?" Colt said with a shrug. "As far as we know, Mr. Pfeffer could be an alien. He kind of looks like one."

Lily laughed.

"Since I'm pretty sure you don't hang out with Mr. Pfeffer all that much, where were you?"

"At a recording studio."

"I'm impressed."

"It wasn't a big deal," Lily said. "I'm supposed to fly out to Nashville in a couple of weeks, and my dad thought that I should bring some of my new songs."

"Nashville? That sounds like a big deal to me."

"We'll see," Lily said.

"Got any big plans this weekend?" Colt cringed as soon as the words came out of his mouth. He didn't want Lily to think he was about to ask her out. "I mean, besides the alien hunting."

"As a matter of fact, I do," she said. "I'm having a few people over on Saturday night. I'd love it if you and Danielle would stop by. Oz will be there."

Colt hadn't been expecting that. "Um, yeah . . . I think I can make it," he said. He was trying not to sound too enthusiastic.

Lily looked at him sideways. "So is that a yes?"

"Sure. I'll be there."

"Don't forget to tell Danielle," Lily said before one of her friends walked over to drag her away.

CHAPTER 32

Does the name Jimbo Tompkins mean anything to you?" Danielle asked at lunch the next day.

"Not me," Oz said with a mouth full of food.

"Should it?" Colt asked.

"He tried to stick you with a syringe full of bubbling blue liquid a couple of days ago."

"How did you find his last name?"

"I called the gas station and asked if they had anyone named Jimbo working there, but they didn't. So I checked their credit card transactions."

"You did what?"

"A friend of mine has access to the credit card verification company's database. He kind of owed me a favor."

"Isn't that illegal?"

"So is turning people into killing machines with biochips," Danielle said. "Anyway, I ran a background check. Jimbo is forty-two years old and he owns a small auto body shop in downtown Chandler. He also has a criminal record."

"You got all that from a credit card transaction?" Oz asked.

Danielle rolled her eyes. "No, that's how I got his name," she said. "I got the information by doing some research."

"Oh."

"Jimbo was convicted of marijuana possession with the intent to distribute," Danielle said. "There were also a couple of domestic violence charges. Apparently he's a heavy drinker, and he gets violent when he's drunk."

"Maybe he was drinking the other day," Colt said.

"I don't think so," Danielle said. "A few years ago Jimbo started to notice tremors in his hands, and as it got worse, he started to drink more."

"So he was self-medicating," Oz said.

"That's my guess," Danielle said. "Anyway, he took part in a clinical trial run by Trident Biotech. They implanted a next-generation biochip to control his Parkinson's."

"It makes sense," Oz said. "If he couldn't use his hands, then he'd lose his business. It's hard to do auto body work if you can't hold any tools."

"There you are," Ms. Skoglund said as she walked over to the table where the three of them were sitting. "I've been meaning to hunt you down all week, but it's been absolutely insane around here. For some reason the school board decided that we needed a new security system. They're installing cameras, metal detectors, and who knows what else. You'd think we were expecting an invasion or something."

"It sounds pretty high-tech," Oz said.

"Oh, it is. All those cameras are going to allow me to monitor every nook and cranny of this school from my desk."

"Let's say you spot someone pouring . . . oh, I don't know, some kind of hot sauce in Mr. Pfeffer's coffee . . ." Oz said.

"If it happens during first period I'll probably be in a meeting with the principal, so I won't be able to do much about it," Ms. Skoglund said with a quick wink.

"By the way, if I haven't told you yet, I'm really digging the new do."

Ms. Skoglund lifted her hands to her hair. "Really? I thought Mauricio cut it too short."

"Nah, it's perfect," Oz said. He flashed her a bright smile.

"Anyway, I really came over to see how you were adjusting to life at Chandler High," Ms. Skoglund said as she turned to Colt, who couldn't stop wondering if she was one of the CHAOS agents in deep cover.

"Everything's been great so far." Without realizing it, Colt's eyes shifted to the far side of the cafeteria.

Ms. Skoglund turned to see what had distracted him. "Oh," she said as Lily Westcott walked over to the cashier to pay for her lunch.

Colt blushed as Oz patted him on the back. "I think he's going to like it here just fine."

"Apparently so." Ms. Skoglund excused herself.

"What do you think, is McAlister going to get the girl?"

"I think we have bigger problems right now," Danielle said.

"I don't know," Oz said. "The homecoming dance isn't that far away. If McAlister doesn't make his move soon, he's going to be stuck on the sidelines."

"I don't know what you're talking about," Colt said.

"Really?" Danielle said. "I thought you two were going together. You know, to share your bromance with the world."

"Maybe we will," Oz said.

Colt looked at him sideways.

"That way we can give all the ladies a chance to dance with us," Oz said. "It's only fair."

"You certainly don't suffer from any self-esteem issues," Danielle said.

"Relax, Salazar. I'm just messing around. Besides, I have my eye on somebody right now."

"Who?" Danielle and Colt said at the same time.

"That's on a need-to-know basis," Oz said, "and right now neither one of you needs to know."

"Do you think that Ms. Skoglund heard what we were talking about?" Colt said, changing the subject before it came back around to Lily.

Oz shrugged and took a deep draught from a carton of chocolate milk. "I doubt it."

"Look, we don't have much time before the bell rings," Danielle said. "I had some free time in my computer lab, so I did a little research on Trident Industries. Apparently their scientists were running mind control experiments before World War II. They were even trying to splice human DNA with wolves to create some kind of hybrid."

"Like werewolves?" Colt asked.

"I guess. Anyway, after World War II Trident Industries was on the verge of bankruptcy. The rest of the world didn't want to do business with Nazi sympathizers, so they had to launch a major public relations campaign.

"Since then their record has been squeaky clean," she continued. "They're environmentally conscious, they've donated billions to charity, and they even offered public apologies for the atrocities that the Nazis committed using Trident innovations."

"If they're still running a mind control program, somebody

has to know about it," Oz said. Then his eyes lit up. "Basil Hyde."

"Who's that?"

"It's kind of . . . well, he's a businessman."

"You're hiding something."

"Maybe," Oz said. "What are you two doing tonight?"

"I was going to get a dress for Lily's party," Danielle said.

"Change of plans," Oz said.

"When am I supposed to buy my dress?"

"How should I know?" Oz said. "I bet you have a closet full of them. Just wear one of those."

"You don't understand girls, do you?" Danielle asked.

"Not really."

"So what are we doing?"

"You'll find out when we get there. Just make sure you wear something nice." Then Oz turned to Colt. "That goes for you too. They won't let us in if you dress like a slob."

"Am I supposed to rent a tux or something?"

"Just comb your hair and put on a decent pair of jeans and a button-up shirt," Oz said. "If you have a sport coat, that wouldn't hurt."

"Are you serious?"

Oz smiled as the bell rang. "And no flip-flops."

:: CHAPTER 33 ::

G'randpa McAlister was mowing the front yard when Danielle dropped Colt off after school. His pale legs were sticking out of a pair of plaid shorts, and he was wearing blue socks and cream-colored shoes that were smeared with grass stains.

"Why don't you let me do that?" Colt said.

"Because I like things done a certain way." Even though the enormous brim of a fishing hat covered Grandpa McAlister's face, he was still bright red. Sweat was pouring off his forehead, and his threadbare golf shirt was soaked through.

"You could always show me how to do it your way."

"You've got enough to worry about right now. Besides, I've got plans for you this afternoon, and I don't need you complaining about how tired you are."

"Whatever you say, Gramps."

"Do you have any homework tonight?"

"A little, but I was going to do it tomorrow. I'm kind of burned-out right now. Besides, Oz wants to hang out later."

"You'll have plenty of time to be with your friends, but I

have something to show you. You'll need to put on some pants, though."

Colt did as he was told, and a few minutes later he was seated in the cab of his grandfather's pickup as they trundled down the highway, heading east. Grandpa McAlister had wrapped something up in a tarp and stuck it in the bed of his truck. Whatever it was, it was big.

"That isn't a body back there, is it?" Colt asked.

"You'll find out soon enough."

When they exited on Signal Butte Road, Colt's eyes shifted from his grandpa to the window. He started drumming his fingers on the armrest.

"What's wrong with you?" Grandpa McAlister asked.

"Nothing, why?"

"You're kind of jumpy."

Colt stopped drumming.

Ten minutes later Grandpa McAlister pulled into the hidden drive that led back to his desert property. "Well, what are you waiting for?" he asked after getting out of the truck. Colt hadn't moved. "Would it kill you to give me a hand?"

Colt stepped out of the cab to help his grandfather. Whatever they had been carrying was heavier than it looked. They set it on the dusty ground, and then Grandpa McAlister pulled out a pocketknife so he could cut the twine that was holding the bundle together. Inside were two tarnished metal tanks connected to thick leather straps, kind of like a parachute.

"Is this what I think it is?" Colt asked with wide eyes.

"That depends on what you think it is." Grandpa McAlister handed Colt what looked like a flight suit. It was olive green with leather patches on the knees and elbows.

"A jet pack?"

"As a matter of fact, it is."

"You're going to teach me how to fly?"

"Somebody has to."

"I think this is going to be too big," Colt said as he held up the flight suit.

"That's because it was mine. It's a bit of an antique, but it'll have to do for now. Most of the reconnaissance crews wear body armor nowadays, but I don't like it. Too restrictive."

Colt zipped it up before rolling up the sleeves and the cuffs of the pant legs so it would fit better. Then his grandpa had him step into a harness that crossed over his chest to form an X.

"Now this might not feel comfortable, but it beats the alternative," Grandpa McAlister said as he cinched the harness tighter than Colt would have preferred. Then he picked up a length of chain and connected it to an eyelet screw that was lodged in a block of cement. He took the other end and fastened it with a carabiner to a ring that was on the harness.

"That'll get you to fifteen feet or so," he said, checking his handiwork to make sure Colt was secure.

Next came the jet pack. Colt had to lean forward just to keep from falling down. There were two armrests connected to the pack, and Colt set his arms on top of them before he grabbed what looked like joysticks.

"Now this is the ignition switch," Grandpa McAlister explained, pointing to a red button on top of the left joystick. "Once you hold it down, you're going to feel those rockets kick in. It'll shake a bit, but that's normal."

Colt nodded.

"Those handles are going to control your throttle and your

pitch," Grandpa McAlister continued. "When you're ready to come down, just keep your thumb on the red button. The longer you press it, the smoother the landing. And whatever you do, don't double tap the darn thing. That cuts the engine, and you'll drop like a rock."

"Don't double tap. Got it."

"There's just one more thing," Grandpa McAlister said before placing a helmet on top of Colt's head. He snapped the chin strap and then pulled out a pair of aviator goggles. "These should keep the bugs out of your eyes."

"So how long will the fuel supply last on this thing?" Colt asked as he slipped the goggles over his helmet.

"On these old models, you'll have about ten minutes . . . maybe less."

"That's it?"

"That's assuming there aren't any leaks." His grandpa took a few steps back. "Now, are you ready?"

Colt nodded.

"Then what are you waiting for?"

Colt hit the ignition switch, and the jet pack sputtered. Then, in a burst, it ignited and Colt started to lift. He was gripping the handles so tightly that his arms shook, but it wasn't long before he started to relax. The ascent was gentle, and moments later Colt was leveling out at fifteen feet, thanks to the tether that kept him from drifting away.

He looked down and saw his grandfather motioning for him to do something more than just hover in place, so he applied gentle pressure to the throttle and pulled to the left. The jet pack obeyed, looping around in a large circle. He did the same thing going right before trying a figure eight.

Colt decided to test the ignition switch. He placed his thumb on the red button and held it down. Just as Grandpa McAlister had promised, he started to descend slowly. As soon as he released the switch, he began to rise again. He flew around in a few more circles before looking up to the sky. It was a perfect day. There were no clouds, and the breeze was gentle. It was a shame to be tethered to this chain when he could be soaring through the air.

Colt looked down at his grandfather and gave him the thumbs-up signal before tapping the ignition switch twice. The engine cut out, and as Colt dropped, the tether drew slack. He reached down and unlatched the carabiner, freeing himself from the chain. Then, right before impact, Colt pressed down on the ignition switch, and the jet pack roared back to life.

He pushed on the throttle and burst into the sky. The wind rushed against his cheeks as Grandpa McAlister disappeared below. The flying motorcycle had been fun, but this was different. It was just Colt and the sky with nothing in between. The slightest hand motion or movement of his leg sent him one way or another. Precision was key. Colt had to maintain his focus, but he loved it. Somehow he felt at home.

He swooped down and watched as two coyotes ran across the desert floor. He followed them for a while before veering toward a rise that was covered in cacti. He circled overhead a few times, easing up on the throttle as he did. Colt didn't want to go back down, but he knew that Grandpa McAlister would be worried. He headed back, and when he spotted the truck, he placed his thumb firmly on the ignition button and held it there. The jet pack descended slowly, and moments later Colt was back on the ground.

"Do you know how foolish that was?" Grandpa McAlister

said as Colt cut the engine. His face was flushed with anger and the veins were popping out on his neck.

Colt flipped the goggles on top of his helmet. "I'm sorry, Grandpa, but I couldn't help myself." His smile was wide.

Grandpa sighed. "I should lock you in your room for a week after pulling a stunt like that," he said. "But I have to admit, that was an impressive piece of flying."

:: CHAPTER 34 ::

You got a flying lesson from the Phantom Flyer?" Oz asked as he drove down the beltway, heading to Scottsdale. "Do you know how incredibly amazing that is?"

Colt shrugged in the passenger's seat. "The flying part was amazing, but I'm still not sure about the whole Phantom Flyer thing. Besides, even if it's true, he's still just my grandpa."

"That man is a living legend," Oz said. He turned his eyes to the rearview mirror so he could see Danielle. "You're awfully quiet back there."

"I don't know about this dress," she said as she pulled the hem down over her knees.

"I think you look great." Oz elbowed Colt in the ribs.

"Yeah," Colt said after turning around. "You look nice."

"Nice?" Oz asked. "What are you, her father?"

"What am I supposed to say?"

"How about that she looks beautiful?"

Colt saw Danielle blush as she locked eyes with Oz through the rearview mirror. Then she turned away.

"So are you going to tell us who this Basil Hyde guy is?" Colt asked, trying to change the subject.

"I already told you," Oz said. "He's a businessman."

"Yeah, I got that part."

"Let's just say he's connected."

"What, like the mafia?"

"Not exactly."

"What's that supposed to mean?" Danielle asked. She leaned forward to stick her head in the front seat with the boys.

"It just means that he knows a lot of people in high places," Oz said. "Whatever Trident Biotech is up to, he's going to know about it."

"How does he get his information?" Danielle asked.

"I've never asked him."

"Is he a criminal or something?"

"That's a bit harsh," Oz said as he glanced at Danielle. "Let's just say he lives in a world that isn't exactly black-and-white."

It wasn't long before they arrived at the Scottsdale Waterfront, a posh collection of high-rise condos, shops, and restaurants that lined a canal bordering Camelback Road. Oz pulled his Jeep up to the valet at a restaurant called the Sanctuary, where a fashionable crowd of beautiful people milled about.

Colt saw a woman who was easily six feet tall without high heels. She was holding a rhinestone purse with a Yorkshire terrier poking its head out as she talked to a man who was at least six inches taller than she was.

"Yeah, he plays for the Phoenix Suns," Oz said when he caught Colt staring. "This is where the who's who come to be seen whenever they're in town. Just try not to gawk, okay?"

It wasn't easy. The street out front was lined with exotic cars that cost more money than most people's houses. There were Rolls Royces, Lamborghinis, Ferraris, and Porsches. Then a limousine pulled up. The driver rushed to get the door for a woman who could have been a supermodel for all Colt knew. Two more who were just as beautiful followed her before another man, taller than the guy Oz said was on the Suns, stepped out. He was wearing a linen suit and sunglasses, and he winked at Colt before flashing a bright smile.

"Come on," Oz said, pulling Colt by the sleeve.

One of the hostesses opened the front door when they approached. "Welcome to the Sanctuary."

The restaurant looked like a gothic cathedral. Servers in formal attire carried trays of food and bottles of wine to tables that were draped in white linen. Thick stone columns stretched from the floor to the top of the vaulted ceiling where at least a dozen iron chandeliers hung. Each was filled with white candles, as were the sconces fixed to the walls and pillars, and the candelabra that sat in the center of each table.

"Hello," Oz said after he walked to the hostess stand. "We have a reservation. It should be listed under Romero."

"Of course," the hostess said. Then, as though rehearsed, she broke into a megawatt smile as she opened a small drawer to pull out three silver wristbands.

"Put these on," Oz said, slipping one on his own wrist.

"What are they?" Colt asked.

"They let you into the VIP section."

"How did we get VIP passes?"

"Come on, McAlister," Oz said. "You're with me, that's how."

"If you follow me, I'll take you right to your table," the hostess said. The three of them followed her as she wound through tables and pillars in the dimly lit room. They passed a stringed quartet, and then headed toward a set of double doors carved from rough wood. A massive iron cross hung on the wall overhead, and two men in dark suits and sunglasses were standing on either side.

"What's with those guys?" Colt asked, trying to whisper so that Oz was the only person who could hear him.

"The guy on the left used to be a CHAOS agent," Oz said. "I think the guy on the right was a Navy SEAL, but I don't remember."

"What are they doing here?"

"Why don't you ask them?"

Colt decided to let it go. He watched as the hostess pulled out a key card. She swiped it on an entry pad, entered a code, and the door clicked open.

"Where are we going?" Colt asked.

"Will you relax?" Oz said. "Trust me, you're going to love it."

"Whenever you smile like that, it means something bad is about to happen."

"O ye of little faith."

The hostess led them through the doors and into a long hallway lined with torches. As Colt watched her walk through the doorway, he could have sworn her body flickered before she passed through. He held back to let Oz go next, and the same thing happened. It was like watching a movie reel skip.

"Did you see that?" Colt asked as he paused at the threshold.

Danielle nodded. "Do you think we should follow?"

"I guess but I'll go first. If anything weird happens, I want you to run."

"Do you see the shoes I'm wearing?" Danielle asked as she looked down at her high heels. "I'm not running anywhere."

Colt closed his eyes and took a deep breath. He felt Danielle grab his hand.

"Let's go together," she said.

As they stepped through the threshold, Colt felt a tingling sensation shoot up his leg. The air around him started to sizzle. He looked down to see what resembled static electricity crackling over his clothes and the same thing was happening to Danielle. Her eyes were wide as she watched the energy travel over her fingers and up her arm.

"What's happening?" she asked.

"You just traveled through a gateway," Oz said.

"Wait, you mean we're not in Arizona?" Colt asked.

"You're not even on Earth."

Danielle narrowed her eyes. "Don't you think you should have warned us or something?"

"Would you have come?"

"Probably not."

"That's why I didn't say anything," Oz said. "Look, I promise nothing will happen to you, okay? I'll even have you home by eleven o'clock. That's your curfew, right?"

"Yes."

"Oh, and McAlister, you might want to take that ring off," Oz said, looking at Colt's Phantom Flyer ring. "Some of the other guests aren't exactly fans of CHAOS, if you know what I mean."

Colt slipped the ring off and put it in his front pocket. Then they hurried down the hallway to catch up with the hostess.

"So if we're not on Earth, where are we?" Danielle asked.

"Think of it as a bridge between two worlds," Oz said.

"Which world are we going to?" Colt asked.

"Technically we're going to stay on the bridge," Oz said. "It's kind of an in-between place, I guess. You two don't have clearance to travel to any other worlds, so this is the best I could do."

Colt looked at Danielle before turning back to Oz.

"By the way," Oz said. "Don't lose those bracelets. You won't be able to get back home without them."

:: CHAPTER 35 ::

Colt's hand went to his bracelet without a thought, making sure it was secure. The last thing he needed was to be locked away in the middle of nowhere with no way to get home, much less anywhere else. He started to wonder if the Thule passed through this hall, not to mention all the other aliens and monsters that populated the twelve worlds that the Earth was supposedly connected to.

"Let's go, McAlister," Oz said when he saw Colt standing there staring at the bracelet. "As long as you stick with me, you'll be fine."

"Oh, sorry," Colt said.

"So is this part of the restaurant?" Danielle asked.

"Kind of," Oz said as he spotted the hostess waiting for them at the end of the hallway. "Come on, we don't want to be late for the fights."

"What are you talking about?" Danielle asked. "You said we were going meet someone who could tell us about Trident's mind-control program. You didn't mention any fights."

"We are," Oz said. "Look, Basil invited us to his luxury box tonight. I mean, how could I pass that up? These fights have been sold out for six months, and more than five million people across twelve planets have ordered it."

"Ordered what?"

"The Intergalactic Heavyweight Championship," Oz said. "It's a big deal, so when you meet Basil, be sure to say thank you."

"Is it boxing?" Colt asked.

"It's more like mixed martial arts."

"Enjoy your evening," the hostess said as she opened the door to Basil Hyde's luxury suite. Inside was an opulent room with overstuffed leather couches, a stone hearth with a blazing fire, a crystal chandelier, and a buffet of savory food where chefs in white hats carved a variety of meats for the guests.

"You're staring again," Oz said as he leaned over to whisper in Colt's ear.

Colt wasn't trying to be rude, but he was having a hard time trusting his eyes. The room was filled with characters straight out of his father's Phantom Flyer comic books. Not five feet away were two Undarians, humanoids who came from a planet that was virtually underwater.

They were tall, with scales of blue and green. Tentacles swept back over their heads like dreadlocks, tied off by leather straps. Goggles covered their large eyes, and a breathing apparatus filled with water was wrapped around their necks and mouths. It was connected to a pair of tanks that hung from their backs like scuba gear.

There were others as well. The Fimorians had smooth gray skin with long necks, and the tiny Ulos looked like children despite the fact that an Ulo didn't reach adulthood until its seventieth birthday. Colt even saw a Nogalar, who looked a bit like a walking rhino, though much more colorful. It wore fanciful robes and its fingers were covered in rings with bright jewels.

"There you are," said a man with a British accent. He wore a charcoal suit with a white shirt and a dark tie. His hair was kept short, he hadn't shaved in days, and his eyes were so blue that it looked like he was wearing colored contacts. "I was starting to think that your father had had second thoughts. It's good to see you, my boy."

"It's good to see you too," Oz said as they embraced.

"I think you've grown another foot since I saw you last," the man said as he broke away to look at Oz from an arm's length. "How long has it been?"

"Almost a year, I think," Oz said.

"How's the old man?"

Oz shrugged. "The same, I suppose."

"I figured as much. He needs to take a vacation."

"No kidding."

"So are you going to introduce me to your friends?"

"Absolutely," Oz said. "Basil Hyde, I'd like you to meet Danielle Salazar."

"A pleasure, young lady," Basil said, taking her hand to kiss it. Then he turned to Colt. "You must be Colonel McAlister's grandson."

"Yes, sir," Colt said. He shook Basil's hand.

"Sir? Clearly this young man has a lot to learn." Basil put his arm around Colt's shoulder as though they had known each other their entire lives. "This is my associate, Mercedes Castro."

Colt hadn't seen the slender woman who was standing behind Basil. She was short, with black hair that was pulled up in a twist.

Her crimson dress made her stand out from the other women in the room, who appeared to prefer black, and her diamond necklace glimmered in the light.

"It's nice to meet you," Colt said.

Mercedes nodded her head slightly before turning her attention to Basil. "Lord Percival has asked to speak with you," she said.

"Ah, yes." Basil patted Colt on the back. "You missed a few of the preliminary fights, but there are plenty more to come. And please, help yourselves to as much food as you can eat." With that he excused himself to walk over and speak to an older man with a sharp nose and sagging eyes.

"Let's do this," Oz said. "I'm starving."

"What about Trident?" Danielle asked.

"We'll get to that, but we have to play the game a bit. When Basil's ready, he'll talk," Oz said. "Right now there're too many people around, but he's going to be watching you. Don't do anything stupid."

"Like what?"

"I don't know, but whatever it is, don't do it." Oz led them to a buffet laden with roast beef, ham, garlic mashed potatoes, and shrimp skewers. There were plenty of surprises as well.

"What's this?" Colt asked as he reached for a fruit that looked a bit like a kiwi, though it was pink and nearly twice as big.

"I forget the name, but it's from an island on Undar," Oz said.

"That's an alcadia fruit," one of the chefs said.

"That's right," Oz said. "There's a grove of them just outside the coliseum."

Colt cringed after Oz scooped what looked like a pile of maggots wriggling around in some kind of gravy.

"Don't knock it until you've tried it," Oz said. "These slugs are amazing. They kind of taste like escargot, but they aren't as chewy."

"I'll take your word for it," Colt said. He continued down the line, watching Oz fill not one but two plates with things that made the slugs look tame. Colt and Danielle stuck to food they were familiar with.

"It looks like they're getting up," Oz said, nodding to a table next to a wall of glass.

As they sat down, Colt could see that they were in some kind of indoor stadium. Below the ring of skyboxes were thousands of seats filled with excited fans, few of which were human. There were clusters of spotlights shining down on the ring, where an announcer was stepping up to a microphone that hung down from above. Video cameras were stationed around the ring, and an army of photographers flashed their cameras.

"What is this place?" Colt asked.

"Hyde Field House," Oz said, "though most of us just call it the Pit."

"As in pit fighting?" Danielle asked.

"Don't get too worked up," Oz said before he stuffed some kind of squid with eight eyeballs into his mouth. "There aren't any dogs, if that's what you're worried about. These are all professional fighters, and it's perfectly legal."

"Then it's more like professional wrestling?"

Oz slurped down the last of a tentacle before smiling. "This is the real deal," he said. "I'm talking the best fighters in the twelve worlds. Can you imagine how amazing it would feel to walk into that ring with everyone chanting your name?"

:: CHAPTER 36 ::

May I offer you a program or some binoculars?"

Colt turned to find a robotic servant standing near their table holding a silver tray. Though it was a machine, there was no denying it had been made to look and sound like a female.

"Thanks," Oz said, reaching for a program. He grabbed one for Colt and another for Danielle. "Do you want the binoculars?"

Danielle looked down at the ring below. The pitch of the stadium was steep, which made it feel like the skybox was almost hanging over the stadium. They had an amazing view. "I can see well enough," she said.

"What about you?" Oz asked, turning to Colt.

"How much are they?"

"Everything here is on the house," Oz said. He took a pair of the binoculars from the tray and handed them to Colt.

"And you, sir?" the robot asked.

"I'm good." He pointed to a series of monitors that were hanging from the ceiling and on the walls. "We get a closed circuit broadcast, which is great for the replays, but I like to watch it live."

The lights in the stadium dimmed before the spotlights flared bright. Loud music started pumping through the speakers. The announcer introduced the first fighter as it came out of the tunnel. The creature looked something like a praying mantis, though its armored hide was bright orange instead of green.

"That's Cho'rex," Oz said. "He's won his last eight fights, six of them by knockout."

Colt had opened his program, where he found bios on all the fighters. "He's almost nine feet tall."

"That's pretty average for a Krilian," Oz said. "Wait until you see who he's fighting . . . it's one of the instructors at the CHAOS academy."

Once Cho'rex was in the ring, the announcer introduced a fighter by the name of Lohr. When he did, the crowd erupted, and so did Oz.

Lohr was a Tharik, though on Earth he would have been called Bigfoot. The difference, at least with Lohr, was that he had robotic components fused to his body. His left arm had been replaced with a mechanical prosthetic, and there was a second head with glowing eyes bolted just to the left of the head he'd been born with.

"That thing is an instructor? What does he teach?"

"Combat."

"I guess that makes sense," Colt said. "What happened to him?"

"His arm got blown off by a Panzer."

"Why the second head?"

"The first one was so ugly, I guess he wanted to try again."

Colt looked sideways at Oz.

"What? That's a great joke," Oz said. "To tell you the truth, I'm not sure why the surgeon decided to give him another head. All

I can tell you is that Cho'rex is about to have his winning streak snapped."

The referee went over the rules as the fighters met in the middle of the ring. From the moment the bell sounded, Cho'rex tried to use a series of jabs, taking advantage of his height to keep Lohr at bay. Lohr was patient as he studied his opponent.

The crowd, however, was growing restless. It wasn't long before they started to boo.

Cho'rex made a clicking sound with his mandibles before he swung with a wild right hook. Lohr ducked under the haymaker and took Cho'rex to the ground. From there, it was only a matter of time. Lohr used his superior strength to keep Cho'rex pinned as he pummeled the Krilian. The referee stopped the fight with more than a minute remaining in the first round.

"What did I tell you?" Oz said.

"You actually like this?" Danielle asked.

"Are you kidding?" Oz said. "It's incredible!"

"It's barbaric."

"Look at the video games you play," Oz said. "They're way more violent than this."

"That's different."

"Why?"

"Because nobody gets hurt in a video game."

"Remember that we're guests, so try not to be too critical, okay?" Oz slid his chair away from the table. "I'll be back in a minute. I need to get some more food."

"What's wrong?" Colt asked once Oz was out of earshot.

"Nothing," Danielle said.

"Come on, I know you better than that. We used to watch wrestling all the time, and I never heard you complain."

"I don't know," Danielle said. She leaned forward to rest her head in her hand. "I guess I just want all of this to end before . . . well, before something really bad happens. That's all."

The lights dimmed once again as the ring was lowered through a trap door in the floor. Then, though Colt had no idea how they did it, a glass tube rose up, replacing the ring. It was at least thirty feet tall and filled with bubbling water that was lighted from below.

"Did I miss anything?" Oz asked as he sat back down with two more plates piled high with food.

"It's just starting," Colt said.

"I've seen underwater fights on television, but never live," Oz said. "You're going to love this."

Colt lifted his binoculars to see that three people were already in the tank. The first was an Undarian, tall and slender with webbed hands and feet. The tendrils on its head waved in the water like snakes on a Gorgon's scalp.

There was a referee wearing scuba gear, as well as a creature that looked like someone had spliced a man and an octopus together. It had six arms that looked like tentacles, with suction cups that lined the underside of each appendage. Its skin was olive green, its head was bald, and its mouth was lined with rows of jagged teeth like a shark's. Colt's eyes shot wide. Was that the creature that had attacked him on his surfboard?

"What's wrong?" Danielle asked.

"Oh . . . um, nothing," he said.

"Undarians and Roraks don't like each other too much," Oz said. "This could get bloody."

The referee must have had a microphone inside of his regulator, because everyone in the arena could hear him giving the instructions. Then, after the bell sounded, the fighters started circling each other. The crowd shouted, encouraging them to engage. They didn't have to wait long.

The Rorak was first. He shot two of his tentacle arms at the Undarian, who slipped out of the way. Then he sent a third to latch around the Undarian's neck. A fourth tentacle shot around one of the Undarian's arms but the Undarian used the tentacles to reel the Rorak in. Then he kicked out, catching the Rorak in the stomach before hitting him in the side of the head with a second kick.

The Rorak was dazed. His tentacles went limp, and then the Undarian went on the offensive. He attempted a number of submission holds, trying to slip around the Rorak's back to choke him out, but the Rorak was too strong and broke free.

"What did I tell you?" Oz said after the first round ended.

"It's amazing."

"Who do you think won that round?"

"I don't know," Colt said. Then he noticed that two Undarian diplomats were seated at the table next to them. "I'd probably give it to the Undarian."

"Me too."

The fight went back and forth for another four rounds, leaving the judges to declare the winner. It was a split decision, but after the results were announced, the referee raised the Rorak's hand in victory as the Undarian bowed his head in shame.

The Undarian diplomats were outraged. One slammed his drink onto the table before all three of them stormed out of the skybox.

"Don't worry," Oz said. "They probably had money riding on the outcome."

CHAPTER 37

From the corner of his eye Colt glimpsed someone walking toward them. He turned to see Mercedes Castro.

"Mr. Hyde will see you now," she said.

They followed Mercedes down a spiral staircase that had been roped off. It led down to a private suite where Basil stood alone, watching out the glass wall as the tank was lowered back into the ground.

"Amazing, isn't it?" he asked without looking at anyone in particular. "I mean, who would have thought that a boy like me, born to a drunken father who left when I was in infant, and a mother who worked three jobs, would have become anything more than a common criminal? Yet here we are."

"Thanks for inviting us," Oz said. "We really appreciate it."

Basil turned from the window holding a tumbler with a honey-colored liquid chilling on ice. Then he looked at Colt. "So tell me," Basil said. "What is it you want to know?"

Colt hesitated. He looked at Oz and then Danielle.

"That's why you came, no?" Basil asked. "You're looking for information."

Colt swallowed. "Someone told us that my parents were murdered by someone working for Trident Industries."

"Yes, I was sorry to hear that. Do you know why?"

"My mom was writing an article about a mind-control program they're running at Trident Biotech, so they killed her before it went to press."

"That wouldn't surprise me," Basil said with a nod. "Tell me what you know about Trident Industries."

"I'm not sure," Colt said. He hadn't expected a pop quiz. "I guess they're one of the largest companies in the world, and they operate out of four main divisions: Trident Defense, Trident Technology, Trident Capital, and Trident Healthcare Systems."

"What else?"

"They partnered with the Nazis during World War II," Danielle said.

"Now we're getting somewhere," Basil said, "though I'm afraid it was more than a partnership. The men that ran Trident weren't just Nazi sympathizers. They breathed life into the Nazi movement."

"How?"

"What if I told you that the board of directors at Trident Industries weren't human? Would that surprise you?"

"Not anymore."

The crowd outside grew raucous as the announcer started to introduce the final combatants of the night. Colt risked a glance to see an enormous creature with red skin covered in tattoos step into the ring. He had a massive set of horns that shot forward before curling back and an enormous gold belt around his waist proclaiming that he was the heavyweight champion of the twelve worlds.

"Are you a fan of Zandarr?" Basil asked.

"Oh, sorry," Colt said. He looked at Basil for a moment, but his eyes kept falling back to the spectacle in the ring. "He's a beast. Has anybody ever beat him?"

"Believe it or not, Zandarr lost his first match," Basil said, "but he's won ninety-seven in a row since then."

"Wait, are those logos tattooed on his chest?" Colt asked.

"Along with his arms, neck, back, and just about everywhere else," Oz said. "The guy is a walking billboard."

"Zandarr is not only the best fighter that we've ever had," Basil said. "He's a savvy businessman. In fact, last year he purchased a minority stake in the IGFL."

"What's that?" Danielle asked.

"The Intergalactic Fighting League," Oz and Colt said at the same time.

As Zandarr's opponent stepped into the ring, there was more applause, but it was mixed with a smattering of boos. The behemoth had a large belly, but his massive chest and shoulders were taut over his cablelike muscles. Mechanical claws with four pinchers had replaced his hands all the way up to his forearms. There were strange iron shields fused to each jaw, along with what looked like exhaust pipes that led from the skin in his neck to his back.

"This should be a good match," Basil said as he joined Oz at the window. "Borog hasn't lost yet, and he has a mean streak to boot. Do you see those patterns on his chest and shoulders?"

Oz nodded.

"Those are tribal markings," Basil said. "They aren't tattooed or branded either. Those were carved into his skin with a knife."

The music stopped playing as the referee went over the rules in the center of the ring. The fighters stared at one another. Zandarr was a bit taller, but not by much. Neither looked intimidated by the other as the house lights went up.

The bell sounded, and the fight was underway. Borog didn't waste time. He lashed out at the champion with one of his clawed hands. Zandarr's head snapped to the right before he staggered back. The crowd cheered and Zandarr smiled as blood poured from the fresh cut on his cheek. He tilted his head to the left and then the right, popping his neck as he stretched. Then he started bouncing up and down.

Borog struck again, but this time Zandarr stepped to the side. He grabbed Borog's outstretched arm before bringing his knee to Borog's elbow. The sound of bone snapping echoed through the arena. The crowd gasped collectively, but Borog didn't stop despite the injury. He wheeled around and struck Zandarr with a back fist, gashing the red behemoth again. Everyone in the arena cheered in appreciation as Zandarr fell into the ropes.

Borog turned to the crowd with a fist raised triumphantly while his broken arm hung uselessly to the side. There were no more jeers. Thousands were chanting his name in unison, which only seemed to infuriate Zandarr. He regained his footing and charged, wrapping his massive arms around Borog's wide midsection before tackling the heavier fighter. The momentum sent them both flying into the ropes, and when they finally untangled, Zandarr had Borog in a choke hold.

Colt was distracted by the fervor, but if Basil noticed he was kind enough not to mention it. "Tell me something," he said to Colt, who tried to focus his attention on the debonair man. "What are you after? Revenge? Justice?"

"I want whoever killed my parents to pay for what they did,"

Colt said. Then he paused, searching for the right words. "And I don't want anyone else to have to go through this."

"It won't be easy," Basil said. "In fact, it may be impossible."

"That doesn't matter. We have to try."

"I told you he was determined," Oz said, though his eyes never left the ring.

"You're familiar with the twelve gateways?" Basil asked.

"I think so," Colt said.

"Around the turn of the century, a team of archaeologists found what they thought were the remains of a lost civilization. There were pictographs of strange creatures that looked like walking lizards, and later they found skeletons that matched. Each had six arms and long skulls almost like an American football."

"The Thule?"

"Very good," Basil said. "As archaeologists are wont to do, they kept digging. Eventually they found a cave that took them to a strange jungle where prehistoric animals roamed."

"Like that book, *Lost World*?"

"Something like that, yes," Basil said. "Now these gentlemen in Greece believed that they had found their own lost world. In a manner of speaking, I suppose they did, but it was much more. What they had stumbled upon was a gateway to another planet . . . one so far away that we could never reach it by spacecraft."

"Why aren't there any books about it?" Danielle asked.

"That's a fair question," Basil said as the crowd cheered. Zandarr had thrown Borog over the top rope, and he was following him to the floor. "A team of seven men crossed over, but only one returned, and he didn't live long to tell his tale. He had a camera filled with photographs of the bizarre land, yet even after they were printed, no one believed the images were real. After all, there were no dinosaurs or lizard men among the living. Such an idea was preposterous."

"Wait, I've seen those photos online," Colt said. "Those are real?"

"I believe so, yes," Basil said. "You see, not long after that, people started seeing what they thought were aliens skulking about places like Athens, London, Tokyo, and New York City. There were even reports that the Americans had caught one of the strange lizard men, and that it could morph into virtually any human shape at will."

"Look at this!" Oz said as he started jumping up and down in excitement.

Zandarr rushed across the ring. His head was lowered and his horns shining under the lights as he crashed into Borog. The air rushed out of Borog's lungs as the fat that padded his stomach rolled in waves under the impact. He left his feet, flying backward into ropes that somehow held, acting as a slingshot before they hurtled Borog back toward Zandarr.

Everyone in the arena was cheering as Zandarr sidestepped. Then he reached out with his arm, wrapping it around Borog's thick neck. Within seconds, Borog was choked out. Zandarr threw his head back and roared. His eyes were crazed as he let Borog's unconscious body fall to the mat.

:: CHAPTER 38 ::

"That was amazing!" Oz shouted, his exuberance matching the crowd as everyone in the arena continued to cheer.

Basil was smiling as he joined Oz at the window, but Colt didn't get up from his seat at the table. "I think we gave them their money's worth tonight," Basil said.

Colt turned back to look at Mercedes, who was standing next to the spiral staircase, her eyes locked on his. She was smaller than Danielle, but there was something about the way she carried herself that made Colt wonder how well she'd fare in the arena—and he had a feeling she could hold her own and then some.

When he turned back around, Basil offered him a drink.

"Come, toast with me to a fabulous evening," Basil said, but Colt simply looked at the glass that Basil was holding. Basil's eyes narrowed, though only for a moment. Then his smile returned. "There's no alcohol, I assure you."

Behind Basil, Oz was glaring at Colt. Then his eyes opened wide and his head bent forward as though he was directing Colt to take the glass.

"There we are," Basil said, raising his own glass as Colt

followed. Oz and Danielle did the same. "To a glorious evening of fighting, food, and friends, both new," he said, motioning to Colt, "and old," he added, nodding toward Oz. "May there be many more in our future."

"I'll drink to that," Oz said, tilting his glass back. He finished the contents in three large gulps and then licked his lips.

A robotic servant came by to remove the empty glasses, though Colt barely sipped his drink. He was trying to look as enthusiastic as Oz, but Colt knew he wasn't doing a good job. He was too distracted by thoughts of his parents, Trident Industries, and the Thule.

Basil placed his empty glass on the robot's tray as he regarded Colt. "I'm being rude," he said, his voice pleasant before he walked back over to take a seat across from Colt. "We were talking about the Thule, were we not?"

Colt nodded. "It's just like the comic book, right? I mean, the planet where the Thule lived was dying, so when those archaeologists reopened the gateway, the Thule were going to cross over to destroy us. That way they could take Earth as their home."

"That was their plan," Basil said. "Thanks to Nikola Tesla and some other scientists, we found a way to close the gateway, but there was no telling how many of the Thule had already crossed over. We think most settled in Germany, where they were plotting to open another door back to their world."

"There're other doorways, though, right?" Colt asked.

"Indeed," Basil said. "Most have been closed, but some remain intact. CHAOS agents keep them under lock and key."

"Not all of them," Oz said.

"I suppose you're right," Basil said. "You see, there are soft spots all over the world—places where the fabric that separates our planet from others has started to weaken. CHAOS has teams whose sole purpose is to discover those weak points and stitch them back together, but they can't possibly find them all. So things slip through from time to time."

"Like Yetis and Bigfoot?" Colt asked.

"Perhaps," Basil said. "Which brings me back to our friends at Trident Industries. You see, it's my belief that their board of directors is composed of members of the Thule who failed to destroy us during World War II. Now, instead of open warfare, they have slowly built their political capital and financial strength to the point where they are one of the most powerful entities in the world. It was a brilliant strategy, really."

"What do they want?" Colt asked.

"To open a floodgate between our world and theirs so their armies can cross over to eradicate mankind. They want our planet."

"How are they going to get through if we shut down the gateway to Gathmara?" Colt asked.

"Trident didn't choose the locations of their corporate campuses based on the price of land or the quality of the community. They chose them because they've found weak spots that they believe will open up to their world."

"Why hasn't CHAOS shut them down?" Colt asked.

"It's not that simple," Oz said.

"How true," Basil said. "The Trident board of directors is cunning. They've allied themselves with powerful political figures from around the world, including the president of the United States. They're well protected."

"Isn't there enough evidence so it wouldn't matter?"

"I believe there is some, but not enough," Basil said. "You

have to remember that the politics in Washington aren't always based on evidence, much less what's good for the people of your fine country. No, I'm afraid that at the moment, Trident is well-fortified against attack."

"What if we could prove the biochips they produce allow them to control people like puppets?" Danielle asked. "If word of that got out, their stock value would take a big hit. I mean, their power is based on financial strength, right?"

"You're a cunning one, aren't you?" Basil said. "I like that."

"Is she right?" Colt asked.

"Perhaps."

"So can you help us?"

"There may be something I can do—after all, Trident may be watching us, but I have an eye on them as well. Still, I need to consider the cost," Basil said. "Going up against the most powerful corporation in the world is never good for business. Then again, if the Thule start wiping out entire planets, I won't have any customers left, will I?"

<hr/>

After all the excitement with Basil Hyde and the Intergalactic Fighting League, Colt nearly forgot about Lily's party the next day. Oz had given him a username and password to watch old matches online . . . and that's what he was doing when Danielle called.

"We're running behind, but we should be there in about an hour," she said. "I need to stop by the mall and get a new pair of shoes first."

Colt had that sick feeling that always showed up when he'd forgotten something important.

"Don't tell me you forgot," Danielle said after a long silence.

"I didn't forget," Colt said. "I just got sidetracked."

"Hurry up, okay?"

After a quick shower, Colt tried on five different shirts before he settled on the first one that he had picked. His hair was still damp when Oz and Danielle showed up. "I'll see you later, Grandpa," he said before dashing out the front door.

Danielle was sitting in the front seat wearing a black dress and matching sweater. Her hair hung around her face, and she was wearing more makeup than usual. Oz was dressed up as well—at least for Oz. He wore a black button-up shirt, jeans, and a pair of shiny square-toed shoes.

"Don't you look nice," Danielle said.

"Is it too much?" Colt asked. "My grandpa told me to put the jacket on."

"It's perfect," Danielle said.

To offset the fact that he was wearing a sport coat, Colt decided not to tuck in his shirt. He was also wearing his favorite pair of blue jeans. They were starting to fray around the cuff, but he didn't want to look like he was trying too hard to impress anyone.

"Flip-flops and a sport coat?" Oz asked when he saw Colt's shoes.

"Leave him alone," Danielle said. "He looks fine."

"I'm going to buy you some cowboy boots for your birthday," Oz said.

"Wait, were we supposed to bring a gift?" Colt asked as he slid into the backseat next to two brightly wrapped packages.

"Are you serious?" Danielle asked.

"Yeah."

"It's Lily's adoption day party."

"Lily was adopted?"

"You might want to do a little more research before you decide to stalk someone, McAlister," Oz said.

Colt asked Oz to pull into a drugstore on the way. If nothing else, he wanted to at least get her a card. Danielle suggested flowers, but that wasn't going to happen—especially since Graham was going to be there.

"It took you long enough," Oz said after Colt returned with a bag in his hand. "How long does it take to get a card?"

"About thirty seconds," Colt said. "Finding a gift was the hard part."

"What did you get her, nail polish remover?" Danielle asked.

"How did you know?"

:: CHAPTER 39 ::

Lily lived in a gated community on a golf course. The one-story house was elegant, but not ostentatious, with a circular front drive that ran under a portico. The palm trees in the front yard were wrapped in white lights, and the stucco exterior was accented with stonework.

"Nice place," Oz said as he parked in the street in front of the house. "What does her dad do?"

"He's an emergency physician," Danielle said, "but I think he owns a chain of urgent care facilities."

"Not bad."

Everyone got out of the Jeep except for Colt, who was staring at the dashboard.

"Are you coming, or what?" Oz asked.

"I don't know."

"What's wrong with you?" Danielle said.

"You're sure this is the right house?"

"Let's see. There's a string of pink and white balloons tied to the lights. Yeah, I think this is it." The door was open, so Danielle walked inside, where she placed her gift on the front table with the others. Oz followed, but Colt was still having second thoughts. Most of the presents looked like they'd been wrapped professionally at a department store, and his pathetic gift bag definitely stood out.

He was about to ask Oz for the keys so he could hide it in the Jeep when Lily walked into the foyer. "Hi, guys," she said cheerfully. "I'm so glad you could make it."

Colt had to fight against his instincts to keep from staring. She was wearing a sleeveless dress with shimmering sequins that spilled down the front like falling stars. Her legs were toned like a dancer's, but thin, and she wore elegant heels that sparkled with rhinestones.

"You look amazing," Danielle said.

"So do you."

"Hey, what about me?" Oz asked, pretending to be hurt.

"You look as handsome as ever," Lily said. She turned back to Colt, who was trying to hide the gift behind his back. "What do you have there?"

"It's nothing."

"Can I open it?" Lily didn't wait for Colt's response before she grabbed the bag out of his hands. First she pulled out the square envelope and tore it open. There was a picture of Elvis Presley on the front of the card, and the caption read: *It's your birthday, and you can do anything . . .*

She opened it, and the foyer echoed with the sound of Elvis singing about his blue suede shoes. "I love singing cards," she said with a wide smile. "Let's see what else I got." She reached inside the bag and pulled out a box of permanent markers.

Colt felt his face flush. "Look, I have to be honest with you . . . I just found out that this was your adoption party, so I didn't have a chance to buy you a real gift."

"What are you talking about?" Lily said. "I've always wanted my very own box of permanent markers."

"I figured you could use them to sign autographs for all your fans."

"You're too sweet," Lily said.

Colt exhaled. It didn't matter if she was just trying to make him feel better. It worked.

"I hope you guys are hungry," Lily said as she led everyone to the kitchen. "There's more food than we know what to do with, so everyone needs to have seconds and probably thirds."

If anything, Lily had understated how much food there was. A local Italian restaurant had catered the party with heaping trays of fettuccini alfredo, mushroom ravioli, veal Parmesan, and angel-hair pasta with shrimp and scallops. And for dessert, there was tiramisu.

Colt was in awe of Oz's capacity to eat. He finished off no less than three full plates and was ready to go back for more. For as small as she was, Danielle ate a full plate and even went back for seconds of the fettucini.

The guests were mostly family, with a few neighbors and some of Lily's friends from school. Lily was busy walking from group to group ensuring that everyone was having a good time. With Oz and Danielle focused on each other, Colt was left to fend for himself. He was about to get something to drink when he felt someone's hand on his shoulder.

Colt spun around, ready to defend himself against one of the Cursed. Instead, he found Lily looking at him with a raised eyebrow.

"Did I scare you?" she asked.

"Sorry, I thought you were Oz," Colt said as his mind raced for a believable excuse. "He likes to sneak up on me and try out new wrestling moves."

"You know, I could see him becoming a professional wrestler."

"He was born for it."

"Do you have a minute? I have something I want to show you."

"Yeah, sure."

Lily led Colt down a hallway off of the family room. "When the social worker brought me here for the first time, I felt like a princess in a fairy tale. I stayed up all night, hiding under my covers and praying that nobody would take me away."

When she turned on the light to her bedroom, Colt realized why. There was a king-size canopy bed draped in white linen, with a thick down comforter. The wood floor had a rich cherry finish, accented by an area rug that reminded Colt of dandelion fluff. She even had her own bathroom, not to mention a walk-in closet that looked bigger than Colt's entire bedroom.

Colt watched as she walked over to a dresser that was covered in framed pictures. "I lived in five foster homes before I turned six," she said. "Every time the phone rang or a door opened, I thought it was my parents coming to rescue me."

"From what?" Colt asked, caught in her sorrow.

Lily looked at him, her sweet face fraught with sadness. "Don't get me wrong. Most of the foster families that I stayed with were wonderful, but . . ."

Colt resisted the urge to reach out and hold her.

"Let's just say that some days were tougher than others," Lily finally said, leaving Colt to paint the details between her words.

Lily picked up one of the pictures and handed it to Colt. "These are my birth parents."

He took the frame, holding it gently in his hands. Lily wasn't much more than a year old as she sat in her mother's lap, clapping her hands while her father strummed a guitar.

"You look just like your mom."

"Her name was Emma, and my dad's name was Waylon," Lily said, forcing a smile. "It's weird, but this picture is the only memory I have of them."

"What happened?"

"He was a disc jockey at a country station, and he'd been laid off. Jobs were hard to come by and times were getting tight, but something finally opened up in Albuquerque." Lily paused while she looked at the picture. "I stayed at my grandma's house so my mom could drive out with him for the interview, but their truck hit a patch of ice. My dad lost control. They ran into a semi and were killed."

"I'm so sorry," Colt said.

Lily stopped and looked into Colt's eyes. Then she stretched on her tiptoes and kissed him on the cheek. Her lips were warm, and Colt felt intoxicated.

"Thank you," she said.

"For what?"

"You're the first person that I've been able to share that with."

"Really? Why?"

"Because you're the only person I've known who could understand."

||||||||||||||||||||||||||||||||||

Colt's head was still swimming with a sense of euphoria when he watched Lily blow out her candles later that night. He could still feel her lips on his cheek and he didn't want the sensation to fade. Not ever.

That kiss wasn't the only thing on his mind, though. While everyone ate cake and ice cream, he decided to slip into the backyard. Talking to Lily had brought back a flood of emotions about his parents. It was odd, but whenever he wasn't depressed he felt guilty. It was as though any joy he felt was a slap in the face to the memory of his parents. He wanted to go back inside and ask Lily if time would make it any easier, but he didn't know if he could handle the answer.

"There you are," he heard Danielle say as the sliding glass door opened behind him. "What are you doing out here?"

Colt sighed. "I don't know. I just needed some fresh air."

"Do you remember how everyone would be inside watching a movie or playing games, and you'd be outside in the hammock looking at the stars?"

"I was a weird kid."

"You weren't weird, just different. It's part of your charm."

"I really wish I were up there right now," Colt said, gazing at the stars. "When I was flying yesterday, it felt like all the problems in the world just melted away."

"They'll be waiting for you when you come back down."

Colt sighed. "Tell me about it."

It was starting to get cooler at night, so Colt took off his jacket and wrapped it around Danielle's shoulders. They sat together, listening to the sound of the automatic sprinklers in the fairway behind the Westcotts' yard.

"So what were you and Lily doing?" she asked.

"What do you mean?"

"Come on, Colt. Everyone saw you disappear together."

"When you say everyone, how many people are we talking about?"

"Enough."

"Graham?"

"I'm sure he'll hear about it."

"Nothing happened."

"Okay, but . . ."

"But what?"

"What do you expect people to think when you disappear into her bedroom?"

"It's not like that," Colt said. "She was . . . look, it doesn't matter. People can say whatever they want."

"You don't really believe that, do you?" Danielle asked. "Colt, you know I love you like a brother, but even if Lily was the one who asked you to go with her . . . and even if nothing happened . . . people are going to assume the worst. That's just the way we're wired. So if you really care about her like I think you do, you need to protect her."

"I guess you're right."

"If it's any consolation, Lily likes you too."

"Did she say something?"

"She didn't have to. You can see it in her eyes. But you have to give her time."

"Do I have a choice?" Colt said. He decided to change the subject. "By the way, what's up with you and Oz?"

Danielle frowned. "What do you mean?"

"There's nothing to be ashamed about," Colt said, lowering his head to hide the smile. "I mean, think of all the girls at school who would do just about anything to be in your shoes right now."

"I think you've lost your mind."

"I see the way you two look at each other."

"If you say another word . . ."

"Don't worry, your secret is safe with me."

:: CHAPTER 40 ::

Danielle refused to talk to Colt for the rest of the party, and from what Colt could see she'd decided to avoid Oz as well. Colt was convinced that her dramatic reaction proved his point. Oz, on the other hand, didn't even seem to realize that he was getting the cold shoulder. He was locked in an unusually competitive game of charades with a group that included Lily's grandparents, her little brother, and a girl named Bailey Anne who Colt recognized from his Spanish class.

At the same time, Colt did his best to make sure that he was never in the same room with Graham. It wasn't that he was scared of the all-state football star. Graham might have been nearly as big as Oz, but compared to shape-shifting aliens and mind-controlled assassins, he wasn't much of a threat.

Colt just didn't want to face the guilt. Oz had told him—on multiple occasions no less—that all was fair in love and war. He also pointed out that Lily wasn't wearing a ring on her finger, and as far as Oz was concerned that meant she was fair game. While Oz may have been technically right, Colt didn't want to reduce Lily to some kind of a prize that went to the winner.

The party started winding down around ten. Lily's mom did her best to send food home with everyone. Some politely declined, while others took paper plates covered in tinfoil. Oz left with two large pans under his arms. He would have taken more if Danielle hadn't stopped him.

"You're being a pig," she said under her breath.

Lily stood in the entryway as everyone left, but when Colt saw Graham hovering close by, he tried to slip out the front door unnoticed.

"Where are you going?" he heard Lily call out.

Colt closed his eyes and sighed before turning around with a fake smile. "Nowhere."

"You know, it's rude not to say good-bye."

"Sorry," Colt said. "I get kind of emotional whenever I say good-bye, and I didn't want to make a scene."

Lily raised an eyebrow.

"Okay, I'm still embarrassed about that stupid present."

"Don't be," Lily said. "I loved it."

"Anyway, I better get going. Oz and Danielle are waiting."

Lily raised her arms out as though she was expecting a hug. Colt looked around to make sure Graham wasn't watching. Then he hurried over and wrapped Lily in an uncomfortable embrace. His forehead knocked into hers, and then his lips grazed her cheek before narrowly missing her mouth.

"Are you okay?" she asked after he pulled away.

Colt could see a red spot on her forehead. "Sure. How about you?"

"I'm fine," Lily said.

They both started laughing.

"Bye," Colt said, his face still flushed as he turned to run down the front steps and across the yard. Oz had the Jeep running and the radio blaring. Danielle was in the backseat with her arms crossed. She looked angry, but Oz was too busy singing along to the music to notice as he pounded on the steering wheel like it was a snare drum.

"Please tell me you weren't doing damage in the bathroom," he said as Colt slid into the passenger's seat.

"What?"

"Then what took you so long?"

"I was just saying good-bye to a few people, that's all."

"Oh really?" Danielle said. "You spent most of the night by yourself in the backyard, so who exactly were you saying good-bye to?"

"Do you even have to ask?" Oz said.

"Is that all you guys think about?" Danielle asked as Oz put the Jeep in gear.

"What?"

"Girls?"

Oz shrugged. "Pretty much."

Colt laughed. "He's just messing with you."

"Wait, you thought I was serious?" Oz asked. "Because we talk about all kinds of stuff, like . . . I don't know. What do we talk about, McAlister?"

"Yesterday you showed me a sleeper hold."

"See?"

"We also talk about stuff like movies and football," Colt said. "Oh yeah, and this afternoon Oz told me about all the poetry he writes."

"Yeah . . . wait, what did you say?" Oz looked like he was on the verge of a panic attack.

"Don't you remember showing me your diary?" Colt asked, as he snuck a peak at Danielle.

She turned away, trying to shield the fact that she was biting her top lip to keep from laughing.

"I swear that isn't true. I've never written a poem in my life," Oz said. Then he looked at Colt and lowered his voice. "What are you doing?"

At that point Danielle was laughing openly. "Don't worry," she said. "I believe you."

Oz exhaled. Then he eased onto the freeway to head back to the McAlisters' house and it wasn't long before he was singing along to the music again.

"Every time I see a full moon, it reminds me of the fight between the Phantom Flyer and Hitler's Dog Soldiers," Colt said. "Can you imagine sitting in a foxhole, knowing that the Germans were coming at you with everything they had?"

"Was that the one with the Nazi K-9 units?" Oz asked.

"Yeah, but instead of dogs, they had wolf men on the end of their leashes."

"Can we talk about something else?" Danielle asked.

"You're not scared, are you?" Oz said.

"I just don't want to talk about wolf men, that's all."

"All right," Oz said. "What should we talk about? Butterflies? Fairies? Unicorns?"

"I think we should hack into Trident Biotech's network," Danielle said.

Oz raised his eyebrows. "I knew there was a reason I liked hanging out with you."

"What about Basil?" Colt asked. "Shouldn't we wait to see what he says?"

"We don't even know if he's going to help us," Danielle said, "and every day that we wait, we risk getting attacked again. I'm sick of being scared."

Colt couldn't argue.

"I want to find out how those biochips work so we can shut them down," Danielle said. "I doubt they're going to hand over the schematics to us, so we're just going to have to take them."

"I don't know," Colt said. "That seems like a big risk."

"All we need to do is get hold of the credentials from a Trident employee who has access to the files," Danielle said. "Once I have that, I can upload a virus into their system that will allow me to make a new username and password."

"Won't a cyber attack raise a red flag?" Colt asked.

"We'll be able to log in any time we want, and they won't have a clue."

"So how do we get the credentials?" Oz asked.

"I'm still working on that part."

"I don't want anything to happen to you," Colt said. "And if Trident Industries thinks that you're snooping around—"

"Dang it," Oz said as he looked in the rearview mirror.

Colt turned and caught sight of the red and blue lights flashing behind them.

"How fast were you going?" Danielle asked.

"Too fast." Oz eased over to the shoulder and put his Jeep in park before reaching for his wallet. "Hey, McAlister, will you grab my registration out of the glove box?"

"You better turn your radio off," Danielle said. "You don't want the officer to think you're a punk."

Oz reached over to turn off the radio before placing both hands on the steering wheel. "My dad is going to kill me."

Moments later the patrol car pulled up behind them with a floodlight pointed at the Jeep. Colt watched the patrolman run Oz's license plate through the system before he approached the Jeep.

"Good evening," he said, shining a flashlight inside the cab. "Do you know why I pulled you over tonight?"

"Yes, sir," Oz said. "I was driving a little fast."

"I guess you could say that," the officer said. "I clocked you at twenty miles per hour over the speed limit. Where are you folks headed?"

"Home, sir," Oz said.

"I'll need your license and registration."

Oz handed them over, squinting in the beam of the flashlight.

"I'll be back in a minute."

Colt watched the patrolman walk back to the car, reading Oz's license with the aid of his flashlight. Then he paused before looking back at the Jeep. "This isn't good," Colt said.

"What's wrong?" Oz asked.

"Look."

The patrolman had sheathed his flashlight and was reaching for the gun in his holster. He drew it out slowly and approached the Jeep, his boots crunching in the gravel. The patrolman's eyes were glowing red.

:: CHAPTER 41 ::

McAlister, listen to me," said Oz. "No matter what happens, your job is to get Danielle out of here. Do you understand?"

"No way," Colt said. "We're not leaving you behind."

"I don't have time to argue. Just do it, okay?"

Oz flared his nostrils as the patrolman took his last few steps to the Jeep. As he raised the barrel of his gun, Oz kicked his door open. The force caught the patrolman on the arm, and the gun went flying. Oz jumped out of the car and launched at the man, tackling him into the gravel.

"Wait . . . where are you going?" Danielle asked as Colt fumbled with the handle, trying to get out.

He managed to open the door and ran over to look for the gun.

The patrolman wasn't a big man, and if his gray hair was any indication, he was only a few years away from retirement. Still, somehow he managed to push Oz away as though Oz were nothing more than a goose-down pillow.

Oz groaned as he hit the gravel, but he rolled to one knee before the patrolman could kick him in the head. He caught the cop's leg and twisted. The motion sent the man off balance, and he fell face-first to the ground as Oz brought his elbow down on the back of the patrolman's thigh. He followed with a strike to the kidney and then one to the back of the neck before climbing on top of the officer.

"I told you to get Danielle out of here," he said. His chest was heaving from the adrenaline as he reached for the cop's handcuffs. In one quick motion he locked the right wrist, then tightened the left so the patrolman's hands were caught behind his back.

Colt was standing over him wide-eyed with the officer's gun in his hands.

"You realize those patrol cars have cameras with live feeds, right?" Oz said as he rolled the man over. He was unconscious, and when Oz lifted his eyelids, the red glow was gone.

Colt hadn't thought about that. "Now what?"

"In the next few minutes this place is going to be crawling with news cameras and cops with itchy trigger fingers," Oz said. "They don't appreciate it when you attack a member of their fraternity."

"But . . . his eyes."

"Until we can prove that Trident Industries can turn anyone with a biochip into an assassin, it's just another conspiracy theory. Think about it," Oz said. "Last week you wouldn't have believed it either."

Colt lowered the gun and turned to Danielle, who was sitting in the backseat on the verge of hyperventilating.

Oz picked up the patrolman and slung him over his shoulder before walking to the cruiser. "Open the door, will you?"

Colt obliged, and Oz set the patrolman in the front seat. "Now let me see that gun."

Colt handed him the firearm, and Oz started wiping away the fingerprints with the tail of his shirt.

"Won't they be able to trace the fibers?"

"First of all, you watch too much television," Oz said without looking up. "And second, if you have a better idea, I'm all ears."

"I don't suppose that CHAOS has access to any time machines? I think we need a do-over."

"Why don't you go check on Danielle? I'll be there in a minute."

"So I guess that would be a no."

At first it was faint, but before long the sound of rotor blades roared overhead. Colt looked up to see an enormous silhouette in the sky. Floodlights shone down, lighting up the desert below. As the airship closed in, the wind picked up and clouds of dust blanketed the freeway. Colt had to shield his face to keep the sand from his mouth and eyes.

"What is that thing?" Colt said as his hair blew.

"The cavalry."

Colt watched as the largest helicopter that he'd ever seen landed in the desert not more than twenty yards away. It looked like an armored whale painted army green. Its tires were taller than Oz's Jeep, and it had a massive propeller jutting out on either side of the tail. The rounded nose was covered in a honeycomb of glass windows. There were rocket launchers mounted on top, and from below, a giant howitzer jutted forward.

"Let's go," Oz said as he slapped Colt on the back. He got in the front seat of his Jeep and started the engine, but Colt didn't move. "Come on, McAlister, those cops are going to be here any minute. Let's go."

Colt shook his head clear before he ran to the passenger seat. At the same time the belly of the airship opened to form a ramp.

Colt hopped into the Jeep, and Oz put it in gear before slamming his foot on the pedal. They shot off in a cloud of dust. Oz steered them between the copter's front tires, up the ramp, and then into a cargo bay that was as big as a gymnasium.

There was a wall of storage crates on the far end, as well as two armored trucks and six ultralights that looked similar to the model Colt had flown. CHAOS soldiers were everywhere, clad in high-tech body armor that matched the hue of the copter.

Helmets covered their faces, making them look like modern-day knights, but the design was sleek instead of bulky. The eyes were backlit by an ambient light. Each carried a rifle with a grenade launcher mounted beneath, and there were jet packs strapped to their backs. Grandpa McAlister was right—his jet pack was a relic.

The hydraulics hissed as the ramp closed behind them, and moments later the helicopter was lifting back into the sky.

"It's a pleasure to see you again, McAlister," Agent Richmond said as he approached Oz's Jeep. Agent D3X was close behind, his single eye flaring bright in the dim cargo bay. "I meant to tell your grandfather that the footage we captured from your memories was most helpful. That was definitely Van Cleve, not some imper-sonator. My goodness, but you had yourself a scare that night, didn't you, son?"

"Yes, sir."

"As for you, Romero," Agent Richmond said. "The trouble you get yourself into never ceases to amaze me."

"I guess I'm just lucky," Oz said.

"I'm not sure that's what I'd call it," Agent Richmond said. "But where are my manners?" He walked over to open the back door so Danielle could get out.

"Thank you."

"My pleasure, Miss . . ."

"Salazar."

"Ah, yes," Agent Richmond said as he closed the door behind her. "The young lady who nearly got herself run off the road the other day. I'm glad to finally make your acquaintance."

Danielle's eyes were locked on the robot.

"Oh, don't mind him," Agent Richmond said. "He's just a big old bucket of bolts . . . kind of like an overgrown toaster with feet, you might say. So long as you're one of the good guys, you have nothing to fear." He paused. "You are one of the good guys, aren't you, Miss Salazar?"

Her lips were moving, but no words came out of her mouth. She had to settle for nodding her head.

"That's wonderful," Agent Richmond said. "Then I'm sure there's a perfectly reasonable explanation why the three of you had a respected highway patrolman handcuffed with a gun pointed at his head."

Danielle looked first to Colt, then to Oz, but she didn't say anything.

"We didn't have a choice," Colt said. "He was going to shoot us."

"I see," Agent Richmond said, after nodding his head a few times. "Now why was he looking to shoot three handsome young teens like yourselves on a night like this?"

"Ask the people at Trident Biotech," Oz said. "They sent him."

"So you believe the patrolman, who has given nearly thirty years of service to the highway patrol, is an agent of Trident Industries?"

"No," Colt said. "At least not by choice. He's one of the Cursed."

"Those biochips are pesky little things, aren't they," Agent Richmond said in a voice that Colt thought was too cavalier. "Well, you three are lucky that we were assigned as part of the security detail tonight. Otherwise you might be in a mess of trouble right now."

"What do you mean?" Colt asked.

"He means that he's been following us around," Oz said.

"Director Romero asked us to keep an eye on you," Agent Richmond said. "I must say, that was some party at the Westcott residence. And who knew you had so much in common with that pretty young lady."

Colt narrowed his eyes. Apparently Trident wasn't the only one watching him.

"I'm just doing my job, son."

"What about the video camera in the patrol car?" Oz asked.

"Oh, we've already taken care of that."

"How?" Colt asked. "I mean, that was a live feed, right?"

"We scrambled the signal before they ever saw it," Agent Richmond said.

"And the patrolman?" Oz asked.

"He'll be fine," Agent Richmond said. "A bit sore, I'd say, but fine. He won't remember a thing, though. They never do. As for the evidence that you left behind, our cleanup crews will take care of it. However, I believe now would be a good time to talk about a curfew for the three of you."

:: CHAPTER 42 ::

To Colt's dismay, his grandfather was in agreement about a curfew, but it didn't end there. Starting Monday, he was going to be driving Colt to and from school every day.

"Can I still go to the comic book shop with Oz on Wednesdays?"

"We'll talk about it."

"What about Danielle's house?"

"Once the Salazars get their new security system installed, I suppose that would be all right."

"The movies?"

"Don't push it."

Colt let it drop. It wasn't like he had much of a personal life anyway. Lily's party was the first time that he'd been out since he moved to Arizona, and his only two friends were destined to become a couple. Since Lily wasn't going to break up with her boyfriend any time soon, that meant Colt would become the dreaded third wheel.

Sunday morning dawned bleak. Colt didn't want to get out of bed, but he promised his grandfather he would start going to church. The service was supposed to start in thirty minutes, and

Colt knew that as far as Grandpa McAlister was concerned, ten minutes early was still too late.

Instead of taking a shower, Colt wetted his hair in the bathroom sink, rolled on some deodorant, and washed his face. He could tell that his grandfather wasn't impressed with his blue jeans and T-shirt, but at least he'd gone with the track shoes instead of flip-flops.

"Are you ready to go?" Grandpa McAlister said, though he didn't wait for a response. He grabbed his powder blue sport coat from the back of the kitchen chair before hurrying to the garage.

As he passed by, Colt could smell the drugstore aftershave that his grandfather had worn for as long as he could remember. "You look nice, Gramps," Colt said.

"Maybe next week I'll let you borrow one of my ties."

They got to church with enough time for Colt to grab a bagel and orange juice from the café. Grandpa McAlister decided to head over to the sanctuary, where he sat toward the front. Pastor Shrader's sermon was about a man named Uriah whom King David had sent to war knowing that he would be killed, all so he could steal Uriah's wife. Colt couldn't help but wonder if he would send Graham off to war if it were in his power.

After the service, Colt was surprised to find Lily in the foyer with her parents and her little brother, Michael. If he hadn't known better, he would have thought the siblings were related by blood instead of adoption. Like Lily, Michael was thin with hair so blond it was almost white.

"I didn't know you went to this church," Lily said.

"My grandpa's been going here for a while, but this is my first week."

"We were just talking about you."

Colt frowned. "Really?"

"I'm singing during the service next week, and . . . well, since you play the guitar—"

"I don't think so," Colt said, cutting her off before she could get to the question.

"Come on," Lily said, grabbing him playfully by the arm. "I don't have anybody else to ask."

"Why do I have a hard time believing that?"

"Look, I'm not going to take no for an answer."

Colt knew he was in trouble.

"I'll e-mail you the music so you'll be ready for practice on Thursday night," she said.

"But—"

"Pick me up at six sharp."

There were so many ways that this was wrong, but before Colt could stop his lips from moving, the word *okay* slipped out.

:: CHAPTER 43 ::

That afternoon Lily e-mailed Colt her arrangement of a hymn called "When I Survey the Wondrous Cross." He had sung it plenty of times over the years, but that was from the anonymity of a pew, not on a stage with a microphone. He sighed and then grabbed his guitar to tune the strings, figuring that he might as well practice in case he wasn't able to come up with a reason to back out.

If that weren't enough, at lunch the next day Danielle shared her plan to break into Trident Biotech's server—and she was going through with it whether Colt and Oz helped her or not. She was tired of wondering where the next attack was going to come from, she declared.

Danielle had never been good at playing the role of the victim. She preferred to be in charge, and if that meant taking the fight to a multinational corporation with more resources than half the countries in the world, then so be it.

"I need to get someone's credentials so I can log into their system," she said. "Once I'm in I can upload a virus that will let me make a new credential, and then we'll be able to get in whenever we want. I'm thinking we could go to the Trident Biotech campus over by the hospital during lunch tomorrow."

"I hate to break this to you," Oz said, "but Chandler High is crawling with undercover CHAOS agents, and they're all under strict orders to keep an eye on us. There's no way we're going to be able to leave . . . And even if we did sneak away, the minute we walk through the doors at Trident Biotech, they're going to recognize us."

"Then I guess we'll have to get creative, won't we?"

Colt had no idea how she managed to pull it off—and in only two days' time, no less—but somehow Danielle arranged for everyone involved with Chandler High's Biotechnology Academy to take a tour of Trident Biotech's corporate headquarters on Thursday. If it was an official school trip, there was nothing the undercover CHAOS agents could do to stop her.

Apparently Danielle discovered that Trident Biotech had underwritten Chandler High's entire biotechnology program, so she'd approached the dean of the academy with her idea. Once Mrs. Barnum signed off, Danielle called Trident's community relations department to book a tour. Their first opening wasn't until February, but after a bit of cajoling, they agreed to squeeze the students in.

Danielle's aunt was a reporter at the *Arizona Republic*, so Danielle promised to pull some strings and turn the tour into a photo op. It didn't hurt that the father of a classmate was a vice president in Trident Biotech's sales department.

Oz wasn't a part of the program, so he had to stay behind— and he wasn't happy about it. Danielle promised him that she'd text updates as often as she could.

"Do you have any idea what they're going to do to you if they find you there?" he asked.

"No, but I suppose you're going to tell me."

"This isn't a game, Danielle."

"Really? Because I was having so much fun fighting off mechanical spiders and getting chased through the streets by a maniac who wanted to run me off the road. Oh, and I almost got shot too. So no, I had no idea that this wasn't a game."

Oz shook his head.

"Look, they would never expect us to walk through their front door," Danielle said. "Besides, Trident Industries has more than 300,000 employees worldwide. Do you think they're all in on the taking-over-the-world thing? I kind of doubt it."

"I still don't like it," he said.

"We'll be fine. I promise."

Thursday morning the buses pulled up to the front of the Trident Biotech tower with forty-seven students, three faculty members, and five parent volunteers, including Danielle's aunt and a photographer from the *Arizona Republic*.

There were twenty buildings in all, on more than forty acres of what used to be dairy farms. Besides a state-of-the-art research facility and an enormous library, employees at Trident Biotech had access to incredible amenities. There was a health club with personal trainers and massage therapists, a salon, a bowling alley, a preschool, a dry cleaner, and five different cafeterias that looked like gourmet restaurants. There was even an indoor rock climbing gym, a swimming pool with a high dive, and a theater that played all the latest movies.

"This is more like a city than a business," Colt said as he looked out the window.

"It's too bad they're trying to take over the world," Danielle said, "because I'd love to work at a place like this one day. It's incredible."

"Now I want everyone to be on your best behavior," Mrs. Barnum said. "Our department exists because of their generous donation, so before you decide to do something that you might regret, remember that." Even though Mrs. Barnum was only five feet tall, her naturally curly hair combined with her predilection for high heels gave her an extra five or six inches depending on the day.

As the students stepped off the bus, a trim man in a pinstripe suit greeted them. Howard Liang was Trident Biotech's Community Relations Director, and members from his staff handed each of their guests a duffel bag. Inside there was a T-shirt, a key chain, a coffee mug, and a variety of other trinkets with Trident Biotech's company logo.

"Welcome, everyone," Mr. Liang said, stretching his arms wide. His theatrics reminded Colt of the ringmaster at a circus, but it was his job to make sure that anyone who visited the facility left feeling enthusiastic about the Trident Biotech brand.

"Inside your gift bag you should find a visitor's badge," he said. "If you would be so kind, we would appreciate it if you would clip it to your shirt or your belt. As you would imagine, there are quite a few secrets locked behind these doors, so we have to take stringent security measures to protect them. Your badge will make sure that our security teams will recognize you as VIP guests instead of corporate spies."

Mr. Liang forced a laugh that went on just a little too long before clapping his hands together. "Oh, and I forgot to mention it, but we don't allow cell phones, cameras, or any other type of recording device. You'll be able to check them in at the security station when we first walk in, and they'll be returned once we're finished. Now please follow me, and we'll begin our tour."

"Sure, Trident can watch us, but we can't watch them."

Danielle ignored him as she took a small device out of her purse, walked over, and slipped it into a pouch on the photographer's unzipped bag. The security team would have to let him take all of his equipment inside, or they weren't going to get the shot for the paper.

The entrance to the building was stunning. There were marble walls that stretched thirty feet into the air, with a waterfall that fell into an infinity pool. Off to the right was some kind of an art gallery with paintings that could rival the world's most prestigious museums. There were pieces from Rembrandt, Van Gogh, and Norman Rockwell, as well as local artists from Arizona.

"They like to flaunt their money, don't they?" Colt said out of the corner of his mouth.

Danielle didn't appear to hear him. She was distracted as she watched the security guard look through the photographer's bag. He opened the main compartment and carefully removed two of the lenses before replacing them.

"It's mostly just batteries and such," the photographer said.

The guard unzipped the pouch containing her device.

CHAPTER 44

The guard zipped the pouch shut and let the photographer through.

Colt watched Danielle breathe again.

"You probably already know that Trident Biotech is the global leader in developing new therapies for grievous illnesses, as well as for victims of paralysis and amputees," Mr. Liang said. "We strive to improve the quality of life for patients around the world."

"By turning them into remote control assassins," Colt whispered, earning a laugh from Danielle.

"Stop that," she said, slapping him on the shoulder. "We don't want to stand out."

For their first stop they were taken to an amphitheater where they watched a promotional video about Trident Biotech. They learned about everything from advances in cancer research to their partnership with Trident Robotics.

The companies were working together to develop prosthetic limbs that not only afforded amputees the ability to walk or hold a pencil once more, but outperformed organic limbs in both strength and dexterity while still offering the sensation of touch.

The video also mentioned how Trident Biotech was pioneering a new future where humans would no longer suffer from things like epileptic seizures, Parkinson's disease, or even paralysis.

"All for the low, low price of your soul," Colt said.

"Would you stop?"

As the video ended, Mr. Liang walked up the steps and onto a small stage. "Now before we begin, are there any questions?"

"Don't you dare," Danielle said as Colt started to raise his hand.

Mr. Liang sidestepped a question about the rumors that Trident Biotech was involved in human cloning experiments, but he was happy to answer questions about salary expectations for research scientists, as well as their corporate commitment to the ethical use of animals in research.

After a tour of the grounds, the students were taken to the offices of Trident Biotech's president, Aldrich Koenig, for a photo op. The front room was opulent, with wood paneling polished to a bright shine and a stone fireplace that looked as though it had never been used. The room was large enough to hold the visitors from Chandler High with plenty of room to spare.

A woman with long blonde hair pulled tightly back into a ponytail sat at a desk near the far wall. She wore stylish glasses, and she stood as the students entered the room.

"This is Gretchen Roth," Mr. Liang said as he escorted Mrs. Barnum over to the woman's desk. "She's Aldrich Koenig's executive assistant."

"It's a pleasure to meet you, Ms. Roth."

"The pleasure is all ours. And please, call me Gretchen."

"Well, Gretchen," Mrs. Barnum said. "I'd like you to meet Ellie Salazar from the *Arizona Republic*."

"Wonderful. Mr. Koenig is on a conference call right now, but he should be finished in a few minutes," Gretchen said. "I wanted to tell you that he's very impressed with the progress of your academy. When he heard that the students would be here today, he wanted to make sure that he greeted them personally."

"Great," Ellie said. "Where would you like to take the picture?"

"I think over here would be nice," Gretchen said as she led Ellie and the photographer to the opposite wall.

"I'm willing to bet that she has access to just about everything that Koenig does," Danielle said as she leaned over so only Colt could hear. "This is our chance."

"How are you going to get her credential?"

"Watch and learn."

Danielle walked across the room as Gretchen handed her aunt a business card. Danielle placed herself between them and stuck out her hand. "Hi, I'm Danielle Salazar, Ellie's niece."

Gretchen frowned at first, but she recovered quickly and accepted Danielle's hand. "It's very pleasant meeting you."

"I wanted to personally thank you and Mr. Koenig for the grant that you gave our school. I've been interested in human therapeutics and biotechnology for as long as I can remember. My grandpa was a double amputee."

"I'm so sorry to hear that."

"He was a prisoner of war in a Nazi camp, and they didn't give him any medical attention," Danielle said. "Luckily he survived, but the frostbite was so bad that they had to cut off his feet and halfway up his shins. He died when I was little, but I still want to develop something that would have allowed him to walk again."

"We've made quite a few advancements in our prosthetics department; it's a shame he wasn't able to benefit from it,"

Gretchen said. "But we're always looking for bright young minds. I'm so glad you were able to join us today."

"Thank you."

Danielle turned to walk away, though not before reaching into her aunt's purse to take Gretchen's business card. Then she walked over to where the photographer was setting up his equipment.

"My parents bought me a new camera for my birthday, but I'm not sure I like the lens that came with it. I really enjoy landscapes—especially in the desert with all the cacti silhouetted against the setting sun—but I never seem to get a wide enough shot. Do you have any recommendations?"

As the photographer discussed some of his favorite models, Danielle looked curiously at his bag. "Do you mind if I look at yours? I promise I'll be careful."

The photographer paused. Then he shrugged. "Sure, why not."

Danielle bent down to take one of the lenses from his bag. She held it up as though investigating for potential flaws. When she saw that the photographer was back working on the lighting, she reached down and unzipped the small pouch where she had hidden her device. She slipped it into her pocket and walked back over to where Colt was standing.

"Listen to me, because we aren't going to have much time before Koenig gets here."

"Okay," Colt said.

"I want you to go find a phone, then you need to call the cell phone number on this card. You have to make her think that whatever you're talking about is really important. Can you handle that?"

"Where am I supposed to find a phone?"

"You're smart," she said. "Improvise."

Colt looked down at the card and then back to Danielle. "Just call this number?"

"Yes, but you need to keep her on the line. Can you handle that?"

He nodded and walked over to Mr. Liang. "Do you think I could use the rest room?"

"Why, of course," Mr. Liang said. "It's out that door and then down the hall to the right."

"Thanks."

Colt headed down the hall, praying that there were no hidden cameras. There were a few offices, but the doors were closed, and Colt could hear people talking inside. He found the rest room, but kept going. Then, at the end of the hall to the left, he found an empty conference room. There was a water pitcher with beads of sweat sitting in the middle of the table, and dirty glassware near most of the chairs that sat askew.

Colt figured that whoever met there had been gone for a while, and it didn't look like they were coming back. There was a phone in the middle of the table that looked like something out of a science fiction movie. It was triangular in shape, with a speaker on top—not what he needed. Then he saw a second phone on a small table next to a leather chair in the corner. He picked it up and dialed 9.

It worked. He got a dial tone and proceeded to call the number on the business card. It rang once . . . then twice. After the third ring, someone picked up.

:: CHAPTER 45 ::

"Excuse me," Gretchen said. "I should take this call."

Danielle watched Gretchen walk away from the conversation with Ellie and back toward her desk, cell phone to her ear. She appeared to be confused, which wasn't surprising. Danielle had no idea what Colt was talking about, but she hoped he could keep Gretchen on the phone long enough for this to work.

She counted to thirty and reached into her pocket to pull out what looked like a garage door opener. The device was covered in black casing, with two small lights sitting between a pair of small antennas that sat at the top.

When Danielle flipped a switch, the red light started to flash before going solid. As though on cue, Gretchen kept repeating "hello," then she hung up the phone. Gretchen tried to reconnect the call, but she clearly couldn't get any reception. Danielle watched as Gretchen pinched the bridge of her nose and sighed.

"Cell phones can be such a pain," Danielle said as she walked over to where the personal assistant was standing. "I have that same phone, and it used to drop calls all the time. Did you know there's a patch that will fix it?"

"No, I guess I didn't," Gretchen said. "I haven't had too many problems, but I can't afford a dropped call if I'm on the line with Mr. Koenig. He can be a bit impatient."

"It only takes a minute to fix," Danielle said. "I'll show you where you can download the patch if you'd like."

Gretchen looked over at the door to Mr. Koenig's office, but it was still closed. "You wouldn't mind?"

"Of course not. I just need the connection cable to plug your phone into the computer, and I'll have it back to you before you know it."

"That's very kind."

Gretchen walked Danielle over to her desk where she reached into one of the drawers and pulled out a length of black cable. "I think this is the one."

"That looks like it."

Danielle sat down in Gretchen's chair and wiggled her mouse to wake the computer up. The monitor flared to life, showing a log-in screen with the Trident Biotech logo. "Oh, I'll just need you to log in so I can get to the Internet."

"Of course."

Danielle swiveled the chair away from the computer in dramatic fashion to show that she wasn't going to try and steal Gretchen's username and password.

"That should do it," Gretchen said.

"Perfect." Danielle reached around and plugged the cord into the tower of Gretchen's computer, but what Gretchen didn't see was that Danielle had slid her flash drive into her hand, and she plugged it into a second USB port.

"Now to plug the other end into your phone," Danielle said, and she did just that. "Believe it or not, that was the hard part."

Gretchen smiled, but she wasn't leaving. There was no way Danielle was going to be able to upload the virus with Koenig's assistant standing there. Then she had an idea.

"Oh, could you do me a favor?" Danielle asked. "I think I left my purse over by the door. I have the URL that we need written down on a business card."

"By the door, you say?"

Danielle nodded, and Gretchen went off to fetch the purse . . . which was still on the bus.

Her first order of business was to gauge what kind of admittance Gretchen had been given on the servers, and thankfully her hunch had been right. Gretchen appeared to have access to everything that Koenig did, including restricted files. Danielle went to work, uploading the virus into the servers. Then she downloaded a new ringtone so that it looked like she had done something.

"I'm sorry, but I couldn't find your purse. What does it look like?"

"Oh, it doesn't matter," Danielle said, handing Gretchen her phone before removing the cord and her flash drive from the back of the computer tower. "I found the website and downloaded it for you. You're all ready to go."

"Are we training a new assistant?"

Danielle looked up to see a man with the most striking blue eyes that she had ever seen. He was tall, with short blond hair combed to the side, and brilliantly white teeth.

"Mr. Koenig," Gretchen said, "I'd like you to meet Danielle Salazar, but I'm afraid she has bigger aspirations than being an assistant. She's going to spearhead the next generation of prosthetics."

"It's a pleasure to meet you," Danielle said, standing up to offer her hand. She was trying to compose herself, but it wasn't easy. Behind Koenig stood a man that she assumed was his bodyguard. He was easily six and a half feet tall, and like Koenig, he was wearing a tailored suit, but it couldn't hide his broad chest and wide shoulders. His eyes were hard as he caught Danielle's stare. She had seen him before—he was the man who was driving the Mercedes that nearly ran her off the road.

"Do I know you from somewhere?" Koenig asked. His accent was slight, but definitely German.

Danielle looked to Gretchen and then back to Mr. Koenig. "I don't think so."

"You have a familiar face." Koenig paused as though accessing his memories. "Either way, it's nice to meet you, Danielle."

"I believe we're ready to take that picture for the newspaper, Mr. Koenig," Gretchen said.

"Very good," he said. "Danielle, if you'll excuse me."

"Of course."

Gretchen pointed to her cell phone and then mouthed the words *thank you* before following Mr. Koenig to where the photographer was waiting. The bodyguard hesitated, his eyes not straying from Danielle.

"Okay now, everyone," Mr. Liang said as he walked into the line of sight between Danielle and the bodyguard, breaking the tension. "We're just about ready for the picture. I'm going to need everyone over here."

As the bodyguard followed Koenig back across the room, Danielle closed her eyes and exhaled.

|||||||||||||||||||||||||||||||||||

After the photo with Mr. Koenig, the students and their chaper-ones were taken to a test facility where they were able to see some of the robot prosthetics in action. When that was over, it was time to head back to school. The students turned in their badges, retrieved their cell phones from the security station, and climbed on the buses. They were back in time for the lunch period, where they found Oz waiting impatiently at their usual table.

"You're sure that was the guy?" Oz asked. He hadn't touched a thing on his plate, which was unusual to say the least.

"I think so," Danielle said. "I was kind of busy weaving in and out of traffic, so I didn't get the greatest look, but if it wasn't Koenig's bodyguard, then it was somebody who looked like him. I mean, it's not like there are a bunch of blond giants walking around."

"And you think he recognized you?"

"I'm not sure. I thought so, but he didn't follow me out the building or anything. Somehow I think Koenig knew who I was, though. He said that I looked familiar."

"He probably put the hit on you," Oz said.

"Maybe I'm just paranoid."

"Did he see you uploading the virus?"

"I don't think so."

Oz looked to the left and then to the right before leaning for-ward. "You said that there was some kind of alien driving that car, but only for a second, right?"

"I don't know," she said. "I think so, but I was so freaked out that it could have been my subconscious playing tricks on me."

"Or Koenig's bodyguard is one of the Thule."

"You think so?" Colt asked.

"Why not?" Oz said. "There aren't that many left, and most of the remaining Thule are supposed to work at Trident. Rumor has it their entire board is made up of Thule."

"By the way," Colt said, dipping an onion ring into a pool of ketchup before he turned to Danielle. "Where did you get a cell phone scrambler?"

"In my Christmas stocking," Danielle said.

"Is it legal?"

"You'll have to ask Santa."

"So when will we know if your big plan worked?" Oz asked.

Danielle felt her cell phone vibrate, and she looked at the display and smiled. "We're in."

"Remind me not to leave anything on my computer that I don't want you to see," Colt said.

"Too late. I hacked your laptop months ago."

"Seriously?"

"I guess you'll never know, will you?"

"You're sure they won't see the virus?" Oz asked.

"They shouldn't," Danielle said, "but even if they did, they won't be able to trace it back to us. Besides, it's not like Gretchen is going tell Koenig that she gave some random high school student access to their servers. She'd probably lose her job." Danielle reached into her purse to pull out a small envelope.

"What's that?" Colt asked.

"SIM cards. As long as we don't stay logged on for too long, we should be fine. Just in case, I'm going to switch these out every ten or fifteen minutes. That way nobody will be able to track the connection back to us."

"You're going to start looking for the files now?"

"Well, yeah."

:: CHAPTER 46 ::

During lunch Danielle was able to download a database with the names and contact information for all the people who were implanted with Trident biochips. She switched out the SIM card in her phone before finding a second database of people who were scheduled to have the operation over the next few months.

"What about documents that show how they control people's minds?" Colt asked.

"There are so many folders in their network, it could take months to find what we need," Danielle said.

"We don't have months."

"I understand that. Look, we'll find it, but it's going to take some time. I got us this far, didn't I? Trust me."

||||||||||||||||||||||||||||||||||

Apparently it didn't take as much time as they thought it would. Between lunch and the end of school, Danielle had forwarded six different documents to Colt's phone, including a confidential memo about the mind control program from Aldrich Koenig to the Trident Industries board of directors, and a document out-lining something called the Eden Project. It amounted to the complete annihilation of the human civilization so the Thule could use Earth as their new home—their garden of Eden.

Colt was too tired to do much of anything after school, so he sat down on the couch and watched an afternoon baseball game. "Don't you have practice with the Westcott girl tonight?" Grandpa McAlister called from the kitchen where he was mixing up a pan of macaroni and cheese. "What time do we need to leave?"

After the excitement at Trident Biotech, Colt had almost for-gotten about the song he was supposed to play with Lily. Grandpa McAlister hadn't been crazy about the idea, but he relented once Colt told him they were going to be performing at church—but only on the condition that he drove them to and from their rehearsal. If Colt wanted to go, he didn't have much of a choice.

They were a few minutes late because Colt decided to take another shower and change his clothes. He spent nearly twenty minutes in front of the mirror trying to make his hair cooperate, and switched shirts three different times. In the end, he settled on a long-sleeved T-shirt with a distressed Celtic cross, his darkest blue jeans, and a pair of black track shoes.

He debated whether or not to use cologne, but he ended up erring on the side of caution. He didn't want to make it come across like they were going on a date. It was important to find that balance between caring and not caring.

When Lily answered the door, Colt could tell that she hadn't expected to see Grandpa McAlister sitting in the driveway. "It's a long story," he said as she looked over his shoulder.

Thankfully she didn't press for any details, because Colt wasn't sure what he would have said. It wasn't like he could tell her that he was on a strict curfew because a race of shape-shifting aliens was trying to kill him.

He carried her guitar down the steps before setting it in the bed of the old pickup with his, and then he opened the passenger door for her. Lily slid in next to his grandpa, and Colt joined them for the most uncomfortable ride of his life. The church wasn't far from Lily's house, so it was only a few minutes before they arrived.

"Wait, what are you doing?" Colt asked as Grandpa pulled into a parking space.

"I thought I might grab a cup of coffee in the café, if that's okay with you."

Colt wanted to tell him that it wasn't remotely close to being okay, but he swallowed the words and grabbed the guitars out of the back. They agreed to meet back up at eight o'clock, and Lily led him to the conference center.

It was a large multipurpose facility filled with hundreds of chairs. The church used the room to help with overflow since the sanctuary wasn't big enough to hold everyone. They showed a closed circuit broadcast of the sermons on three large screens.

"This place is amazing," Colt said as he walked up to the stage.

"And just think, in a few days it will be packed with all the girls from Chandler High chanting your name and screaming for more."

"Yeah, right."

"So you're telling me you don't see the way they melt when you walk by?"

"You must have me confused with Oz."

"I don't think so," Lily said. "When they hear that you're going to be playing the guitar this weekend, they're going to go crazy. You're definitely the most eligible bachelor at school."

Colt could feel his neck turning red, so he decided to change the subject. "I've never actually performed in front of anybody before."

"Never?"

"Not like this anyway. So don't blame me if I ruin your music career before it starts."

"I'm sure you'll do fine," she said. "Besides, that's why we're practicing tonight."

Colt followed Lily up the steps and onto the stage. It was all set for Sunday morning, with microphones and stands, a drum kit, two stacks of amplifiers, an electric keyboard, a bass, and a rack of guitars, including a vintage electric Gibson with a sunburst finish.

Colt flicked his case open and pulled out an old acoustic. The finish was coming off around the bridge and the sound hole, but it had been a gift from his parents and he wasn't about to trade it in no matter how worn it looked.

"I don't have an input for the amplifier," he said.

"You aren't getting out of this, so you might as well stop trying."

A door opened, and a large man with a beard entered without a word before slinking though the shadows and into the sound booth. Colt frowned.

"That's just Tim. He runs the board," Lily said.

Colt narrowed his eyes, but then he relaxed. "Sorry, I guess I've been a little jumpy lately. It's probably all that UFO stuff they keep talking about on the news."

"Mr. Pfeffer is rubbing off on you, but I don't think we'll have to worry about little green men tonight. Want to get started?"

Lily took her guitar out, threw the strap over her shoulder, and reached down to plug a cord into the amplifier's input jack. She strummed a few chords and the sound came out of the speakers before echoing through the empty hall. Lily took a moment to tune her strings. Colt decided to do the same.

"Can you turn his mic up a bit?" Colt heard her ask.

"Sure thing," Tim said.

"Play something," she said, turning back to look at Colt.

"Like what?"

"Anything. We just need to do a sound check."

Colt ran his fingers down the strings. It made a screeching noise that reverberated through the speakers before he launched into the first few notes of "Dueling Banjos."

"Okay," Lily said, after laughing. "Anything but that."

He smiled before turning back to his guitar. Then Colt tapped his foot and counted, "One . . . two . . . three . . . four." He picked a gentle melody that repeated for a few bars.

"I think we got it," Tim said from the back.

"Okay, you're going to start it out with the intro, and I'll come in before the first lyric. We may have to make some adjustments along the way, so don't get upset with me if I stop."

"You're the boss."

"We'll see how you feel about that once we're done with rehearsal."

It didn't take Colt long to figure out that Lily was a perfectionist. She would stop frequently to adjust the harmony or experiment with an a cappella section, only to go back to full accompaniment. He sat patiently, taking her instruction, and in the end they were both happy with the progress.

"Not bad," she said as she unplugged her guitar. "So what time can you be here Sunday morning?"

"It's not like I get to sleep in. My grandpa starts banging around in the kitchen at five thirty, so I'm up pretty early."

"Can you meet me at seven? That way we can go over every-thing before the service."

"Sure," Colt said. The phone that Oz had given him rang then, and he reached into his pocket to shut it off. "Sorry about that."

Lily looked up at the clock that hung on the wall over the sound board. "We still have half an hour. Do you want to grab a cup of coffee?"

:: CHAPTER 47 ::

A t first Colt was relieved that Grandpa McAlister wasn't in the café, but then his imagination kicked in. He pictured his grandfather fighting six-armed aliens, and the barista's eyes flaring red as she attacked him.

"Are you okay?" Lily asked before she ordered a mocha cappuccino. "You seem distracted."

"Sorry," Colt said. Then he turned to the barista. "You didn't happen to see an old guy in here earlier, did you?"

"Mr. McAlister?"

"Yeah. He's my grandpa."

"He left a few minutes ago, but he said he'd be back."

Colt felt relief, but then his phone vibrated again. He looked down and saw a text message from Oz: **Call me. It's about Dani.** The last thing Colt wanted to talk about was Oz's budding relationship with a girl who was practically Colt's sister, so he put the phone back in his pocket and followed Lily to a table.

The café had vaulted ceilings and an entire wall of windows that opened up like garage doors to a grassy area. There were a few college students gathered at one of the tables, but other than that, Colt and Lily had the place to themselves.

The music was soft, the lights were dim, and each table had a lit candle that was flickering as the air-conditioner blew. It would have been romantic if it weren't for the fact that Lily was dating someone else. Then again, if Colt cared about that he wouldn't have been alone with her to begin with.

"Are you ready for Nashville?" he asked as Lily stirred her drink.

"I'm a nervous wreck."

"Why?"

"This is my shot, and I don't want to mess it up," she said. "I mean, what if my voice cracks, or . . . I know it sounds ridiculous, but I've worked so hard. I just want my parents to be proud of me. They've done so much to help make this dream come true."

"Relax," Colt said. "Your parents are going to be proud of you no matter what. Besides, you're only sixteen. I'm not in the music business or anything, but I'm pretty sure that you'll get another chance if it doesn't work out."

"I doubt it."

"Your biggest problem is going to be deciding which offer to accept."

Lily stared at him. Her lips were on the verge of a smile.

"What?" Colt asked.

"It's just that whenever I'm around you it feels like everything is going to be all right."

Colt frowned. "Are you in trouble or something?"

"No, it's nothing like that," she said. "I'm sorry, I probably shouldn't have said anything."

Colt swirled the bottle of water he had ordered as he stared at the flame on the candlewick. "Can I ask you something?"

"Of course."

"Does it ever get easier? I mean, in some ways it seems like my parents have been gone for years already, but I don't know. I could be sitting in the middle of class and I'll think about something stupid, like how my mom used to make such a big deal about my birthday. She'd wait until I was asleep and then stay up half the night decorating. Then she'd wake up early the next morning to make me those pancakes with the smiley faces."

"The kind with bacon for the mouth?"

"Yep, and sliced banana for the eyes. She'd even add raisins for eyebrows. Then she insisted on reading my birthday story, and as I got older I complained because I thought it was embarrassing, but now . . . well, I'd give just about anything to hear her read it one more time." Colt turned away, afraid that Lily might see the emotion he was feeling. "It's just that I miss them so much, and I'm afraid I'm going to forget them."

Lily reached out to grab his hand. When he finally looked up, he could see her eyes were misted over.

"You'll never forget them," she said. "And I promise, it will get easier."

"I hope so."

"What were they like?"

Colt shrugged. "My dad was the most generous person I've ever known. When he retired from the navy he started his own charter service. In the beginning he was the janitor, secretary, mechanic, and pilot. He worked around the clock to make it successful, but I think he ended up giving away more money than he kept. Anytime somebody needed a loan, they'd call him. I don't think he said no once."

"What about your mom?"

"She was amazing," Colt said, smiling at a forgotten memory. "I have no idea how she did it, but she managed to raise eight sons, go to all of our games, feed us, and still have time to be a writer. We used to say that she was a vampire, because we didn't think she ever slept."

"You should write some of your memories down."

"Have you been talking to Dani or something?"

Lily raised an eyebrow.

"Sorry," Colt said. "It's just that she got me a journal so I could write my feelings down, and I wasn't exactly receptive."

"I'm not conspiring with her, if that's what you mean."

"Good." Colt took a sip from his water bottle. "Can I ask you another question?"

"I suppose." Lily brought the mug to her lips, but her eyes never strayed from Colt's.

"Does Graham know?"

"Know what?"

"That you're with me tonight," Colt said. "I mean, not with me, but . . ."

Lily smiled and set her coffee mug back on the table before licking a bit of foam from the top of her lip. "I don't think he'd care."

"Really?"

She sighed. "We broke up."

"What happened?"

"He's been cheating on me."

That wasn't the response he expected. "I'm sorry."

"He met up with his old girlfriend after my party," Lily said as she ran her finger in a circular pattern around the lip of her mug. "I can't blame him. She's beautiful."

"Are you sure?"

"That she's beautiful? Yeah, I'm sure."

"No," Colt said. "That he was cheating on you. Maybe they were just hanging out or something."

"I don't think so. A friend of mine saw them over at the Coffee Rush holding hands. Well, that and they kissed good-bye, and it wasn't a peck on the cheek." Lily took a deep breath and exhaled before forcing a smile. "Oh well, it's not like it was going to last anyway. Graham is going to Idaho State next year, and long distance relationships never work, right?"

"It's funny you should mention it, because I just broke up with a girl who goes to Idaho State. Maybe I could introduce her to Graham."

Lily laughed. "You're a dork."

"What can I say?"

"So do you have your eye on anybody?"

"I don't know," Colt said. "I mean, I met this girl in one of my classes, and she's—"

"Are you two ready to go?" Grandpa McAlister asked from the other side of the room. It was loud enough that he drew the attention of the barista and the table filled with loud college students as well.

Colt lingered a moment, looking at Lily before he stood up. Then he smiled. "We better get you home."

:: CHAPTER 48 ::

The ride to Lily's house was fairly quiet. There wasn't much to say—at least not with Grandpa McAlister sitting in the truck with them. The windows were rolled down and, as always, the radio was tuned to a local news station. Distracted by his own thoughts, Colt hadn't been paying much attention until he heard an update about a missing person. He reached across the cab to turn up the volume.

". . . Again, Dr. Albert Van Cleve, the Nobel Prize-winning research scientist credited for Trident Biotech's breakthrough bio-chip technology, has been reported missing. According to police, he was last seen on the night of September thirteenth at his home in Chandler. He was expected to speak at a conference in Vienna the following day, but he never made the flight . . ."

Colt turned the radio down before looking over to his grandfather, but Grandpa McAlister kept his eyes on the road.

A few minutes later they pulled into Lily's driveway. Colt got out and walked her to the door. There was an awkward moment where he didn't know if he should hug her, shake her hand, or just turn around and walk back to the truck. Thankfully Lily made it easy. She wrapped her arms around his neck and pulled Colt close. It wasn't a long embrace, but it felt like the perfect end to the evening.

"What's going to happen now that the police are involved?" Colt asked once he was back inside the cab. "Am I going to be a suspect?"

"I wouldn't worry about that," Grandpa McAlister said.

"I'm probably the last person who saw him alive."

"You don't know that he's dead."

:::::::::::::::::::::::::::::::::::::::

Colt knew he was going to have a hard time falling asleep. He couldn't stop thinking about Lily. After a quick shower and a bowl of butter pecan ice cream, he was about to sit down on the bed with his guitar when the phone rang. He looked at the caller ID hoping it was Lily, but it was Danielle. "What's going on?"

"Colt . . ."

"Dani, is that you?"

"I . . . I'm so tired."

"What?"

"I can barely keep my eyes open."

"Where are you?"

"I'm not sure. It's really dark, and I . . . I don't know how they found me."

"Wait, who found you?"

"Don't be mad at me . . . please, just promise me you won't be mad."

"Have you been drinking?"

"I didn't want to tell them, but they made me."

"Dani, you aren't making any sense."

"What did you do with the files that I sent you . . . the files from the Trident server?"

"Nothing. They're still on my phone."

"Good. You need to bring it to Trident Biotech. Just promise me you won't back the files up or send them to anybody else, okay? You can't even print them . . . they'll know."

"What are you talking about?"

"If you don't come alone in the next hour they're going to—"

The phone went dead.

Colt wanted to give way to the panic, but he didn't have the luxury. Sixty minutes wasn't much time. He looked at the phone. The files that Danielle found were his only chance to bring Trident to its knees. Without them, an innocent man was going to go to prison for killing his parents and thousands of others with Trident biochips would continue to be at risk.

But all Colt could think about was Danielle. If he didn't turn the files over, they were going to kill her. Colt knew they weren't bluffing either. Human life meant little to them, considering the ultimate goal of the Thule was to wipe mankind from existence. So they could use Earth as a new home.

"We'll have to find another way," Colt said. Then he dialed Oz's number.

"I've been trying to reach you all night," Oz said by way of greeting. "I finally got Zombie Extermination Squad, and I need you to help me level up so I can play with Dani."

"Sorry, I've been at church."

"On a Thursday?"

"It's a long story."

"Let me guess. You were practicing that song with Lily."

"It doesn't matter," Colt said. "I just got a call from Dani. They have her."

"Who?"

"Trident."

There was a long pause. "I thought she said the plan was foolproof."

"Apparently it wasn't."

"Are they asking for a ransom?"

"I have less than an hour to bring my phone to Trident Biotech," Colt said. "They want the files Dani sent me, and if I don't deliver them, I think they're going to kill her."

"They're going to kill her anyway."

"So what do we do?"

"Have you told anybody else?"

"Not yet."

"Keep it that way," Oz said.

||||||||||||||||||||||||||||||||||||||||

It should have taken Oz twenty minutes to get from his house to Grandpa McAlister's. Instead, he was there in a little over ten.

"Where's your grandpa?" Oz asked after Colt answered the door.

"At the grocery store."

"Good. Basil agreed to help us."

"What about CHAOS?"

"I'll get to that in a minute." Oz walked into the kitchen where he pulled out his phone, pressed a few buttons, and set it on the table. A three-dimensional hologram of the Trident Biotech campus shot out from the display, hovering in the air. Each building, tree, and road was perfectly scaled, glowing in bright shades of green.

"Wait, can my phone do that too?"

"Focus, McAlister," Oz said. "Basil has people inside Trident, and they're going to help us break in so we can find Danielle."

"Wouldn't it be easier if I went through the front door and gave them my phone?"

"Yeah, if you both want to die. Look, they aren't going to let either one of you walk. You're liabilities because you know too much."

"Then why not let CHAOS agents go in and get her? They're more qualified than I'll ever be."

"Remember what Basil said? Trident executives have friends in high places, and my dad isn't going to storm their fortress without permission from his board of directors. And they aren't going to do anything without talking to the president and the joint chiefs."

"That's ridiculous."

Oz shrugged. "He's not going to hack off the people who sign his paycheck, and he doesn't want the U.S. government breathing down his neck—especially since they're his biggest client."

Colt took a deep breath. "What about my grandpa?"

"We can't tell him either . . . at least not yet."

"So what are you thinking?"

"Trident's security system is as advanced as it gets," Oz said. "They have cameras, dogs, motion and heat sensors, and armed guards. For all we know they have missile systems and a nuclear bomb too. There's only one way to get in without being detected."

"Do I want to hear it?"

"Basil found some old records in the city archives. Apparently they built their corporate offices on top of what used to be a military installation. There's a series of tunnels and bunkers under the entire campus. The only problem is that they're flooded."

"So how are we supposed to get in?"

"Do you scuba dive?"

"You're kidding, right?"

"There's an entry point outside the wall here," Oz said, tapping a small building. It lit up, showing a trapdoor that led down to one of the bunkers.

"That's a taco shop," Colt said.

"They close at three."

"If it's underground, we won't be able to see where we're going."

"I brought flashlights."

"It doesn't sound very safe."

"We're breaking into a company owned by aliens who want to wipe humans off the map. It's not supposed to be safe."

"I guess you have a point."

"So are you in?"

"Let's do it."

:: CHAPTER 49 ::

Oz tapped in a number and then placed his phone into a rack on his dashboard. The phone rang twice before a holographic image of Basil Hyde shot up from the touch screen. It was about the size of a vintage Star Wars action figure, and the image was crystal clear, though slightly transparent.

"You decided to go through with it then?" Basil said as Oz pulled his Jeep out of Grandpa McAlister's driveway.

"We're on our way to the entry point," Oz said. "We'll be there in a few minutes."

"Excellent," Basil said. "We'll have the security system shut down in exactly twenty-three minutes and ten seconds, but you'll only have a thirty-second window to break through. If you miss it . . . well, let's just say you'll be in a bit of hot water."

"You know where they have Danielle?" Colt asked.

Basil nodded. "We believe Koenig has locked her in the main tower on the thirteenth floor, but if we're going to make this count, we need to do more than rescue her. We need to knock their satellite system off-line. Without that, they won't be able to control anyone's mind."

At the mention of Koenig's name, Colt felt such a strong emotional reaction that his chest started to heave. If everything they believed was true—if his parents were murdered because someone at Trident Biotech made the order—that meant Koenig was responsible. He either gave the order himself or he gave the approval. Either way, Colt decided then and there that he wouldn't rest until Koenig was brought to justice.

"Piece of cake," Oz said.

"Once you're inside, we'll have supplies waiting for you. There'll also be a drive with a virus we created just for this purpose. You'll need to upload it into their servers, but the only point of access is through their data center on the top floor."

"Top floor, got it," Oz said, but he was looking at Colt. "Are you okay?"

"Yeah, I'm fine," Colt said, his eyes locked on Basil. "How did you get this lined up so fast?"

Basil smiled. "We've been on high alert since the night I met you," he said. "Besides, I've had people on the inside for years. Nothing happens inside Trident Industries—or just about anywhere—that I don't know about."

Colt wanted to ask Basil if his people had infiltrated the CHAOS agency as well, but he decided against it. There would be time for more questions later.

"I hope you don't mind," Basil said, "but I also sent copies of your mother's article to a select number of news outlets. With any luck, when the markets open up tomorrow we'll bring Trident Biotech to its knees, and that's going to hurt their parent company as well. Investors aren't going to want any part of the Trident empire."

"Can I ask you a question?" Colt said.

"Of course."

"Why are you helping us?"

"Maybe one day you can return the favor." With that he hung up, and the hologram disappeared.

Oz turned into the lot of a small taco shop called Rico's. He pulled around back and parked next to a garbage Dumpster.

"Do you trust him?" Colt asked.

"Not especially," Oz said. He turned off the lights before cutting the engine. "But he's our only chance to save Danielle." He handed Colt a duffel bag.

"What's this?"

"Your gear."

Both boys slipped into what looked like armored scuba gear. It had a black and gray camouflage pattern, and the fit was snug. Oz helped Colt strap the oxygen tanks to his back, then slid into his own.

"What about weapons?"

"Here," Oz said, handing Colt an ammunition belt. Then he strapped one around his waist and fished out a metal sphere from one of the pouches. "This is a concussion grenade. All you do is punch in the code and you'll have ten seconds to detonation. Same with these."

Oz was holding what looked like a silver hockey puck. "They're electrical charges, and they pack enough power to knock an elephant on its butt, so make sure you have some distance before you set one off."

"What about guns?" Colt asked, as he thought about Koenig's bodyguard. Colt was certain that the man was going to play a role in all of this before the night was over, and that would have been hard enough if he were just a human. Unfortunately, it looked like he was one of the Thule.

"Let's hope we won't need them, but I wouldn't worry about it. Basil probably has some surprises waiting for us inside. Do you have your phone?"

"It's right here." Colt zipped it up inside his wet suit.

"Good. Then let's go." Oz led him across the parking lot to the back of the restaurant. They were carrying their flippers and masks. He stood at the door, listening to see if anyone was inside. "Stand back."

"Before you kick it in, let me give it a try," Colt said. He reached over to twist the doorknob. "It's open."

"My way would have been more exciting."

"Tell that to the poor guy who would have had to pay for a replacement," Colt said. "Besides, this isn't an action movie."

"You never know," Oz said. "CHAOS has cameras everywhere."

Colt frowned.

"Don't worry about it," Oz said. Then he paused, looking at Colt thoughtfully. "You're a good kid, McAlister."

The boys walked into a small kitchen that smelled like cooking oil and corn tortillas. The lights were off and the only noise was coming from the motor of the walk-in refrigerator.

"Where's the secret passage?" Colt asked.

Oz looked down at a visual display that was attached to his wrist. "According to the map, it should be right here." He set his mask and flippers aside before reaching down to pull up a rubber mat. Beneath was a manhole cover. Oz looked around, found a mop, and unscrewed the handle. Then he stuck one end into a notch in the manhole cover and pried it open. A mass of cockroaches poured out.

"That's disgusting," Colt said as he tried to sidestep the insects.

Oz stepped on one before grinding it with the heel of his

boot. "I guess the breakfast burritos are going to have some extra protein in the morning."

Colt looked into the darkness. "I can't see the bottom."

"You will soon enough," Oz said. He pulled his phone back out to dial a number before he set it on the ground.

"What are you doing?"

"Letting the cavalry know where they can find us."

"What about Agent Richmond? I thought he put a homing device on your Jeep. I'm surprised he isn't here yet."

"He thinks I don't know it's there, but I took it off," Oz said. He dropped his flippers down the hole. It was a long time before they hit the bottom. Then he put his goggles over his forehead and lowered himself into the hole on metal rungs that formed a ladder. "Watch your step. It's slippery."

Before long they were in the bunker. The room was shaped like a shoe box, with cement walls, a cement floor, and a low cement ceiling where a single lightbulb hung. Water was seeping through cracks in the wall, and everything was covered in mildew.

Oz walked over to flip the switch, but it didn't work.

They could see metal shelves that had once held supplies in case of a nuclear attack. Something scampered across the floor, and Colt felt his heart race. He shined his flashlight in the direction of the sound where a rat cowered in the corner.

Oz smiled. "If that's going to make you jumpy, we're in for a long night."

"I thought this place was supposed to be underwater."

"Give it a minute. It will be." Oz slipped into his flippers and Colt did the same.

Oz walked over to a metal door that looked like a bank vault, with a five-pronged spindle wheel. He gripped two of the prongs and tried to twist the door open. It wouldn't budge. He let go to shake his hands, and then tried again. Still nothing. "Give me a hand."

Colt walked over and grasped two other prongs, and the boys strained until veins popped out of their necks. The spindle still wouldn't budge.

"I don't suppose you have any lubricant in your utility belt?"

"Where would I keep it?" Oz looked down at his watch. "We have a little over nine minutes before they shut off the security system."

"So now what?"

"We improvise." Oz reached into his pouch to pull out what looked like modeling clay.

"Is that what I think it is?"

"Plastic explosives." He kneaded it before slapping it near the spindle. Then he applied a small digital display and set it with a combination.

"You have stuff like that lying around your house?"

"Doesn't everybody?" Oz smiled as he walked to the far corner of the bunker, dragging Colt with him. Ten seconds later there was a small explosion. The metal around the door crumpled. Water started to seep through the cracks. It was slow at first, but it didn't take long to pick up speed.

"Brace yourself," Oz said. He pulled his mask over his eyes. Then he flicked a switch. Two lights flared to life on either side of his goggles. The water was up to his knees when he stuck the regulator into his mouth.

Colt already had his goggles on when he bit onto his regulator. He was looking for something to grab. There weren't many choices. All he could think of was the shelving, but that wasn't going to do much good. It wasn't bolted to the floor.

As the pressure built up, the cement around the door started to crumble. It fell away, splashing into the water and the door burst open and a wall of water rushed through like a tidal wave. The force sent the boys pummeling into the back wall.

The air burst out of Colt's lungs as his regulator was yanked from his mouth. Pain shot through his ribs. He gasped and water went down his throat. Something hit him. In the swirl of chaos he couldn't tell if it was Oz, the shelving, or something else from the other side of the door. His head slammed against something hard.

In the distance he could see two small lights. The water started to calm. Colt grabbed his regulator and placed it back into his mouth. The oxygen helped calm his nerves. As long as he could breathe, he'd survive. Now all he needed was to find Oz.

:: CHAPTER 50 ::

Colt reached up to turn on the flashlights built into his goggles and kicked off the wall, launching into the murky water. He skimmed passed a floating chair before cutting through the shelves where he found Oz waiting at the door. Oz pointed to his watch, then to his eyes.

Navigating the tunnels would have been impossible without Basil's map. The endless maze was lined with cinder-block walls and everything looked the same. Their only light came from the flashlights lodged onto their masks, and Colt was starting to feel claustrophobic.

They were in a room filled with old desks, chairs, and filing cabinets. Broken picture frames littered the ground next to office supplies. Staplers. Scissors. A T-square. Oz stopped to check his bearings, then looked at Colt before pointing straight up.

Colt was about to give the thumbs-up, but something caught his eye. There was movement. A silhouette was creeping out from the darkness. Colt turned. He could see bubbles rising in the glow of his flashlight.

He felt it before he saw it. Something large. Something terrible.

He spun around, looking to find whatever was down there with them. All he could see were the bubbles as something grabbed his shoulder. Colt kicked with his leg before pushing off, and then he turned to find Oz looking at him.

After pointing to his eyes, Colt made a motion with his hand and arm to show that there was something swimming through the water. Oz raised an eyebrow as Colt's eyes shot wide. Something was coming at them from over Oz's shoulder.

Colt ducked to the side and yanked Oz by the arm, pulling him out of the way. Whatever it was swam past and Colt saw yellow eyes and a serpentine body. It was big. Oz grimaced as he gripped his shoulder. When he pulled his hand away, a stream of blood floated through the water like a red cloud on a gentle breeze.

Oz grabbed something that looked like a conductor's baton from his belt. He pulled on the tip and it expanded until it was nearly a meter long. Oz pointed up but Colt shook his head. He wasn't going to leave Oz behind, but Oz took him by the front of his wet suit and pushed him to the side.

The creature came in fast. It was as long as a school bus with a head that looked like a crocodile. Its body reminded Colt of an eel, though it had three sets of arms that all ended in clawed hands.

It battered Oz with its tail and disappeared into the darkness, but it wasn't gone long. Oz didn't have enough time to turn around before the creature bit him on the shoulder. He dropped the baton. Without thinking, Colt shot toward it. He dug his thumbs into its eyeballs, and the creature let go. It shook its head back and forth as Colt pulled Oz out of the way, then it disappeared.

Colt could feel the creature behind him before he saw it. He spotted a desk pressed against the wall and didn't hesitate. He jammed Oz beneath the desk. The monster lashed out, raking its claws against Colt's back. He could feel fabric and skin being torn.

Colt clenched his jaw against the searing pain. He turned around and pulled out one of the electrical charges from the pouch on his belt, hoping it would work underwater. He waited, but he didn't have to wait long. The monster came at him, mouth agape.

Colt set the charge and watched as the green light blinked four times, then five. *Six. Seven.* He plunged the device into the monster's mouth. *Eight.* Colt let go of the charge and quickly pulled his hand out. *Nine.* He ducked beneath the desk where Oz was hiding. *Ten.*

The charge exploded in the monster's mouth. Its body convulsed as crackling light shot over its scales. It went stiff, its eyes charred and its jaw slack as it sank to the bottom.

Colt looked down at Oz. Blood continued to seep from his shoulder, but his eyes were open. Grabbing Oz by the collar, Colt swam to the surface, where he could see a hatch. He looked down at his watch. The security system was supposed to go off-line in less than a minute.

Seconds ticked slowly by and Colt thought he saw something in the distance. He wanted to dismiss it as a hallucination, but he couldn't—not after what just happened. He looked down at his watch. *Five seconds. Four. Three. Two. One.*

Colt grabbed Oz around the neck. He was heavy, even in the water but Colt managed to make it to the hatch. It was already open. He hesitated, but then he figured one of Basil's men on the inside must have helped them.

Colt climbed out of the water and pulled with everything he had. Soon both boys were lying on the tiled floor of a small, windowless room. Barrels marked *Toxic Waste* stood against one wall as Colt propped Oz up against another. "Come on. You can't quit on me now."

Oz groaned and opened his eyes. "Are we inside?"

"I think so."

"Where?"

"I'm not sure, but there's a bunch of toxic waste. We better get out of here."

"It's not toxic waste."

Colt frowned.

"Go ahead," Oz said. "Look inside."

Slowly, carefully, Colt removed the lid of the closest barrel. He expected to find bubbling green goop. Instead, there were two duffel bags. He lifted one out before unzipping it to see what was inside. "More gifts from Basil?"

Oz answered with a nod as his face grimaced in pain.

"I still don't get why he's helping us?"

"Like I said, it's good for business."

"That's it?"

"Basil used to be a CHAOS agent," Oz said. "He and my dad go way back, and he knows it's smart to keep on my dad's good side."

"I'm going to say that this is yours," Colt said as he pulled a size twelve boot out of the duffel bag. He put it back inside before sliding the bag over to Oz. "How's your shoulder?"

"It hurts." Oz had peeled off his wet suit as well as his shirt. Colt could see the bite marks. They were seeping with blood and puss.

"You need a doctor."

Oz looked at his watch. "I'm more worried about Danielle. We only have six minutes to find her."

:: CHAPTER 51 ::

Oz gritted his teeth as he changed into the clothes that Basil's men had left. Besides the boots, there was a black T-shirt, matching cargo pants, goggles, and an ammunition belt with more grenades.

"What was that thing in the tunnels?"

"I didn't get a good look, but I think it was a Gorem," Oz said. "They live in the swamps on Gathmara."

"Are they poisonous?"

"A little bit."

"What's that supposed to mean? It's either poisonous or it isn't."

"Look, it doesn't matter because we need to hurry." Oz made his way to another barrel before peeling off the lid. He reached in to pull out a large canvas sack.

"What's that?"

"Our ticket out of here." He handed it to Colt.

Inside was a jet pack. It was smaller than Grandpa McAlister's, and there were two retractable wings jutting out from the sides.

"How does it work?"

"Just like that antique you practiced with the other day. It's just faster, that's all," Oz said.

Colt could see that his friend's shoulder was bothering him as he strapped the jet pack on and cinched the buckles across his chest.

As Colt struggled to slide into his own jet pack, Oz punched a series of commands into his watch. A small holographic replica of the Trident Biotech tower sprang to life, hovering in the air.

"We have a little over four minutes to get to the thirteenth floor."

"I thought buildings didn't have thirteenth floors."

"That's why it's the perfect place to hide," Oz said. "Let's go." He cracked the door open and peered out, before slipping into the hall with his back against the wall.

"What about security cameras?" Colt asked.

"Basil took care of them."

"How?"

"He hacked into the system. Instead of showing a live feed, all Trident security will see is a loop of empty rooms and hallways. As far as they're concerned, we're not even here."

"What about the motion sensors?"

"Hopefully those were shut down too."

Oz used the hologram map to navigate the hallways. The three-dimensional image showed more than the layout of the building. Red dots represented Trident employees. Oz and Colt showed up as green. So did Danielle, and it looked as though wherever they had her, she was alone.

They were able to duck into empty offices or boardrooms when anyone got too close, though they had a close call when a janitor followed them into a bathroom. He left before he discovered the boys hiding in the stalls.

The lights flickered once, then twice. Then they went out. The red glow of an exit sign at the end of the hallway was the only source of light. Colt couldn't see Oz, even though he was standing next to him.

"What was that?" Colt asked.

"I don't know."

"Do you think it was Basil?"

"I doubt it."

Before they could pull out a flashlight, there was a sound like an engine powering up and the lights came back on. Colt looked at Oz. His skin was pale, and his forehead was beaded with sweat.

"Are you sure you're okay?"

"The stairwell should be just around the next corner," Oz said, ignoring the question as he walked away. When he got to the corner, though, he pulled back.

"What?"

Oz put his hand over Colt's mouth. "We have company," he whispered.

"I don't see anything on the map."

"There's no heat signature because it's not human."

Colt peered around the corner to find a robot. Its narrow head sat on top of broad shoulders and a wide breastplate, all painted red. Colt could see exposed wiring in its midsection, though its thighs, shins, and feet were fully plated. It had a single eye that glowed amber. One hand was a claw, and the other held an oversized pistol.

"What is that thing?"

"The Thule call it a Wächter," Oz said. "It's German for watchman, but we just call it a Sentry." Oz reached into a pouch to pull out what looked like a handful of silver marbles. Then he raised a finger to his lips and stepped into the hall.

"Identify yourself," the robot said as a beam from its eye scanned Oz.

"You can call me the grim reaper," Oz said with a wicked smile. He tossed the marbles, which stuck to the robot's metal casing. It looked down as Oz stepped back behind the wall.

Colt could hear a beeping sound. It was slow at first, but it picked up speed.

"You might want to cover your ears," Oz said.

There was an explosion. Light flashed and the walls and floor shook before everything went quiet. Oz stepped into the cloud of smoke wafting down the hall. He started to cough. "All clear."

The robot was lying on the ground with its head a few feet away. Its chest was riddled with holes and scorch marks.

"Nice trick," Colt said.

"Thanks." Oz coughed again and stepped over the robot. He placed his fingertips on a sensor pad next to the door, and each lit up with green circles as a picture of his face appeared on the touch screen. The door opened.

"How did you get clearance?"

"Guess."

"Basil."

The door led to an empty stairwell with cameras everywhere. Colt hoped that Basil's video feed was still working, not that it mattered. After that explosion, everyone in the building was going to know there was a break-in.

"Why didn't we take the elevator?" Colt asked.

"I needed the exercise," Oz said. He was leaning over with his hands on his knees, and his breathing was heavy.

Colt could see the blood seeping through Oz's shirt, and his skin was chalky white. "We need to find a first aid kit or something."

"I don't think a bandage is going to do much good."

"Probably not, but you need to clean those wounds."

"It's already in my bloodstream," Oz said. "The sooner we finish this, the sooner I can get to the emergency room."

It wasn't long before they reached the thirteenth floor. Oz placed his fingertips on the sensor pad and it lit green before the door opened.

"According to this," Oz said, referring to the hologram map, "Danielle should be in a room at the end of this hallway . . . but—"

"But what?" Colt asked, agitated.

"She's not alone."

"Who's with her?"

"I don't know, but it looks like somebody from Trident."

"It's probably Koenig," Colt said through clenched teeth. His pulse had quickened, his fists were clenched.

"Maybe, but no matter who it is we have to hurry. We only have about three minutes until you were supposed to meet with Koenig. If we don't find Danielle before then, he's going to kill her."

:: CHAPTER 52 ::

Where is everyone?" Colt asked as they crept down the hallway to where Danielle was supposed to be hidden. "This
is too easy."

Oz coughed so hard his face turned red. "It's not over yet.
Besides, don't forget about Koenig's bodyguard. He's got to be
around here somewhere."

"Trust me, I haven't forgotten about that goon," Colt said as
the boys made their way to the end of the hall.

"This is the door," Oz said before leaning against the wall. His
head was thrown back, his breathing looked pained as he shut his
hologram watch down. "Are you ready?"

Colt nodded, though he wasn't sure. He had never been a violent person, but all he could think about was wrapping his fingers
around Koenig's throat and watching the head of Trident Biotech
fight to breathe. He was torn between guilt and rage, knowing
that killing Koenig wouldn't bring his parents back, but wanting
Koenig to pay a heavy price for what he had done.

"Listen," Oz said. "If this goes sideways, I want you to get out
of here."

"No way. We're in this to the end."

"Don't be an idiot." Oz didn't wait for Colt to respond as he tried the handle. It was unlocked. "One . . . two . . . three." He twisted it before pushing the door open.

Aldrich Koenig, or what appeared to be a holographic representation of him, was seated behind a large desk. Colt felt robbed. He couldn't exact revenge on a hologram.

Danielle appeared to be flesh and blood as she stood next to Koenig's bodyguard. He looked all too real as he towered over her. Oz was big, but the bodyguard was enormous and Colt started to wonder if they were going to get out of there alive.

"Welcome," Koenig said, his voice strong despite the fact that he wasn't sitting there—at least not really. "Would you like to take a seat?"

"We want Danielle," Colt said through a clenched jaw.

"All in due time. Please," Koenig said as he gestured for Colt and Oz to sit down. "Do you know something? I'm curious, what did you expect to gain by all of this?"

"What do you mean?" Colt asked. He could see Oz eyeing the bodyguard.

"Did you come to avenge the death of your parents? Or are you simply trying to play superhero like your grandfather?"

Colt ignored the question as he turned his attention to Danielle. She looked tired. Her face was drained of color, and it looked like she was struggling to stand.

"Ah, you've come to rescue your lady fair," Koenig said as he followed Colt's gaze. "It's rather romantic, isn't it?"

"We're going to take Dani home, that's all. And you're going to let us."

Koenig smiled, as though taken aback by Colt's bravado. "What do you know about us, I wonder," he said, his hands positioned so that his fingertips were touching. "I mean, beyond the propaganda, of course. What do you truly know about my kind."

"I know enough."

"Yes, of course," Koenig said dismissively. "But were you aware that when the first humans crossed into Gathmara, they took our children back to Earth? Scientists dissected and studied them like animals."

"Give me a break," Oz said.

"Perhaps you knew that your forefathers released a viral epidemic in an attempt to kill off every living creature on my home world?" Koenig said. "Of course they failed, but they wanted to turn our world into a settlement for humans. That way your wretched species would have a place to go once you destroyed your planet. It's rather monstrous, even for a society as primitive as yours."

"You should talk," Colt said. "I mean, you're the one who killed my parents. What do you call that?"

"A necessary evil, I'm afraid," Koenig replied far too casually for Colt's liking. There wasn't an ounce of remorse in his voice.

Colt seethed as he stood before Koenig's hologram. "What about the Eden Project?"

Koenig smiled as he stood up. His hologram was only slightly transparent as he walked in front of his desk to stand in front of Colt. "So you did read the files," he said. "It's a pity your mother had to die because of them. Because of her—well, let's call it persistence—she took your father with her, and now it appears that her noble son will suffer the same fate."

"I wouldn't count on it."

"You have your grandfather's courage, I'll give you that," Koenig said.

"What you're doing? It'll never work," Colt said.

"Oh, but it will," Koenig said. "Even as we speak, our forces are gathering on the other side. The wall that separates our worlds is crumbling, and soon this planet will be ours."

"We'll fight back, just like the last time. You won't win."

"There's that American bravado I've come to admire, wouldn't you say, Rainer?"

Koenig's bodyguard smiled.

"Come on, Dani," Colt said, ignoring Koenig. He took a step toward her with his hand outstretched.

Danielle didn't move.

"Such an obedient one, she is," Koenig said. "And I haven't even activated her yet."

"What are you talking about?"

Rainer reached into the interior breast pocket of his suit to pull out a small device that reminded Colt of a television remote control. "You see, I wasn't convinced that you were going to cooperate, so I had one of our biochips implanted into Ms. Salazar's head."

Koenig's bodyguard entered a code into the device, and Danielle's eyes flared red, her posture changed. No longer tired, she was like a soldier standing at attention. "I can have Rainer shut her cerebral cortex down from anywhere in the world. Once that happens, she'll stop breathing. Then her heart will stop beating."

"No!" Oz shouted.

Colt looked at Koenig's bodyguard, then at Danielle. He hit the ignition switch on his jet pack, and it roared to life. He leapt. His shoulder rammed into Rainer's midsection. The impact sent them both smashing into the wall as the remote device flew out of the bodyguard's hand.

"You idiot!" Koenig shouted as Oz scooped it up.

Colt tried to push away from the bodyguard, but the massive man was gone. In his place was a wicked creature wrapped in blue scales. Its head was vaguely reptilian, ending in horns that swept back like exhaust pipes. It had six arms, each ending in clawed hands.

"Does his true form bother you?" Koenig asked as Rainer threw Colt across the room.

"The smell does," Oz said. He was holding three concussion grenades in each hand, all of them blinking green. "Grab Danielle and get out of here," he told Colt.

Colt was woozy as he tried to stand up.

"Now!" Oz shouted.

Before Rainer could reach them, Colt managed to grab Danielle around the waist. He threw her over his shoulder and ignited his jet pack. Her weight was throwing them off balance, making it hard for Colt to control where he was flying. The low ceiling and narrow walls weren't helping, and neither was the giant reptilian creature that was trying to grab them.

Colt managed to make it out the doorway just as Oz rolled the grenades toward Koenig's shape-shifting bodyguard. Seconds later the first grenade exploded. Two more followed, detonating in rapid succession as Oz jumped into the hallway.

The roof fell, trapping Koenig's bodyguard inside as alarms sounded and the sprinkler system spit out water. Colt landed clumsily and fell forward, dumping Danielle on the ground. Her head bounced off the carpet as Colt flipped over. The engines of his jet pack were still engaged, sending him reeling into the wall. He double clicked the red button and the engines shut down.

"Are you okay?" Oz asked from across the hall. He was running toward them as water fell from the ceiling.

"Yeah. Fine," Colt said, though he felt dizzy. "Dani's not conscious—can you shut her biochip down?"

"I don't know. The stupid remote isn't in English."

Danielle's eyes popped open and her hand shot out to grab Oz around the throat. Before he could react, she kicked him in the ribs. He fell back and she turned her attention to Colt.

"Dani, what are you doing?" Colt asked. She was walking toward him, her eyes glowing red.

Oz ran up behind her and snaked his arms beneath hers, locking his fingers behind her neck. "I'll take care of her. You go to the control room and shut them down."

"Don't hurt her!"

"Go!"

Danielle fought to break free, but Oz held tight. She slammed the back of her head against his nose and there was a loud crack. Blood flew. Oz staggered back, his eyes tearing up as Danielle walked toward Colt again.

"I said get out of here!" Oz shouted. He launched at Danielle, tackling her around the knees. She fell, but scrambled around so she was lying on her back. Oz tried to pin her, but she kicked at him with both feet and he flew backward, smashing into the wall, breaking the drywall.

Colt fled.

    |||||||||||||||||||||||||||||||||||||

Guilt gripped at Colt as he made his way through the halls. It took every ounce of concentration to move forward. He wanted to go back and help Oz, though as he thought about it, if he wanted to be honest, Colt really just wanted to make sure that Oz didn't hurt Dani.

He hoped that Koenig's bodyguard truly was trapped, but even if he was, that still left Koenig. With each step toward the control room, anger grew inside of him, all of it focused on the president of Trident Biotech.

Reaching the control room undetected wasn't easy. With the alarms sounding, the halls were wild with activity. Most of the employees were running for the stairs, hoping to get out of the building before it burned down. Colt looked in a few rooms to see if he could find Koenig, but they were all empty.

When he finally got to the control room, there was a touch pad hanging on the wall near the door. Colt lifted his fingertips to the screen, and green circles lit up. The door clicked open.

Inside, the room was empty. Colt couldn't stop thinking that something was off. He glanced around the room, though he had no idea what he was looking for ... Koenig's bodyguard ... one of the Thule ... maybe even Koenig himself. There was nothing, so Colt sat down at a control console.

He reached into his pocket to pull out the flash drive with the virus, then placed it into a USB port. A folder popped up on the screen and Colt double clicked on the icon. As he activated the virus, the door opened behind him. Instead of Koenig's bodyguard, another crimson Sentry, just like the robot near the stairwell, burst into the room holding a gun. It took aim at Colt and pulled the trigger, releasing a ball of energy that burst from the barrel.

Colt ducked and dove off the chair before rolling on his shoulder across the floor. *Boom!* A monitor blew up. Colt came up on one knee before reaching into a pouch to pull out a grenade. As he punched the sequence, the robot came after him, tossing chairs aside and leaping over a console filled with monitors.

Colt ran, trying to activate the grenade, but it slipped out of his hands. The robot was closing in and Colt pushed a rolling chair in front of it.

"Stop!" the robot commanded as it leveled its gun. Colt ducked and the shot flew past him to shatter a window. He reached into his pouch to pull out another concussion grenade, and this time he was able to set it. He rolled it toward the robot before reaching for another.

Waves of energy shot from the robot's weapon. Colt looked at the open window, knowing there was only one way out. He hoped the virus was done uploading, but there was no way he could check—not without getting his head blown off. He set two more grenades, tossed them over his shoulder, and ran toward the broken window. Blasts from the robot's energy weapon burst against the wall as the first grenade exploded.

Colt looked over his shoulder. The blast had sent the robot hurtling into the air.

The window was only a few feet away and Colt didn't stop. He leapt through the broken window and his stomach lurched as he fell. He hit the ignition switch on the jet pack, but it sputtered. Flames leapt out of the jets as Colt shot into the night . . . but it wasn't far enough.

There were two more explosions, and the force from the blasts sent him flying head over heels. The jet pack sputtered and then stalled. Colt fell, punching the ignition switch in desperation before it sputtered again.

:: CHAPTER 53 ::

Sparks flew out of the jets, but they didn't start. Colt hit the ignition switch once more, and it sputtered again. The ground was closing in and he tried again. There were more sparks, and then, with a whoosh, the jets ignited. Colt was heading toward the pavement.

He arched his back and braced for an impact that never happened. As he shot back into the sky, he risked a glance and saw the world growing smaller below him. He spun and whooped as the rush of wind pulled at his cheeks and whipped through his hair.

Then he remembered Danielle, and elation turned to fear. Colt circled back toward the main tower, hoping that Oz had found a way to shut her biochip down.

One explosion followed another as flares of light lit up the sky. The corporate headquarters of Trident Biotech had turned into a war zone. Smoke billowed from the guard tower at the front entry as a convoy of black trucks sped through the gate and toward the main building.

People were running across the lawn, trying to get as far away as they could. White lights flashed like dotted lines in the darkness as men fired strange weapons. Colt looked for Koenig, but from that altitude everyone looked like tiny dots.

All that Colt could see in detail were a pair of machines that were at least twenty feet tall. He recognized them from the hologram game at Oz's house. They were called Trackers, and the Thule used them to round up humans that had escaped from internment camps.

The Trackers were rough like relics from the Second World War, with dents and scratches. Still they were menacing as they towered over the lawn. Inside, Colt knew, a team of mechanics, engineers, drivers, and soldiers manned each machine. The Trackers' enormous eyes shone like floodlights as men fired at them, the ammunition bouncing off their iron hides.

Each Tracker had a gun turret with a cannon mounted on top. One took aim at an approaching truck. There was an explosion as the truck was blown off the road. The battered vehicle spun as it flew into the lawn, rolling before it smashed into a tree.

The second Tracker took aim at another truck. Its first shot missed, but not the second. The front end of the truck burst into flame as the windshield shattered. Its back end lifted off the ground before it bounced on the pavement. Somehow the driver managed to open his door and stumble into the circular drive. He took three steps before he fell.

Colt could see that the men in those trucks were CHAOS agents. It was an impressive response time, but they were outgunned. Trident assassins were pouring out of the building, joining the Trackers. Colt thought that he saw one of the Thule, and he wondered if Koenig's assistant had escaped from the wreckage in his office. Then he saw another, running amidst a horde of corporate employees. The janitor who nearly spotted Colt and Oz in the rest room was there as well, and they all looked terrified.

As Colt scanned the bedlam looking for Oz and Danielle, he saw a CHAOS agent take aim at a Sentry. The blast from his pulse rifle hit the robot in the chest. It stumbled back but kept its footing and raised a clawed hand. A sphere of crackling energy formed between the prongs. Then it fired. The plasma charge enveloped the CHAOS agent before expanding. In a flash it was gone, and so was the agent.

Bolts of light burst in the sky all around Colt. He looked down to see another Sentry shooting at him. He spun like a corkscrew as he climbed in the air, trying to get out of range. The Sentry turned its attention to easier prey.

Not far away, smoke was streaming from the windows of the control center where Colt had detonated the concussion grenades. He thought about going back in through the window to look for his friends, but the roar of helicopter blades distracted him.

Colt turned to see the airship that Agent Richmond had used to rescue them from the highway patrolman. The gun that jutted out from under its belly opened fire, chewing up the ground around one of the Trackers. The robot's gun turret swiveled before it took aim. Bolts of energy raced toward the airship, but none found a target.

One by one, CHAOS agents dove from an open door in the side of the airship, igniting their jet packs. The glow from their exhaust dotted the sky like fireflies on a summer's night. Then the propellers on the airship rotated forty-five degrees until it was hovering in place.

It sent two missiles rocketing toward one of the giant robots. The first hit the Tracker in one of its eyes. An explosion sent glass flying and the second missile caught the Tracker on the knee. There was a loud pop followed by a bang. The leg crumpled and the Tracker fell.

The cannon on top of the second Tracker unleashed a relentless volley at the airship. Sparks flew from its iron hide, and the cockpit windows shattered. One of the engines burst into flame before it started to fall. One propeller wasn't enough to keep the airship afloat. More CHAOS agents jumped as the airship started to spin.

The body of the airship crumpled as it crashed into the lawn. Colt flew toward the wreck as someone emerged from the flames. It was D3X, with Agent Richmond limping at his side. One of the Thule took aim at them with two plasma rifles. D3X pushed Agent Richmond to the ground before absorbing the punishment. The energy blasts hit the robot's shoulder, then its chest. D3X raised an arm and a beam of light shot out from its palm, knocking the Thule to the ground. It didn't get up.

CHAOS agents in jet packs swarmed around the last Tracker like bees attacking a grizzly, but their weapons were useless. Its iron hide was too thick. Without the airship, there wasn't much they could do. The cannon on the robot's turret erupted and trucks exploded as asphalt and metal shot into the air.

Colt spotted two figures on the front steps of the tower. They were tucked behind a pillar, hiding. Oz was holding Danielle in his arms.

Colt sped toward them. A Sentry robot took aim, releasing a volley that followed Colt across the sky, but nothing connected. Colt risked a glance just as a CHAOS agent shot a grenade launcher. The Sentry exploded in a cloud of metal and circuitry.

Colt lost track of where he was, and when he turned back around he had to cut the engine of his jetpack. He was going too fast and the landing was hard. Something popped in his ankle before he fell, sliding across the pavement. His shoulder took the brunt of the punishment, but his ankle flared when he tried to stand. Colt had to hop on one foot until he could keep his balance.

Danielle's head was flopped back, and her arms and legs were dangling. "Is she . . . ?" Colt didn't dare finish the sentence.

"She's alive," Oz said. His face was grim and his arms were shaking as he set her down.

"What happened?"

"I have no idea. I just kept hitting buttons until her eyes faded."

"Have you seen Koenig?"

Oz shook his head, but his eyes lit up when he spotted the Tracker.

Colt followed his gaze.

"That's not supposed to be on our side of the gateway," Oz said.

"Do you think Trident found another opening?"

"I didn't think they could tear the fabric enough to let stuff that big cross over."

"Wait, do you think they reopened the bridge between our worlds?"

"Let's hope not," Oz said. "Or this might be our last night on Earth."

An errant blast struck the building above where they were

standing. Oz hunched protectively over Danielle as they were showered with debris.

"We have to get you out of here," Colt said.

Oz was looking past Colt, to the sky. At first his eyes were narrowed, but then he smiled. The Phantom Flyer was descending into the mayhem.

:: CHAPTER 54 ::

J ust like when he appeared in his comic books, the Phantom
   Flyer was clad in army green with a white star on the front
   of his helmet and a green gas mask covering his face. He
took aim with his pulse rifle at one of the Sentries and with one
shot, the robot was obliterated.

"I wish I had a video camera," Oz said.

A Trident assassin shot at the Phantom Flyer, hitting one of
the tanks on his jet pack. Sparks flew as the wartime hero was
knocked off course. He tumbled through the air, but quickly
gained control. When he spotted the assassin, he dove.

The assassin fired again, but the Phantom Flyer dipped to
the left and the shot went errant. As he flew past the assassin, he
brought the butt of his rifle down on the man's head. The Trident
assassin fell to the ground, unconscious.

Two crimson ultralights came into view. Their guns fired
at the Phantom Flyer, but missed. The errant shots tore into the
ground as the Phantom Flyer burst straight up. The Trident assassins gave chase.

Colt could see the glow of the Phantom Flyer's jet pack as it cut through the night. The ultralights spat rounds of ammunition, but the Phantom Flyer kept going. Left then right. Up then down. It was an erratic pattern, but the ultralights kept pace.

The Phantom Flyer cut his engine. He started to fall, but when the ultralights blew past him, he reignited the engine and gave chase. The men on the ultralights looked over their shoulders, trying to spot their pursuer. One banked hard to the right while the other dipped to left with the Phantom Flyer following close behind.

When he caught up with the ultralight, the Phantom Flyer grabbed the pilot under his arms and lifted him into the air. The ultralight fell away as the Phantom Flyer let go. The pilot kicked his legs and waved his arms as he fell, but once the panic lifted, he pulled the rip cord on his parachute. The ultralight crashed into the ground in a fury of fire.

The second ultralight came back around, screaming toward the Phantom Flyer as bolts of energy shot from the guns beneath its wings. The Phantom Flyer hovered in place as it approached and somehow the bolts missed.

Then, at the last possible second, the Phantom Flyer shot straight up. The ultralight passed below him, but not before the Phantom Flyer grabbed the pilot by the straps of his parachute. In a burst, the Phantom Flyer shot toward the ground, where he let go of the pilot. The man tried to land on his feet, but he ended up tumbling before he came to a hard stop against a fence.

The Phantom Flyer pulled up, stopping to make sure the man was okay. Then he turned—and a blast from the Tracker's cannon struck his jet pack. There was a spark of light as he lost control, flying erratically as smoke issued from his tanks. Then he fell.

Colt turned to Oz. "Can you carry Danielle to one of the CHAOS trucks?"

"I think so."

"I'll be there in a minute." Colt ignited the engine on his jet pack and launched into the air. He spotted the smoke coming from the Phantom Flyer's engine. Landing was going to be painful. He slowed, then hovered for a moment before he cut the engine.

Pain shot up his leg when he hit the ground. Colt lay there, holding his ankle as he gritted his teeth. Then he rolled over, deciding it would be easier to crawl than to walk.

Colt found the Phantom Flyer lying on his side in the grass. His helmet had fallen away and he had pulled off his leather mask, revealing silver hair. There was blood flowing from a cut above his eye and his gas mask was askew, but he was breathing.

The Phantom Flyer groaned as Colt reached to gently pull the gas mask away. "Grandpa?"

His grandfather opened his eyes and took Colt's hand. "Did you find Dani?"

Colt nodded. There was a lump in his throat. He couldn't speak.

"Good." Grandpa McAlister coughed before wincing in pain.

"Grandpa . . ."

"I'll be fine."

The ground shook and Colt looked up to see the Tracker approaching. It took another step and the ground shook again as its bright eyes scanned the grounds like floodlights.

Grandpa McAlister tried to sit up, but he didn't have the strength. "We have to take it out."

"How?"

"Where's my rifle?"

Colt strained, but it was too dark. He couldn't see it.

"Here," Grandpa said after reaching into a pouch on his ammunition belt. "It's a magnetic grenade. Find my gun and load it into the launcher under the barrel. I only have one, so you need to make it count."

Colt took the grenade in his hand. It looked like a giant bullet with a shiny metal casing. Then he looked at his grandpa, wondering if the doubt he felt was evident on his face.

"You'll do just fine," Grandpa McAlister said.

Colt tried to stand, but his ankle wouldn't bear his weight. He crawled again, searching for the gun with his hands. The ground rattled as the Tracker drew near. It was close enough for Colt to see the rivets holding it together. He looked at his grandfather. "I'll be right back."

"Colt, wait!"

It was too late. Colt ignited the engine on his jet pack before he burst into the sky. Laser blasts followed him, each missing its target as Colt flew toward the Tracker. The gun turret turned toward him as the cannon lowered. Colt dipped down, and the cannon followed as a spray of energy bolts erupted from the barrel. Colt rolled away before banking hard to the right.

More gunfire shot at him from below and the sky was alive with ammunition. Colt gripped the magnetic grenade in his hand as he pulled up. The turret spun toward him once more and as Colt activated the grenade, the cannon took aim. Colt pulled his arm back. The turret stopped. Colt threw the grenade as the cannon fired.

If his throwing motion hadn't made his head drop, Colt would have been decapitated. Instead, the bolt from the cannon fizzled in the sky before it dissipated. Colt looked up to see that the grenade was stuck to the Tracker's head. He could hear it start to beep. It was slow at first, but it sped up.

Colt burst into the sky as the grenade exploded. He turned so he could see the Tracker's casing buckle as fire and smoke erupted. The cannon bent and the lights shattered as the Tracker teetered and fell. The earth shook. Moments later the engines caught on fire, followed by a chain of explosions as sheets of metal burst into the sky.

Three more CHAOS airships descended from above with guns flared as agents in jet packs poured out from the doorways. Below, the flashing lights from emergency vehicles approached Trident's campus. They weren't alone. News trucks filled with reporters and cameramen were on the scene. Average citizens had come as well. People were lined around the fence trying to get a look at the commotion inside.

Colt saw one of the Thule standing with two hands behind its head while the others were held straight out as CHAOS agents approached with handcuffs. Another Sentry exploded in front of a cameraman.

"Did you get that?" Colt heard a reporter ask as a limousine pulled around to the back of the main building. The driver got out and ran to open the back door as Aldrich Koenig approached the vehicle.

:: CHAPTER 55 ::

Colt didn't hesitate. He dove toward the limousine as Koenig slipped into the back. Any hope of a sneak attack was destroyed when the driver looked up to see Colt flying toward them. He jumped into the front seat and slammed on the gas pedal before shutting his door. The tires spun and the back end swerved as the limo shot forward.

The driver finally pulled his door shut and Colt reached into one of the pouches on his belt to grab one of the concussion grenades. Setting the trigger mechanism as he flew wasn't easy, but after fumbling once or twice, he managed to activate it.

He watched as the green light flashed. It was slow at first but as the countdown continued, it picked up pace. The beeping was loud, even over the rush of wind, and Colt started to worry that he wasn't going to get close enough to the limo before it detonated.

The limo wound around a bend up ahead and Colt tried to follow, but a wall of trees cut him off. With a burst, he flew over the branches and continued his chase. The limo had to stick to the road, but the jet pack let Colt cut a straight course through the sky. With the seconds ticking, he got close enough to read the license plate before he threw the grenade.

His aim was off, but not by much. The grenade bounced off the asphalt and under the back bumper where it exploded. The impact sent the rear of the car bouncing into the air as the trunk flew open, spilling the contents across the road.

The rear tires bounced and the driver fought to regain control as the broken bumper—or what was left of it—dragged across the asphalt. Sparks flew as the driver pulled hard to the left and then to the right but he was going too fast. The rear whipped around until the car was perpendicular to the road. It sped over the curve, tearing through the grass until it smashed into a tree.

The front end crumpled. Steam, or maybe it was smoke, poured out from under the hood as the horn blared. Colt swung around to the front where he saw the driver lying across a deflated airbag that covered the steering wheel. His eyes were closed, but he was breathing as blood poured from a gash across his forehead. It covered his face as though someone had dropped a bucket of crimson paint over his head.

The back door opened, and Colt watched Koenig step out from the limo and onto the road. Despite the destruction around him, Koenig's smile was intact—though his suit coat was singed, his tie was askew, and there was a small cut under his eye where blood the color of seaweed trickled down his cheek.

You know, you're becoming more of a problem than I had anticipated. Koenig wiped at the blood before straightening the cuffs of his shirt.

Colt stopped, hovering over the wreckage. Koenig hadn't actually moved his mouth when he spoke. His voice had somehow invaded Colt's thoughts.

"Come now, why the surprise?" Koenig asked. "Surely you've read enough of your comic books to know that we Thule use telepathy."

There was an explosion behind them, followed by another. Colt turned to watch a third Tracker fall as a swarm of airships hung in the airspace overhead.

"That wasn't the only rift that was open," Koenig said as a plume of fiery orange burst into the sky, followed by a billowing cloud of thick smoke that rose from the Tracker's iron hide.

"It doesn't matter, because you lost," Colt said with satisfaction, figuring that even if Koenig couldn't hear him, he'd be able to read Colt's mind.

"Hardly," Koenig replied, unperturbed as he glanced at the battlefield.

"Look around. It's bad enough that you're outgunned, but did you see all the camera crews? By morning, the whole world is going to know who you really are and what you've been doing. It's over."

Koenig crossed his arms. His smile widened as he shook his head. "This is but a blip," he said. "We've put things in motion that can't be undone, and soon enough this world will be ours." He reached into the breast pocket of his suit coat. "Don't worry," he said as Colt tensed. "I'm not armed. It's just a phone. After all, thanks to your handiwork, I'll need a ride."

"I don't think so," Colt said.

Fire burst from the jet pack as Colt shot toward Koenig, but the head of Trident Biotech sidestepped and brought his fists down on the back of Colt's head. "I was content to let you go . . . at least for now," Koenig said as Colt flipped through the air, head over feet until he crashed into the ground, tearing a path in the grass as he skidded out of control. "That won't be possible now, of course."

Koenig closed the distance quicker than a human should have been able. With outrageous strength, he picked Colt up by the collar and flung him into a tree trunk. Colt groaned as his ribs cracked and the air rushed out of his lungs.

"I take no joy in killing a child, but I'm afraid you've left me no choice," Koenig said as he approached Colt once more.

With his back against the tree, Colt fought to retain consciousness. His head was swimming and pain wracked his body. The aviator goggles he wore were off kilter and as he opened his eyes, Koenig was little more than a blur of motion. Colt tried to stand but he couldn't. Instead, he raised his arms to block the blow.

Koenig reached down and grabbed Colt by his hair, pulling him to his feet. Colt grabbed his wrist, trying to pry him away. He struck Koenig's arm, but it didn't matter. Koenig took Colt's head and smashed it against the tree.

Colt fell, slumped against the trunk. He felt the back of his head, and when he pulled his hand away, it was covered in blood.

"It's a shame you're paying for the sins of your parents," Koenig said as he kicked Colt in the ribs.

Colt gritted as fiery pain shot through his side. He pressed his hands against the ground, trying to find the strength to stand. His fingers fell on something cold. He probed. It was metal, long and solid. Without looking, Colt knew it was a tire iron. He figured it must have flown out of the trunk when the concussion grenade exploded.

Koenig's fist slammed into Colt's face, and he could feel his eye swell shut. Koenig punched him again, this time splitting

Colt's lip. Each punch felt like a cinderblock bashing against his skull.

Through his good eye, Colt could see Koenig reel back to strike again. With his jaw clenched and nostrils flared, Colt swung the tire iron.

Somehow Koenig managed to shift his weight as he went from throwing a punch to dodging out of the way. Still, as quick as he was, he wasn't quick enough. The tire iron struck him on the jaw with a loud crack, sending Koenig reeling backward.

:: CHAPTER 56 ::

For a moment, Colt worried that he may have killed Koenig. All he wanted to do was turn him over to the police. He didn't have to worry for long.

Koenig smiled, and his tongue found its way to the stream of green blood. It lingered for a moment as though he were savoring a decadent treat. "I'm impressed," he finally said, rising to one knee. "But I wonder, do you have more where that came from?"

Colt didn't know where the strength had come from, but he managed to stand on shaky legs. Then he took a step.

"Come on then," Koenig said, chiding him. "That's it."

Colt took a second step, then another. Each felt impossible. The pain was unbearable, but he had to stop Koenig. He raised his arm to bring the tire iron down, but in a blur, Koenig's hand caught Colt's wrist. He squeezed, and Colt yelped as he dropped the makeshift weapon.

"You may beg for your life if you wish," Koenig said. "I may even show mercy, though I doubt it. I'm afraid I've grown tired of our little game."

With his free hand, Koenig slapped Colt across the face. Tears filled his eyes, which is why Colt didn't trust what he was seeing—at least not at first. The air shimmered, like heat rising from the asphalt on a blistering summer day. Then Koenig was gone, and in his place stood one of the Thule.

"Who are you, boy, to think that you can challenge me?" Koenig asked in a mocking tone. His armored hide was covered in scales of blue and green and his snout was long, making Colt think of a dragon. A set of spiraling horns swept into the air behind the monster, and each of his six hands ended in claws that looked like they had been carved from stone.

One of those hands slipped around Colt's neck before hefting him into the air. The grip was tight, forcing Colt to fight for each labored breath. His face turned red, then purple, and though Colt couldn't be sure, he thought that the monster was smiling.

Colt clawed at Koenig's arms. He kicked, but no matter what he did, Koenig wouldn't relent. Then, just before Colt passed out, Koenig dropped him. The monster stood over Colt, looking down with placid curiosity. Colt gasped for breath as he reached for the tire iron, but it was out of his reach.

"Really?" Koenig asked as he kicked the weapon so Colt could take it. "Do you think that will help, or is this your survival instinct? You truly are a curious people."

Colt's hand touched the iron, but he didn't have the strength to grasp it.

"It's pathetic, really," Koenig said. "Though I must admit that I'm impressed by your valor. Stronger men than you have given up much earlier. In fact, most of your kind start babbling, even crying as they beg for their pathetic lives."

Colt looked up at Koenig. "You killed my parents," he managed to say, though his voice was hoarse.

"Yes, I suppose I did," Koenig said in an offhand manner. "Not directly of course, but you must understand, we warned your mother not to move forward with that article. I even had our corporate lawyers send her a threatening letter, but she ignored it. I suppose that must be where you get your spunk, no?"

Grimacing, Colt rose to his hands and knees.

Koenig sighed. "Clearly it is," he said, and Colt thought he heard a tinge of admiration, odd though it seemed.

Koenig reached down, grasping Colt by his ankles. Colt could feel the blood rush to his head as he dangled in the air and he finally understood what a wishbone must feel like before it's ripped in two.

"It's a pity," Koenig said. "Though, on the other hand, you would have been exterminated anyway."

Colt wasn't sure where the idea had come from, but it was all he had. He pressed the ignition switch of his jet pack, and though it sputtered for a moment, flames leapt from the engines, spraying Koenig in a horrible conflagration.

Koenig screamed, the sound as terrifying as it was shrill. He dropped Colt, bringing a set of hands to his charred eyes. "I can't see!" he wailed as Colt cut the engine before rolling out of reach.

The scaled monster staggered as it cried out in agony. That's when Colt saw the black truck speeding toward them. At first he thought it might be some of Koenig's henchmen come to save their master, but as it neared, Colt saw that the driver was a CHAOS agent. He was wearing a ski mask, his eyes protected by heavy goggles and a gas mask strapped over his nose and mouth.

The brakes screamed as the truck skidded to a halt. A dozen soldiers poured out from the back, forming a ring around Koenig. The man-turned-monster hissed as he bared his teeth in a threatening posture. His eyes were bloodshot and filled with tears, but he was ready to fight.

One of the agents brought a rifle to his shoulder. When he pulled the trigger, a tranquilizer dart struck Koenig in the neck. Three other CHAOS agents did the same, and moments later Koenig was brought to his knees.

"You're all fools," Koenig said, though his speech was slurred as the drugs took hold. He fell to the ground, unconscious.

The agents didn't waste time as they bound all six of Koenig's hands. Then one slipped some kind of collar around the monster's neck before they hefted him into the back of the truck. The door was shut and locked.

"We need to get you to a doctor," one of the agents told Colt.

"I'll be okay," Colt said as he stared at the back of the truck. Koenig was in custody, but it didn't matter. There was no relief. His parents were still dead.

Colt wasn't ready to go with them—at least not yet. He hit the ignition on his jet pack and roared into the sky, leaving the confused CHAOS agent behind as he went to find Grandpa McAlister.

The old man was lying in the grass. His eyes were closed and it didn't look like he was breathing. Colt felt his chest constrict as emotion welled inside him. His eyes filled with tears. Losing his parents was hard enough, but he wasn't ready to bury his grandpa too.

Then Grandpa McAlister coughed and it was the most glorious sound that Colt had ever heard.

:: CHAPTER 57 ::

Before the dust had settled, video footage from the battle had found its way to the Internet. A Trident Biotech marketing executive got footage of one of the Trackers from his tenth-story window. He used the recording device in his phone, so the picture quality wasn't great, but there was no denying it. Giant robots had landed in Chandler, Arizona.

He posted the video on a social networking site, and it received more than a million hits in less an hour. Then news agencies picked up the footage. It wasn't long before military consultants and political pundits were on the air talking about what they thought had happened. The opinions ranged from the wild to the mundane, but nobody had real answers.

Someone even managed to get a video of the Phantom Flyer as the ultralights chased him. There was another video of a Sentry exploding. At first most everyone dismissed everything as a hoax. There were even rumblings that it was all part of a preview for a new summer blockbuster. Either way, just as Colt had predicted, by morning the whole world was talking about it.

After a long night in the emergency room, Colt sat on the

couch at Grandpa's house watching television. The sun hadn't come up yet and he couldn't sleep. Not after everything he had just been through. His ankle was wrapped so tightly he couldn't move it, his eye was swollen shut, and his chest was wrapped in bandages thanks to three broken ribs.

Grandpa was seated next to him in his favorite chair. His arm was in a sling and there were stitches beneath the gauze on his forehead. He couldn't sleep either.

"If giant robots weren't strange enough, we're just getting word that Trident Biotech has allegedly been running a mind control program using their biochip technology," a news reporter said through the speakers on the television. "Apparently chips once thought to cure epilepsy and Parkinson's disease were actually receivers that turned unsuspecting patients into sleeper-cell agents forced to do the bidding of Trident executives."

The image on the television shifted from the reporter to footage of Aldrich Koenig being led into the police station. He raised his cuffed hands to try and hide his face, but it didn't do much good.

"Their parent company, Trident Industries, has already seen its stock drop 60 percent within the first hour of trading, and it doesn't look like it's hit bottom yet," the reporter continued. "Global markets are taking a beating as investors dump stocks in the face of what some are calling Armageddon. The Dow Jones has dropped over three hundred points since the opening bell."

"What do you think, Grandpa? Is this Armageddon?" Colt asked as videos of panicked mobs roaming the streets of major cities around the world played on the screen.

Grandpa McAlister rubbed his temples with his thumb and forefinger. "I'm not sure."

"We stopped them, though, right? I mean, Agent Richmond said that the virus worked. We shut down Trident's satellite, so they won't be able to control people any more."

"That's what I've been told anyway," Grandpa McAlister said, "I'm afraid we just waited too long."

"So there's going to be an invasion?"

"I wish I knew the answer, but I don't." Grandpa McAlister stared out the window and up at the sky.

"Yes, you do," Colt said, though he meant no disrespect. He knew his grandfather was trying to protect him, but overnight the world had changed. The safety of mankind had always been an illusion, but now everyone knew. Colt knew. It was only a matter of time before a horde of aliens streamed into their world, and Colt felt helpless to stop it.

"After the war," Grandpa McAlister said, his voice heavy with emotion, "we hunted them down. They called us exterminators, and I guess that makes us no better than the monsters we killed. But even then, we didn't kill enough of them."

"That's not true," Colt said. He winced as he sat up. The pills they gave him dulled the pain, but his ribs still ached. "I can't imagine how many lives you must have saved because of what you did."

"Maybe." Grandpa McAlister's eyes brimmed with tears. "War is a terrible thing. All those books . . . all the movies they've made. And now video games? They've tried to make it glamorous, but it's not. We weren't heroes, Colt. The boys who died over in Europe and the Pacific? They were the heroes. We were just lucky enough to survive. No, if you ask me, there are no winners when it comes to war, and there's no glory in taking another life."

As he turned to Colt, a single tear escaped, streaming down

the stubble on his cheek. "The best you can do is pray that you're fighting for a righteous cause, but it'll change you. Once you've killed someone, you'll never be the same." He paused, pulling out a handkerchief to wipe his eyes before he blew his nose. "I fought so your folks . . . you and your brothers . . . for Dani and Oz . . . I fought so none of you ever had to . . . so this world would be safe from monsters like Koenig and his like . . . and here we've come full circle."

Colt sat there, letting the words sink in. "Now what?" he finally asked.

Grandpa McAlister folded the handkerchief and stuffed it back into his pocket. "Senator Bishop called a few minutes ago. He wants you to transfer to CHAOS Military Academy as soon as you're up to snuff."

"But I just got here."

"I know," Grandpa said. "I don't like it any more than you do, but we're running out of time. The brass in Washington seem to think that you're going to be the one to pull us out of this mess, and they won't take no for an answer."

"I still don't get it," Colt said as he eased back into the chair. "Why me?"

"We all have a calling, and as much as I hate to say it, this might be yours."

"It's not that I'm scared to die," Colt said, trying to process his feelings. "It's just that . . . I don't know. I don't want to leave you alone. Or maybe I don't want to be alone. I guess I just want my old life back."

"I'm afraid it's too late for that," Grandpa McAlister said as more footage of strange aliens flashed on the television screen.

"I guess," Colt said. "What about Oz?"

"He's going with you."

"But not Danielle?"

Grandpa McAlister sighed.

"I can't leave without her," Colt said. "Not now . . . not like this. What if they can't remove the biochip?"

"CHAOS is bringing in a team of surgeons. They're the best in the world at what they do, and that's all we can ask for." Grandpa McAlister reached over to touch Colt on the arm. "She'll be fine."

Colt hoped that his grandfather was right, but how could he be certain? For all they knew, Koenig could have ordered an explosive device implanted with the biochip. What if it detonated when someone tried to remove it? He closed his eyes. Exhaustion was making him paranoid.

"Look," Colt said before yawning. "If they want me to go to the academy, they have to take Danielle, or I'm not going."

"I'm afraid it doesn't work that way," Grandpa McAlister said. "I know it's not fair, son, but your country needs you . . . the entire planet needs you."

Colt wasn't sure that he was ready to save the world, much less pack his things and move again—at least not this soon. He knew he'd probably go away for college, but that was two years away. Then he remembered Lily, and how amazing it felt whenever she was near. She was—at least it seemed—the only person who could really understand what he was going through, and now he was supposed to leave her too?

"If I refuse?"

Grandpa McAlister offered a tired smile. "You won't."

READING GROUP GUIDE

1. Colt's life was turned upside down when his parents were murdered. Has your life ever been turned upside down? What happened and how did you cope?

2. Change can be a painful experience. Colt had to leave his friends behind and transfer to a new school in a different state. Have you ever transferred to a new school? What was the biggest challenge? What was the greatest benefit?

3. When Colt first meets Lily, she has a boyfriend. When it comes to dating, do you believe that 'all is fair in love and war,' or should he have backed off?

4. Colt gets embarrassed when Lily sees his father's Phantom Flyer Ring. What do you hide from people because you fear they'll judge you? What is the worst thing that could happen if you would share it?

5. Grandpa McAlister was part of a special unit in World War II that was sent to assassinate Adolph Hitler. What interesting stories are there in your family history?

6. At Lily's adoption party, Danielle cautions Colt it wasn't wise for him to be alone with Lily because people will infer something happened even if nothing did. Do you stop to think about how your actions appear to other people?

7. Many people believe there is intelligent life on other planets. Do you? Why or why not?

8. In the book, Trident Biotech developed biochips that help regulate seizures and control Parkinson's disease. There are robots that can record memories, flying motorcycles with wings that fold up, and people zipping through the sky in jet-packs. Do you think any of that will be possible in the near future? What is the most outlandish technology you can dream up? Do you think it will ever exist?

9. Colt wasn't qualified to face down Aldrich Koenig and the Thule, but he was willing to risk his life to save Danielle. What do you think is more important when it comes to achieving the impossible: skill, experience, or a willingness to risk everything?

CHAOS
SKETCHBOOK

Colt,

I served with your father in Vietnam, and though I may get in trouble for this, I don't care. Roger saved my life . . . more than once, actually. This is the least I can do.

Enclosed is a sketchbook I've kept through the years. These illustrations will verify some of the strange happenings that have taken place over the last few months, including the existence of the Thule. I hope you don't mind, but I included a sketch of you that was created from the most recent picture your parents sent me.

I'll be in touch as soon as I can. Keep your eyes open and stick close to your grandfather. If anybody can get us through the coming storm, it's Murdoch McAlister.

With great sorrow,

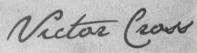

COLT McALISTER SKETCH BY KYLE LATINO.

PHANTOM FLYER: MORE THAN A PULP HERO?

Bastogne, Belgium. As Hitler's troops continue to march through Europe, rumors of augmented supersoldiers created in laboratories abound. Some G.Is insist they have seen wolfmen, and others claim Hitler's foes have robot soldiers with guns in place of hands. Does the United States Army have it's own team of super soldiers? Is the Phantom Flyer more than pulp hero?

"I
sou
a

THE PHANTOM FLYER SKETCH BY KYLE LATINO.

IS THIS NIKOLA TESLA'S MECHANICAL MAN?

New York, New York. There have been multiple reports of witnesses spotting a man with shiny metal skin, clawed hands and a single glowing eye. Could this be the mechanical man rumored as the creation of Nikola Tesla?

Lizard man spotted in Hudson River
Sept 27, 1939

BIG FOOT SPOTTED ON MT. SI IN WASHINGTON

North Bend, Washington. Hikers spotted a large creature covered in golden fur. The beast was thought to be at least eight feet tall, with long arms and a broad chest.

LOHR WAS INJURED BY A GERMAN TANK DURING THE SECOND WORLD WAR. DOCTORS REBUILT HIS ARM AND LEG WITH ROBOTICS DESIGNED BY THE ECCENTRIC INVENTOR, NIKOLA TESLA.

COMMONLY KNOWN AS BIG FOOT OR A SASQUATCH, LOHR IS ACTUALLY A THARIK FROM THE FORESTED PLANET OF NEMUS.

LOHR ILLUSTRATION BY REZA ILYASA.

BOROG, THE ARCONIAN

BOROG IS ONE OF THE DOMINANT PRIZE FIGHTERS
FROM THE INTERGALACTIC FIGHTING LEAGUE (IGFL).
IT FEATURES ELITE FIGHTERS FROM THE TWELVE
KNOWN PLANETS INHABITED BY LIFE FORMS. THE
LEAGUE IS RUN BY A FORMER CHAOS AGENT BY THE
NAME OF BASIL HYDE, A PRESUMED SPY.

MECHANICAL COMPONENTS
HAVE BEEN FUSED TO
BOROG'S BODY, A COMMON
MILITARY PRACTICE
FOR HIS TRIBE.
IT'S SAID THAT
AN ARCONIAN
WILL NEVER
RETREAT
REGARDLESS
OF THE
ODDS.
THEY ARE A
WARRING
PEOPLE.

TRIBAL MARKINGS
ARE NOT TATTOOS.
THEY HAVE BEEN
CARVED INTO
HIS CHEST.

HANDS (OR WHAT'S LEFT OF THEM) WORK
BOTH AS A KIND OF ENERGY CANNON AS WELL AS A
SLICING WEAPON IN HAND-TO-HAND COMBAT.

BOROG ILLUSTRATION BY THAM HOI MUN.

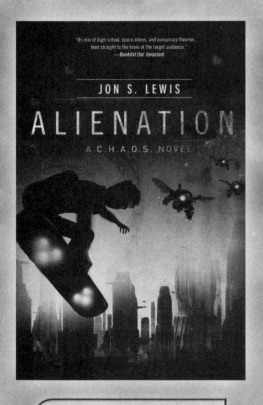